LIFERAY
Enterprise. Open Source. For Life.

LIFERAY ADMINISTRATOR'S GUIDE

Rich Sezov, General Editor

Liferay Administrator's Guide

Richard L. Sezov, Jr., General Editor and main author

Copyright © 2008 by Liferay, Inc.

ISBN 978-0-6151-9648-0

Contributors:

Ray Auge, Jian Cao (Steven), Brian Chan, Shepherd Ching, Bryan Cheung, Ivan Cheung, Alexander Chow, Jorge Ferrer, JR Houn, Scott Lee, Wei Hong Ma (Sai), Charles May, James Min, Alberto Montero, Jerry Niu, Michael Saechang, Li Ji Shan (Dale), Rich Sezov, Ed Shin, Joseph Shum, Michael Young

Table of Contents

Preface

This book was written with the server administrator in mind. It is a guide for anyone who wants to get a Liferay Portal server up and running, and is the only book of its kind. You won't get information from any other source as detailed as what you'll find here.

The information contained herein has been organized in a way that hopefully makes it easy to locate information. We start at the beginning: downloading Liferay as a bundle. From there, we work all the way through the multiple ways of installing Liferay to configuring the portal's many properties, to integrating it with other services, to optimizing performance, and finally to managing and backing up a Liferay installation.

Conventions

Sections are broken up into multiple levels of headings, and these make it easy to find information.

```
Source code and configuration file directives are presented like this.
```

Italics are used to represent links or buttons to be clicked on in a user interface and to indicate a label or a name of a Java class.

Bold is used to describe field labels.

Page headers denote the chapters, and footers denote the particular section within the chapter.

Notes

It is our hope that this book will be valuable to you, and that it will be an indispensable resource as you begin to administer a Liferay portal server. If you need any assistance beyond what is covered in this book, Liferay, Inc. offers training, consulting, and support services to fill any need that you might have. Please see http://www.liferay.com/web/guest/services for further information about the services we can provide.

As always, we welcome any feedback. If there is any way you think we could make this book better, please feel free to mention it on our forums. You can also use any of the email addresses on our *Contact Us* page (http://www.liferay.com/web/guest/about_us/contact_us). We are here to serve you, our users and customers, and to help make your experience using Liferay Portal the best it can be.

1. Introduction

Liferay Portal is the world's leading open source enterprise portal solution using the latest in Java, Java EE, and Web 2.0 technologies to deliver solutions for enterprises across both public and private sectors.

- Runs on all major application servers and servlet containers, databases, and operating systems with over 700 deployment combinations
- JSR-168 Compliant
- Out-of-the-box usability with over 60 portlets pre-bundled.
- Built in Content Management System (CMS)
- Collaboration suite
- Personalized pages for all users
- Benchmarked as among the most secure portal platforms using LogicLibrary's Logiscan suite

User-Friendly Features

Easy AJAX UI

Liferay Portal features a rich user interface that includes

- Drag-and-drop portlet re-positioning
- Dynamic portlet loader
- Portlet stylizer that allows end users to customize colors, fonts, and links without editing style sheets or HTML.

One-Click Look and Feel Change

- Hot-deployable theme architecture allows portal administrators to deploy new portal GUIs that can be selected by end-users without modifying core code.
- New themes can be added instantly using Liferay's Software Update Manager.

Freeform Portlets / WebOS

After pioneering drag-and-drop portlet repositioning, Liferay Portal now offers a free-form layout that mimics the look and feel of a desktop environment.

WebDAV Support

- Users will be more productive managing portal content with familiar operating system conventions for documents and folders.
- Full support for Windows and Linux.

Just In Time Portlet Rendering

Portlets load independently as they become ready so users don't have to wait to start using the portal.

Context-Sensitive Help

Portal users can access information specific to the tool they are using at any given time by clicking on a "question mark" icon.

AJAX Interface Tools

Liferay-tailored Javascript client libraries based on jQuery with support for JSON Web Services to help create rich user interfaces.

Developer-Friendly Features

Service Builder

Liferay's exclusive tool helps developers get their code enabled for Web Services, Spring, AJAX, and data access so they can focus on writing the business logic.

CSS Compliance

- All Liferay Portal pages are coded to CSS standards to simplify new theme development for developers and designers.
- All themes are CSS-driven to make changing the look and feel even easier.

Themes/Layout Enhancements

Liferay 4.3 includes enhancements such as:

- Role-based theme management
- Standardization on jQuery JavaScript Framework
- Simplified theme development process
- Semantic and non-obtrusive markup

- Standards compliance
- LAR Import / Export for Theme

Fine-Grained Permissions System

- Get the right information and application functions to the right people.

- A reusable, extensible authorization architecture is used throughout the portal and is applicable to individual portlet elements such as buttons, messages, portlets and users.

Workflow Capability

- Reduce the time it takes to update applications to reflect how your business changes.

- Easily update processes such as e-commerce checkout, user registration, content publishing, and document approval.

- Default installation of jBPM can be replaced with Intalio or other workflow engines.

What is a portal?

A portal is a web-based gateway for users to locate relevant content and use the applications they commonly need to be productive.

Portals offer compelling benefits to today's enterprises: reduced operational costs, improved customer satisfaction, and streamlined business processes.

Liferay Portal is one of the most mature portal frameworks on the market (in development since 2000) and offers these basic benefits and more.

Key Business Benefits:

PROVIDE AN INTUITIVE AND COLLABORATIVE EXPERIENCE

Maximize the productivity gains of portal users—a good user experience is key to capturing the highest return on an enterprise's portal investment

- Liferay Portal was the first to allow users to drag-and-drop portlets to customize the experience to the unique preferences of a user or community.
- Use one of the 20+ out-of-the-box themes to change the look and feel of the portal without dealing with complex code.
- Individual community members can be given their own pages with a user-defined friendly URL. This option gives users a better sense of ownership over the technology, thus enhancing their experience and generating user loyalty.
- Collaborative tools such as Instant Messaging, Message Boards, Blogs & Wikis allow you to create true communities of users.

CONSOLIDATE, ORGANIZE AND ACCESS ALL YOUR DATA AND APPLICATIONS VIA A SINGLE POINT OF ACCESS

Liferay portal provides you a single point of access to all your organization's data, content, and information from both existing in-house applications (i.e., HR, CRM) and external sources. Single-sign-on lets users log in once to access all their information needs.

After signing in, our fine-grained permissions system allows you to customize and control who can access sensitive information and functionality.

Users get an intuitive front-end while behind the scenes our support of ServiceMix technology simplifies the integration, upgrade, and substitution of disparate applications for the developer.

OPTIMIZE EXISTING IT INVESTMENTS

Leverage your existing IT environment.

Liferay Portal is the only open source portal that works with any application server, database server, or operating system with over 700 deployment configurations in any combination of the components below.

Application Servers	Servlet Containers	Databases
BES Borland ES 6.5	**JET** Jetty 5.1.4	**AD** Apache Derby
GER Apache Geronimo 1.1	**RES** Resin 3.0.14	**DB2** IBM DB2
GLF Sun GlassFish 2.0	**TOM** Tomcat 5.0.x/5.5.x, 6	**FIRE** Firebird
JB JBoss 4.0.3SP1, 4.0.4, 4.0.5, 4.2.X		**HYP** Hypersonic
JON JOnAS 4.8.5		**INF** Informix
JR JRun 4 Updater 3		**INT** InterBase
O OracleAS 10.1.3	Operating System	**JDS** JDataStore
ORI Orion 2.0.6	AIX	**MY** MySQL
P Pramati 5.0	BSD	**O** Oracle
REX RexIP 2.5	LINUX	**PSQL** PostgresSQL
SUN SUN JSAS 8.01	SOLARIS	**SAP** SAP
WL WebLogic 8.1 SP4, 9.2, 10	WINDOWS	**SQL** SQL Server
WS WebSphere 5.1, 6.0.x, 6.1	MAC OS X	**SYB** Sybase

Be assured that existing technology investments are not jettisoned and that future changes will not require an overhaul of an existing Liferay Portal installation.

ADAPT TO THE DEMANDS OF A CHANGING MARKET

Liferay's workflow engine allows organizations of all sizes to be more nimble. Flexible IT makes business processes more dynamic, modular, and adaptable to the demands of fast-changing markets.

No matter how your processes change, Liferay was benchmarked as among the most secure portal platforms on the market using LogicLibrary's Logiscan suite, so you can always be confident in the security of your data.

Scale your business without worrying about your IT

Liferay grows with your organization.

Because our technology is among the few that allows for clustering (the addition of hardware to meet growing usage demands) Liferay Portal's capacity for content and applications is limitless!

Liferay Portal also accommodates today's global business environment with multi-lingual support, including: Arabic, Chinese, Dutch, English, Finnish, French, German, Greek, Italian, Japanese, Korean, Portuguese, Spanish, Turkish, and Vietnamese.

Add Liferay's language portlet to any page and allow end-users to quickly select a different localization with one click.

Gain the lowest TCO.

Liferay Portal provides the highest value and lowest costs at every level.

Open source products promise more freedom and flexibility, but not all open source licenses are the same.

Liferay Portal is offered under the MIT License, the most liberal and business friendly license available with absolutely no license fees or reciprocity clauses.

Hardware and Software– Strict adherence to standards allows Liferay Portal to be deployed in any of over 700 combinations of application server or servlet container, database, and operating system, reaping these additional value benefits:

- Helps your organization avoid "vendor lock-in" or dependence on a single third-party.

- Eliminates the incidental cost of new database or application server licenses a proprietary portal solution might require.

- Allows organizations to leverage existing in-house expertise for application server / database / operating system with no need to hire or train IT staff on new hardware / software.

Implementation – Liferay Portal's included portlet suite (over 60) and built-in web publishing and content management system (CMS) reduce or eliminate the initial cost of custom development.

Should development be needed, the MIT license allows in-house development teams to customize the portal instead of using third party developers.

Training and support are also available to jump start those efforts when needed. Because Liferay Portal is standards-based, developer familiarity with the key technologies in Liferay's architecture will shorten the development cycle.

Maintenance – Liferay Portal is supported by a wide range of 24/7 business critical support offerings. Choose the level of support that meets your needs.

2. INITIAL SETUP

You will find that because Liferay is extremely flexible in its deployment options, it is easy to install as well. If you already have an application server, you simply use the tools for deployment that came with your application server. If you do not have an application server, Liferay provides several application server bundles from which to choose. These are very easy to install and with a small amount of configuration can be made into production-ready systems.

Obtaining Liferay

Liferay is freely downloadable from our web site at http://www.liferay.com. Click on the *Downloads*

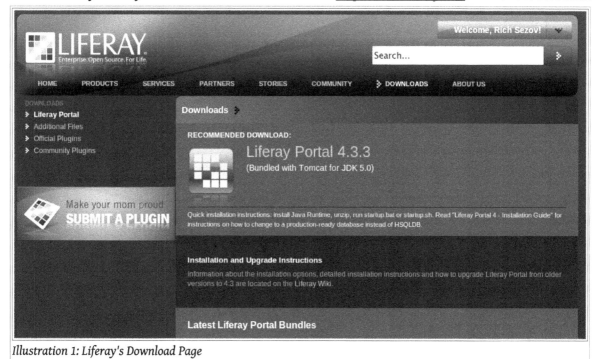

Illustration 1: Liferay's Download Page

link at the top of the page, and you will be presented with multiple options for getting a copy of Liferay.

If you want to install a bundle, there is a list of bundles available on the first download page, with a recommended bundle at the top. If you do not currently have an application server, it is best to download the bundle that Liferay recommends at the top of the page. If you have an application server preference, you can also choose the server you prefer from the available Liferay Portal bundles. Having a JDK (Java Development Kit) already installed is a prerequisite to running any of the bundles.

Please note that Liferay is not able to provide application server bundles for proprietary application servers such as WebLogic, WebSphere, or Oracle Application Server because the licenses for these servers do not allow for redistribution. Liferay Portal, however, runs just as well on these application servers as it does on open source application servers; it just needs to be installed manually.

If you wish to obtain a copy of Liferay Portal for a manual install, you can click on the *Additional Files* link on the left side of the *Downloads* page. Here you will find Liferay .war files as well as links to Liferay's dependency .jars that need to be on your application server's class path. Later in this chapter are instructions for installing Liferay on many of the major application servers available today.

Installing a Bundle

In most cases, installing a bundle is as easy as uncompressing the archive and then starting the application server. For example, if you were to install the recommended bundle (Liferay Portal on Tomcat), you would create a folder to store the uncompressed application server and then uncompress the archive into this folder.

What you wind up with after this is the following directory structure:

Now you would simply start Tomcat in the same way as you would if you had downloaded it manually. Tomcat is launched by way of a script which is found in the *bin* folder. If you drop to a command prompt and go to this folder, you can launch Tomcat via the following command on Windows:

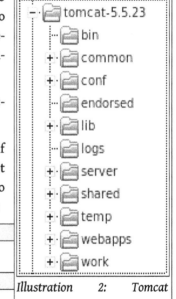

Illustration 2: Tomcat Directory Structure

```
startup
```

or the following command on Linux / Unix:

```
./startup.sh
```

The Liferay / Tomcat bundle will then launch. If you are on Windows, you will see another command prompt window appear with Tomcat's console in it. If you are on Linux, you can see the Tomcat console by issuing the following command:

```
tail -f ../logs/catalina.out
```

Once Tomcat has completed launching, you can then view your Liferay bundle in a web browser. Launch your web browser and then go to the following address: http://localhost:8080. The default Liferay home page will then appear in your web browser. It will be using an embedded database for its configuration, but it is fully functional. You can now begin exploring the various features of Liferay.

Installing a different bundle is done in exactly the same way: unzip the bundle into the folder of your choice, launch the application server, and then view the portal in your web browser. There is only one bundle that differs from this procedure. The Pramati bundle is currently the only bundle that is available from Liferay's web site that uses an installer. If you wish to use the Pramati bundle, you need to launch it via its installer.

The Pramati installer will have a file name such as liferay-portal-pramati-<version number>.jar. Download this file from Liferay's web site. Once it has been downloaded, you can launch the installer from the command prompt by issuing the following command:

```
java -jar <name of bundle file>
```

For example, if you downloaded liferay-portal-pramati-4.3.3.jar, you would issue the following command:

```
java -jar liferay-portal-pramati-4.3.3.jar
```

You will then see the Pramati installer appear on your screen.

Illustration 3: Pramati Installer, Initial Screen

Select the folder to which you wish to to install the bundle and click the *Next* button. There is only one other screen in the installer:

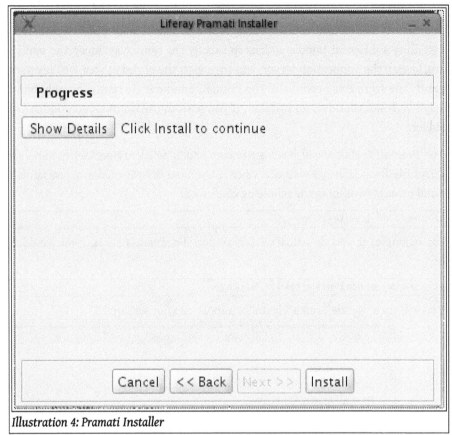

Illustration 4: Pramati Installer

Click the *install* button and the bundle will then be installed. Please note that the Pramati bundle is supported on Windows operating systems only.

As you can see, bundles are the easiest way to get started with Liferay. They come pre-configured with a running Liferay that can be used immediately to explore all of the things that Liferay can do. And with minimal extra configuration (which we will see later), bundles can be converted into full production-ready systems.

Installing Liferay for a Developer

If you are beginning a Liferay-based project, chances are you will need to get your developers up and running before your production systems are ready. In order for a developer to do his or her work, an instance of Liferay needs to be running on his or her machine. Additionally, to prevent file-locking issues, a developer's version of Liferay should not use the embedded database, so a separate database will need to be installed.

Liferay Portal is an open source project, so it makes use of many open source tools for development. This has two benefits: 1) It removes any barriers to entry, as there are no expensive tools to purchase in order to make use of Liferay, and 2) It allows Liferay to remain as tool-agnostic as possible. If developers wish to use an IDE to work on Liferay, great. If developers want to use a text editor and the command line, that's great too. Developers can choose the tools they are most comfortable with to write code on Liferay's platform.

There are, however, some tools that are required in order to develop with Liferay. These are at a minimum:

- Apache Ant 1.7.0 or above

- A Java Development Kit

- A Liferay-supported database (MySQL recommended for a developer machine)

- The IDE or development environment of your choice

If you will be customizing Liferay via the Extension Environment (please see the *Liferay Developer's Guide* for further details), you will need a few more tools:

- Jikes

- A Subversion client (optional: you can also download the Liferay source from the web site)

Standalone Liferay

Installing a standalone Liferay for a developer is a straightforward process:

1. Download the Tomcat bundle from the Liferay web site

2. Uncompress the bundle to a suitable location on the developer's local machine

3. Install a lightweight SQL database that Liferay supports (MySQL recommended)

4. Connect the local Liferay to the SQL database

5. Launch Liferay!

Download the Tomcat Bundle

We recommend using the Tomcat bundle from the Liferay web site for several reasons:

1. Tomcat is small and fast. Because it is a servlet container only and not a full Java EE container, it requires less resources than a full application server, yet it provides all of the resources Liferay needs to run.

2. Tomcat is open source, and so is easy to bundle with Liferay, as the licenses are compatible.

3. Liferay will have to share resources on the developer machine with an SQL database as well as with other tools. Running it in Tomcat ensures that it has as lightweight a footprint as possible.

With that said, if your developers have sufficient resources on their machines to run a different application server (such as Glassfish or JBoss), there is no reason besides the performance reasons mentioned above why they could not do that. Simply substitute the instructions below that reference the

Liferay-Tomcat bundle with the bundle that more closely resembles the application server your developers want to use.

UNCOMPRESS THE BUNDLE

Uncompress the Tomcat bundle to a suitable location on the developer's machine. It is best to use a local directory, and not a networked drive for performance reasons. Liferay will run from a networked drive, but IO issues may cause it to perform poorly.

INSTALL A LIGHTWEIGHT SQL DATABASE

Liferay is database-agnostic, but it needs a database in order to run. The embedded database is fine for demoing Liferay, but for development a real SQL database server should be used. We recommend that you use MySQL for this purpose, as it is small, free, and very fast. If your developers use Linux, it generally comes with their Linux distribution of choice. If your developers use Windows, there is an easy graphical installer that automatically configures it.

Again, if your organization has standardized on a different database, there is no reason not to use that database on your developers' machines as long as those machines have the resources to run it. Liferay supports any database that your application server can provide access to via a JDBC data source.

To install MySQL for a developer, you will need four components: *MySQL Server, MySQL Query Browser, MySQL Administrator, and MySQL Connector/J*, which is the JDBC driver for MySQL. The first component is the server itself, which on Windows will get installed as a service. The second component is a database browsing and querying tool, and the third is an administration utility that enables the end user to create databases and user IDs graphically. If your developer is running Windows, download these three components from MySQL's web site (http://www.mysql.com). Run through the graphical installers for each, accepting the defaults. If your developer is running Linux, have him / her install these tools via the package management tool in his / her distribution.

Once you have a running MySQL database server, drop to a command line and launch the MySQL command line utility. You can find this in the *bin* directory where MySQL is installed, or in the case of Linux, it will be on your system's *path*. Launch it via the following command:

```
mysql -u root
```

By default, MySQL does not have an administrative (root) password set, and this is fine for a developer's machine. If you have set an administrative password, issue the following command instead:

```
mysql -u root -p
```

Once you launch it, it will display some messages and then a MySQL prompt:

```
Welcome to the MySQL monitor.  Commands end with ; or \g.
Your MySQL connection id is 1478
Server version: 5.0.45 Mandriva Linux - MySQL Standard Edition (GPL)

Type 'help;' or '\h' for help. Type '\c' to clear the buffer.
```

```
mysql>
```

At the command prompt, type the following command:

```
create database lportal character set utf8;
```

MySQL should return the following message:

```
Query OK, 1 row affected (0.12 sec)
```

You will be back at the MySQL prompt. You can type *quit* and press enter, and you will return to your operating system's command prompt.

Note that on some Linux distributions MySQL is configured so that it will not listen on the network for connections. This is done for security reasons, but it prevents Java from being able to connect to MySQL via the JDBC driver. To fix this, search for your *my.cnf* file (it is probably in */etc* or */etc/sysconfig*) and comment out the directive *skip-networking* by putting a hash mark (#) in front of it. Save the file and then restart MySQL.

CONNECT LIFERAY TO THE SQL DATABASE

Next, you will need to copy the MySQL JDBC driver—a .jar file—to the proper location in the Tomcat server, so that the Tomcat server can find it. This file should be copied to the common/lib/ext folder of your Tomcat installation. This makes it available on Tomcat's global class path. If you are using a different application server, copy the driver to a location on the server's global class path.

Once this file is copied, you will need to change a configuration file in Tomcat to point it to your new database. Navigate to the following folder in Tomcat:

```
<Tomcat Home>/conf/Catalina/localhost
```

In this folder is a file called *ROOT.xml*. Open this file in a text editor. You should see two Resource tags in this file; one of them defines where the Liferay database is; the other defines where the mail server(s) are. You will be modifying the database Resource tag. Make it look like this:

```
<Resource
        name="jdbc/LiferayPool"
        auth="Container"
        type="javax.sql.DataSource"
        driverClassName="com.mysql.jdbc.Driver"
        url="jdbc:mysql://localhost/lportal?useUnicode=true&amp;characterEncoding=UTF-8"
        username="root"
        password=""
        maxActive="20"
/>
```

Save and close the file.

Again, if you are using a different application server, modify the LiferayPool data source so that it uses the MySQL driver and points to your MySQL database.

LAUNCH LIFERAY!

You are now ready to launch Liferay. Navigate to your <Tomcat Home>/bin folder in your command prompt. On Windows, type:

```
startup
```

On Linux, type:

```
./startup.sh
```

Press Enter. On Windows, another command prompt window should appear with the Tomcat console in it. On Linux, you will need to issue another command to see the console:

```
tail -f ../logs/catalina.out
```

Liferay will start as usual. Because this is the first time Liferay will be launched against your new MySQL database, it will take some extra time creating all of the tables it needs in the database. Once the messages have stopped scrolling, navigate to the following URL in your web browser:

```
http://localhost:8080
```

The default Liferay home page will be displayed.

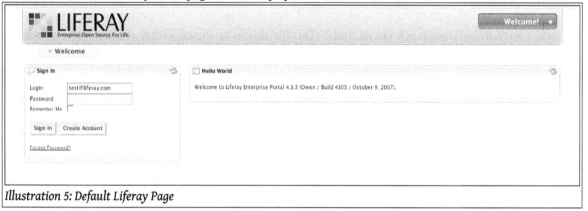

Illustration 5: Default Liferay Page

To log in to your new portal, use the default administrative credentials:

```
Login: test@liferay.com
Password: test
```

Your developer now has a standalone version of Liferay installed on his / her machine, and can use the tools of his / her choice to launch a completely local Liferay instance in order to test code. Additionally, he / she is free to point whatever development tool (IDE, text editor, etc.) at this Tomcat instance in order to start it in debug mode. This Liferay instance can be used to develop, deploy, and test portal plugins (portlet .war files and Liferay themes).

Installing the Liferay Extension Environment

Because Liferay Portal is an open source project, all of its source code is available for developers to view and modify if they wish. Because many of Liferay's customers wish to extend the functionality of the portal, Liferay has provided a means of customization which enables clear separation of customized code from the Liferay core source. This provides several benefits:

- The upgrade path is kept clear, as customizations are kept separate from the Liferay source

- Organization or environment specific customizations don't need to be contributed back to the Liferay project

- One, separate project for all customizations can be checked in to an organization's source code repository and applied to multiple instances of Liferay, or the reverse: an organization can have several instances of Liferay with different customizations

Just like installing a standalone Liferay, the extension environment is tool-agnostic. Developers can use whatever tools they are most comfortable with. This allows them to be as productive as possible, right out of the gate.

The procedure for installing a Liferay extension environment is as follows:

- Install the necessary tools

- Obtain the Liferay source

- Create configuration files

- Create the extension environment

- Install an application server in which to debug

- Deploy the extension environment

Install the Necessary Tools

You will need the full list of development tools (all open source and freely available) to customize Liferay in the extension environment:

- A Java Development Kit

- Apache Ant 1.7.0 or above

- A Liferay-supported database (MySQL recommended for a developer machine)

- Jikes

- A Subversion client (optional: you can also download the Liferay source from the web site)

- The IDE or development environment of your choice

Java Development Kit

Download and install JDK 1.4 or above. Once the install has completed, set an environment variable called JAVA_HOME which points to your JDK directory. This differs from operating system to operating system.

Apache Ant 1.7.0 or Above

Download the latest version of Ant from http://ant.apache.org. This is the build tool that is used extensively by the extension environment. Uncompress the archive into an appropriate folder of your choosing.

Next, set an environment variable called ANT_HOME which points to the folder to which you installed Ant. Use this variable to add the binaries for Ant to your PATH by adding ANT_HOME/bin to your PATH environment variable.

To do this on a Windows platform, go to Start -> Control Panel, and double-click the System icon. Go to Advanced, and then click the Environment Variables button. Under System Variables, select *New*. Make the **Variable Name** *ANT_HOME* and the **Variable Value** *<Path To>\apache-ant-1.7.0* (e.g., *C:\Java\apache-ant-1.7.0*), and click *OK*.

Select *New* again. This time name the **Variable Name** *ANT_OPTS* and the **Variable Value** *-Xms256M -Xmx512M*

Scroll down until you find the PATH environment variable. Select it and select *Edit*. Add %ANT_HOME%\bin to the end or beginning of the Path. Select *OK*, and then select *OK* again. Open a command prompt and type *ant* and press Enter. If you get a build file not found error, you have correctly installed Ant. If not, check your environment variable settings and make sure they are pointing to the directory to which you unzipped Ant.

To do this on a Linux or Mac system, navigate to your home folder and edit the file called *.bash_profile*. It is a hidden file that resides in the root of your home folder. Add the following lines to it, substituting the path to which you installed Ant:

```
ANT_HOME=/java/apache-ant-1.7.0
ANT_OPTS="-Xms256M -Xmx512M"
PATH=$PATH:$HOME/bin:$ANT_HOME/bin
export ANT_HOME ANT_OPTS PATH
```

Save the file and then open a new terminal window and type *ant* and press Enter. If you get a build file not found error, you have correctly installed Ant. If not, check your environment variable settings and make sure they are pointing to the directory to which you unzipped Ant.

A Liferay-supported Database

As above, we recommend that if you don't have a standard for local development databases, you should use MySQL for this, as it is small, free, and very fast. If your developers use Linux, it generally comes with their Linux distribution of choice. If your developers use Windows, there is an easy graphical installer that automatically configures it.

To install MySQL for a developer, you will need four components: *MySQL Server, MySQL Query Browser, MySQL Administrator, and MySQL Connector/J*, which is the JDBC driver for MySQL. The first component is the server itself, which on Windows will get installed as a service. The second component is a database browsing and querying tool, and the third is an administration utility that enables the end user to create databases and user IDs graphically. If your developer is running Windows, download these three components from MySQL's web site (http://www.mysql.com). Run through the graphical installers for each, accepting the defaults. If your developer is running Linux, have him / her install these tools via the package management tool in his / her distribution.

Once you have a running MySQL database server, drop to a command line and launch the MySQL command line utility. You can find this in the *bin* directory where MySQL is installed, or in the case of Linux, it will be on your system's *path*. Launch it via the following command:

```
mysql -u root
```

By default, MySQL does not have an administrative (root) password set, and this is fine for a developer's machine. If you have set an administrative password, issue the following command instead:

```
mysql -u root -p
```

Once you launch it, it will display some messages and then a MySQL prompt:

```
Welcome to the MySQL monitor.  Commands end with ; or \g.
Your MySQL connection id is 1478
Server version: 5.0.45 Mandriva Linux - MySQL Standard Edition (GPL)

Type 'help;' or '\h' for help. Type '\c' to clear the buffer.

mysql>
```

At the command prompt, type the following command:

```
create database lportal character set utf8;
```

MySQL should return the following message:

```
Query OK, 1 row affected (0.12 sec)
```

You will be back at the MySQL prompt. You can type *quit* and press enter, and you will return to your operating system's command prompt.

Note that on some Linux distributions MySQL is configured so that it will not listen on the network for connections. This is done for security reasons, but it prevents Java from being able to connect to MySQL via the JDBC driver. To fix this, search for your *my.cnf* file (it is probably in */etc* or */etc/sysconfig*) and comment out the directive *skip-networking* by putting a hash mark (#) in front of it. Save the file and then restart MySQL.

You will next be using the MySQL JDBC driver to connect your local application server to your MySQL database, but we will need to perform several other steps first. So take note of where you have downloaded this: we will need to use it later.

Jikes

Jikes is a Java compiler that was originally created by IBM and is now open source. It compiles Java

---

code much faster than the default Java compiler does, and so developers find that it can increase their productivity. Liferay 4.3 uses Jikes by default, so we will install it, though it is completely optional. If you do not wish to use it, please see the *Liferay Developer's Guide* to see how you can switch to another Java compiler.

Download Jikes from its web site: http://jikes.sourceforge.net. As you did with Ant, uncompress it into the appropriate folder of your choosing. Create an environment variable called JIKES_HOME which points to where you uncompressed Jikes, and add the Jikes binaries to your path in the same way you did with the Ant binaries, by adding JIKES_HOME/bin to your PATH variable.

A Subversion Client (optional)

In order to work in the extension environment, you will need to obtain a copy of the Liferay source code. You can do this in two ways: you can download a particular release from Liferay's web site, or you can check out the source from the Subversion repository at Sourceforge. One benefit of using a Subversion client is that you can switch easily to newer versions of the Portal source when they become available. Or, if you wish to keep up with a particular branch of code, you can connect to the latest branch to obtain bug fixes as quickly as possible. If you are really adventurous, you can connect to the trunk and run the latest bleeding-edge code.

If you don't want to use a Subversion client, then getting the source code is easy: download the latest source release from Liferay's web site and unzip it to where you are going to store your Liferay development projects.

If you would like to use a Subversion client, both GUI clients and command line clients are available for just about every operating system, such as TortoiseSVN (for Windows), KDESVN (for Linux), or RapidSVN (for Mac). Select the one you think is most appropriate and then install it.

The IDE or Development Environment of Your Choice

Liferay is IDE-agnostic. Developers can use anything from a simple text editor and command line tools to a full-blown IDE such as Eclipse or Netbeans. Your developer should decide what environment he / she is most productive in once the Liferay source and extension environment have been installed on his / her machine. If your developer(s) do not have a particular tool of choice, we recommend starting with Eclipse or Netbeans. Both of them are open-source IDEs with lots of functionality to help streamline development. Additionally, both of them have plugins for Subversion (Netbeans has it built-in, the one for Eclipse is called *Subclipse* and needs to be installed separately) which allows developers to connect to Liferay's code repository directly from within the IDE. Please see the *Liferay Developer's Guide* for further information.

OBTAIN THE LIFERAY SOURCE

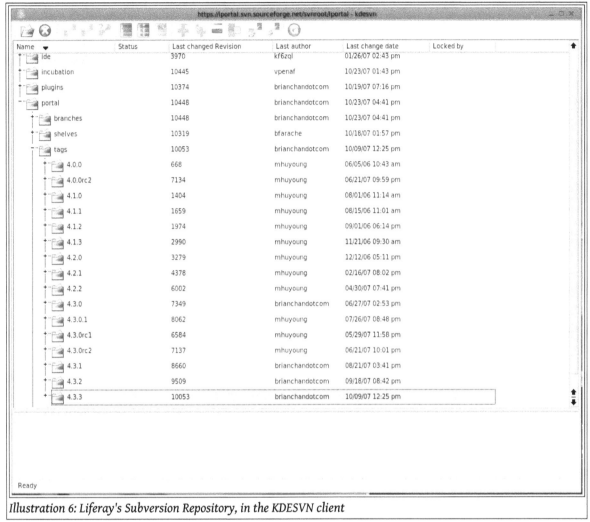

Illustration 6: Liferay's Subversion Repository, in the KDESVN client

If you are not using a Subversion client, you will need to download the Liferay source from Liferay's download page. Unzip the source code into a folder called *portal*.

If you are using a Subversion client, point your client to the following repository:

```
https://lportal.svn.sourceforge.net/svnroot/lportal
```

From there, you should be able to browse to the version of the source you want. Open the top level project called *portal*. If you want to download a particular release of the portal, you'll then want to open the folder called *tags*. From there, you can see the various versions of the software that have been tagged.

If you would rather work from a branch, open the *branches* folder. Here you will see the development branches for the various releases, such as 4.1.x, 4.2.x, and 4.3.x. Bug fixes are back ported to these branches when they become available, and so it is likely that if a support ticket for a particular bug has been closed, but the fix has not yet been part of a release of the software, you will find the fix in the branch. Once a good number of bug fixes have been checked into a branch, the development team creates another release, which you'll then see in the *tags* folder.

If you want to work from the bleeding-edge development version of the code, go to the *trunk* folder. There are no sub folders here; this is the latest version of the code. Note that this code (likely) has bugs and unimplemented features, and you will probably want to update from the repository regularly. Also note that any extensions that are developed against this version of the code will likely need refactoring as the Liferay code itself is refactored. For this reason, unless your developers really know the Liferay source well, it is best to stick with a tagged version of the code or a branch.

Check out the code using the Subversion client of your choice into a folder on your developer's local machine called *portal*. This could take a while, as the Liferay code base has become rather large. You may want to have it run in the background while you perform other tasks.

CREATE CONFIGURATION FILES

The Liferay source project consists of a number of top level folders (some with sub folders), some properties files, and a number of Ant build scripts. Rather than modify the properties files directly (and thus potentially lose their default values), Liferay allows the developer to *override* these defaults by creating new properties files based on the developer's user name. This is generally the name one would use to log in to his / her machine (e.g., jsmith).

Navigate to the folder in which you have now stored the Liferay source code. Inside this folder you will find several properties files (they have the extension *.properties*). There are two of them that will need to be customized, but you won't have to edit them. Instead, you will create new versions of the files that have your user name in them.

The two files that need to be customized are *release.properties* and *app.server.properties.* You will create new versions of these files with the user name inserted in a dot-delimited fashion. For example, if your user name is *jsmith*, you will create *release.jsmith.properties* and *app.server.jsmith.properties.*

We'll start with the customized version of *release.properties.* Open your custom version (the one with your user name in the file name) and the default version at the same time. There are at least two properties that we will need to customize:

```
##
## Release Source
##


lp.source.dir=D:/Projects/liferay/portal/release


##
## Extension Environment
##
```

```
lp.ext.dir=D:/Projects/liferay/portal/ext
```

Copy this from the original file into your new file. The first property defines where you are storing the Liferay Portal source on your local machine. Change this value from what it is to the full path to the folder where you have stored the Liferay portal source. For example, on a Windows machine, a typical developer might have it stored in *C:\java\code\liferay\portal*. If this were where you had unzipped or checked out the portal source from Subversion, you would change the property to read like this:

```
lp.source.dir=C:/java/code/liferay/portal
```

The slashes on a Windows box are changed from backslashes to forward slashes because backslashes are generally used to escape out another character. Since Java knows what operating system it is running on, it can transparently convert the forward slashes in the properties file to backslashes.

On a Linux box, a developer might have the portal source stored in his / her home directory. A typical developer on Linux, then, might put this in his / her properties file:

```
lp.source.dir=/home/jsmith/java/code/liferay/portal
```

The second property defines where you want to store the extension environment you are going to create. Usually it is best to have the extension environment project folder in the same place as the portal project folder. So taking the examples above, the Windows developer would define the second property like this:

```
lp.ext.dir=C:/java/code/liferay/ext
```

And the Linux developer would define the second property like this:

```
lp.ext.dir=/home/jsmith/java/code/liferay/ext
```

Once you have changed the *release.<username>.properties* file to define where you have placed the portal project and where you will place the extension environment project, save it and close it.

Next, you will do the same for the *app.server.properties* file. Open that file and your custom version (the one with your user name in the file name). Again, there are two properties that we will want to customize. The original file allows for the extension environment to be deployed to many different kinds of application servers. The default value is fine: we will be installing Tomcat as part of the extension environment, but we will paste it into our customized file anyway to enable us to switch application servers later if we wish:

```
app.server.type=tomcat
```

The other property we will need to customize is the folder where we want to store our application server(s). This is called the Server Directory. The default is this:

```
##
## Server Directory
##

app.server.parent.dir=D:/Java
```

Copy this and paste it into your custom properties file. You will be changing this to a folder called *servers* that will be inside your new extension environment when it is created. Using the examples above, the Windows developer would change it to the following:

```
app.server.parent.dir=C:/java/code/liferay/ext/servers
```

And the Linux developer would change it to the following:

```
app.server.parent.dir=/home/jsmith/java/code/liferay/ext/servers
```

If you scroll down in the original file, you will see that near the bottom are defined a number of Sourceforge mirror sites. If you know of one that is closer to you than the one which is *not* commented out, copy the property and paste it into your custom file. For example, the Easy News mirror is located in Arizona, USA. If that is a fast mirror for you, paste its property into your custom *app.server.<username>.properties* file:

```
sourceforge.mirror=http://easynews.dl.sourceforge.net/sourceforge/lportal
```

When you are finished, save and close the file.

CREATE THE EXTENSION ENVIRONMENT

You are now ready to create your extension environment. Open up a command window in your operating system and navigate to your *portal* project folder. This is the folder into which you just put the customized properties files. Issue the following command:

```
ant clean start build-ext
```

Ant will use the build script in this folder (called *build.xml*) to compile Liferay and create a clean extension environment in the folder you specified in the properties files. When it finishes, you should have a new folder called *ext* in the same location as your *portal* folder.

Copy your customized properties files from your *portal* folder into your new *ext* folder. The same properties apply to the extension environment that apply to the portal source project.

INSTALL AN APPLICATION SERVER

Your final step is to install an application server in which to run and debug the extension environment code. This is also done by using Ant.

Open a command window and navigate to your *ext/servers* folder. You will see that inside this folder is another Ant script. Issue the following command:

```
ant install-tomcat
```

The script will automatically download and install a Liferay-Tomcat bundle from the Sourceforge mirror that is defined in your properties file. If you have customized this value, it will use the value from your user name-based properties file; otherwise, it will use the default. It can take quite a bit of time to download the bundle and install it; you might want to perform this task in the background while you do something else. When it is finished, you will have a new Tomcat folder in your *ext/servers* folder.

You can install any application server for which Liferay provides a bundle in this way. If you open the original *app.server.properties* file, you will see a number of different application servers defined. They all have properties which look like *app.server.<server name>*. If you want to install and use a different application server, simply modify the *app.server.type* property in your customized *app.server.username.properties* file to reference one of the other application servers that are supported, such as *glassfish* or *jboss-tomcat*.

Once this is done, save the file and run an Ant command similar to the one above, substituting the application server you have chosen on the command line. For example, if you want to use the Glassfish bundle, you would type:

```
ant install-glassfish
```

The script will then automatically download and install the application server bundle you have specified. You can have as many of the application servers installed at one time as you like. When you want to deploy your extension environment to a particular application server that you have installed, all you need to do is modify the *app.server.type* property to reference the application server you have chosen. This provides an easy way to test your code on a multitude of application servers.

Now that you have installed an application server, you now need to point it to your MySQL database. If you are using Tomcat, copy the MySQL JDBC driver (called *MySQL Connector/J*) into your *ext/lib/global* folder. This will ensure that the driver gets deployed to your application server instance (regardless of what that application server is) when you deploy your extension environment.

You now need to modify the data source in your Tomcat instance to point to the MySQL database you created earlier. Navigate to the new Tomcat folder that is inside your *ext/servers* folder. Inside this folder are a number of sub folders. Navigate to the *conf/Catalina/localhost* folder. Inside this folder is a file called *ROOT.xml*. Open this file in a text editor. You should see two Resource tags in this file; one of them defines where the Liferay database is; the other defines where the mail server(s) are. You will be modifying the database Resource tag. Make it look like this:

```
<Resource
        name="jdbc/LiferayPool"
        auth="Container"
        type="javax.sql.DataSource"
        driverClassName="com.mysql.jdbc.Driver"
        url="jdbc:mysql://localhost/lportal?useUnicode=true&amp;characterEncoding=UTF-8"
        username="root"
        password=""
        maxActive="20"
/>
```

If your root user has a password, put that password in the file.

Save and close the file.

Deploy the Extension Environment

You are now ready to deploy the extension environment to your Tomcat instance for the first time. Open a command window and navigate to your *ext* folder. While in this folder, issue the following command:

```
ant clean deploy
```

The contents of the *portal* project will be merged with the contents of the *ext* project and the result will be deployed to your new Tomcat instance. Since you don't currently have any customizations in the extension environment, the end result will be that you will have deployed the version of Liferay whose source you downloaded, plus the sample Reports portlet that is in the extension environment by default.

You can start Tomcat by navigating to the directory in *ext/servers* to which Tomcat was installed. Inside this directory is another directory called *bin.* Navigate to this directory. To start Tomcat on Windows, type:

```
startup
```

On Linux, type:

```
./startup.sh
```

Press Enter. On Windows, another command prompt window should appear with the Tomcat console in it. On Linux, you will need to issue another command to see the console:

```
tail -f ../logs/catalina.out
```

Liferay will start as usual. Because this is the first time Liferay will be launched against your new MySQL database, it will take some extra time creating all of the tables it needs in the database. Once the messages have stopped scrolling, navigate to the following URL in your web browser:

```
http://localhost:8080
```

The default Liferay home page will be displayed.

To log in to your new portal, use the default administrative credentials:

```
Login: test@liferay.com
Password: test
```

Please see the *Liferay Developer's Guide* for further information on how to customize Liferay by use of the extension environment.

Installing Liferay for an Enterprise

Eventually, you will want to install Liferay onto a real server, rather than on a developer's machine. It is easiest to do this by starting with a bundle and then reconfiguring that bundle so that it is enterprise-ready, by connecting it to a database which resides on another server. Because this is by far the quickest and easiest method to get a production Liferay system running, we will look at this first. Often, however, enterprises will have an established Java EE infrastructure upon which they would like to install Liferay. In this situation, a bundle will not suffice. Most of this section, therefore, will focus on installing Liferay onto an already-established application server.

Database Setup

Regardless of which method is used to install Liferay, you will need to configure the Liferay database first. Even though Liferay can now create its database automatically, most enterprises prefer *not* to allow the user ID configured in an application server to have that many permissions over the database. For security reasons, Select, Insert, Update, and Delete are generally all the permissions that most DBAs will grant, and so we will go over how to set up the database manually. If your organization's DBAs *are* willing to grant the Liferay user ID permissions to create and drop tables in the database, you can skip this section.

One other caveat to this: Liferay has an automatic database upgrade function which runs when the version of Liferay is upgraded to a new release. If the user ID that accesses the database does not have enough rights to create / modify / drop tables in the database, you will need to grant those rights to the ID before you start your upgraded Liferay for the first time. Once the upgrade is complete, you can remove those rights until the next upgrade.

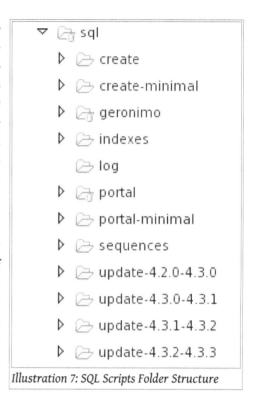

Illustration 7: SQL Scripts Folder Structure

Liferay provides an SQL script archive download on the web site. It is in the *Additional Files* section of the Downloads page. Download this file and unzip it. You will find that it contains a folder structure that is broken down by the type of script (full, minimal, or upgrade), and then further by database vendor type.

It is best to use the *create-minimal* script if you are installing a fresh version of Liferay on development, QA, or production server. This script creates the necessary Liferay tables in the database, with a minimum configuration. This is most appropriate for a new installation of Liferay.

The *create* script, by contrast, configures a Liferay database with a portion of the content from http://www.liferay.com embedded in it. This can be useful from a development perspective, as it contains working examples of the use of many of Liferay's features, including the Journal Content Management System.

Inside the *create* or *create-minimal* folders are scripts for every database that Liferay supports. A DBA can use the script provided to create the Liferay database, complete with the indexes necessary for optimal performance. Once this is done, be sure that the ID that the portal will use to connect to the database has at least Select, Insert, Update, and Delete permissions. Preferably, however, the ID should also have rights to create, modify, and drop tables and indexes, as this makes upgrading easier. This, however, is not necessary for the daily operation of Liferay.

Once your DBA has created the database and provided the credentials for accessing it, you are ready to begin 1) making a bundle enterprise-ready or 2) manually installing Liferay on your application server.

Turning a Bundle into an Enterprise Portal

Liferay Portal is distributed with the following bundle options for servlet containers and full JavaEE application servers:

- Geronimo+Tomcat
- Glassfish
- JBoss+Jetty 4.0
- JBoss+Tomcat 4.0
- JBoss+Tomcat 4.2
- Jetty
- JOnAS+Jetty
- JOnAS+Tomcat
- Pramati
- Resin
- Tomcat 5.5 for JDK 1.4
- Tomcat 5.5 for JDK 5.0
- Tomcat 6.0

Choose your preferred bundle and download it from the downloads page on Liferay's web site. A prerequisite for running any of the bundles is that you have the proper version of Java (1.4 or 1.5) installed on the machine to which you are installing Liferay. Make sure that you have also created the JAVA_HOME variable and have pointed it to your Java installation.

Unzip the bundle to the location from which you are going to run it. For example, you might use c:\apps in Windows or /usr/local/ in Linux or UNIX variants. The default bundle installation of Liferay Portal uses an embedded database. While this is a good method to have it up and running fast for reviewing or developing, it has several drawbacks:

- Only one user can access it at a time. This is because the data is stored on a file on disk and HSQL locks it when doing changes.
- The data is stored inside the application server and might be lost on redeployment.

Obviously, you do not want to be running Liferay against the embedded database. Fortunately,

Liferay has great support for a good number of production-ready databases, and it is easy to configure Liferay to use them. The exact instructions will depend on the application server and database, but can be summarized as:

1. Create the database in your DBMS manager of choice (see the above section labeled *Database Setup* for further information)

2. Reconfigure the Data Source named LiferayPool in your Application Server or servlet container to point to the recently created database. The bundles by default have this configured to go to the embedded database

3. Start Liferay. If your DBAs have given the Create Table permissions to the user ID Liferay will be using to connect to the database, Liferay will create the tables automatically and start. Otherwise, you will have had to prepare the database first by running the appropriate *create* script.

Refer to the manual installation instructions below for further details on configuring the various application servers. There is no difference between the Liferay bundles and the regular distribution archives of the application servers as they are available from their own sites, with the exception that Liferay is pre-installed in them.

FURTHER CONFIGURATION

The configuration in the bundle is set to connect to a mail server installed on the same machine as the application server (referred to as localhost in the configuration). It also assumes that certain paths are present in the system. You will likely need to customize these settings for your particular environment. We will go over these settings in Chapter Two.

Installing Liferay on an Existing Application Server

This section contains detailed instructions for installing Liferay Portal using its WAR distribution. This allows system administrators to deploy Liferay in existing application server installations. It is recommended that you have a good understanding of how to deploy Java EE applications in your application server of choice.

Please note that while Liferay Portal supports a wide rage of databases, for brevity this section assumes MySQL as the database and that the database has already been created. To use other databases, substitute that database JDBC driver and URL for those required by your database. Liferay will automatically create the tables and populate the database the first time it starts. We also assume you have properly configured your server to have Java installed and that your application server is already installed and running successfully.

The following instructions assume an installation on a local machine. When installing to a remote server, substitute localhost with the host name or IP of the server.

GERONIMO 1.1 WITH TOMCAT 5.0.28 / 5.5.17

1. Download and install Geronimo/Tomcat into your preferred directory. From now on, the directory where you installed Geronimo will be referred to as GERONIMO_HOME.

2. Download and install JDK 5. Set an environment variable called JAVA_HOME to point to your JDK directory.

3. Download the WAR for the latest available version of Liferay Portal.

4. Edit GERONIMO_HOME\bin\geronimo.bat (Windows), geronimo.sh (Linux). Insert at approximately line 219:

```
set JAVA_OPTS=-Xms128m -Xmx512m -Dfile.encoding=UTF8 -Duser.timezone=GMT
```

5. Download the Portal 4.3 Dependencies.

6. Point browser to localhost:8080/console to enter Administration Console. Login in as User: system and Password: manager.

7. Click Common Libs under Services. Click Browse, find portal-kernel.jar and add

   Group: Liferay

   Artifact: Portal-kernel

   Version: enter version number of jar

   Type: Jar

   Click *Install*

8. Repeat the last step for each of the libraries in the dependencies ZIP file.

9. Click *Database Pools* under *Services*. Click *Using the Geronimo database pool* wizard.

   Name of Database Pool: LiferayPool

   Database Type: MySQL

   Click *Next*

   Driver Jar: click Download a Driver and select MySQL Connector/J3.0.17

   Click *Next*

   DB User Name: <none>

   DB Password: <none>

   Port: 3306 (default)

   Host: localhost

   Database: lportal

Click *Next*

Click *Test Connection*

Click *Deploy*

10. Click *Deploy New* under *Applications*.

    Archive: Browse for liferay-portal-4.3.x.war (substitute x with the version you've downloaded)

    Click *Install*

11. Click *Web App WARs*.

    Uninstall geronimo/welcome-tomcat/1.1/car

    Start -default/liferayportal/xxxxxxx.../war

12. Open your browser to http://localhost:8080. You should see the default Liferay home page.

GLASSFISH

1. Download the latest liferay-portal-xxx.war and dependencies.

2. Copy the dependencies .jars into *$GLASSFISH_HOME/domains/domain1/lib*, where *$GLASSFISH_HOME* is the directory where Glassfish is installed.

3. Copy *xercesImpl.jar* and JDBC driver into the same place.

4. Start Glassfish if it hasn't already been started. Go to the Glassfish Administration Console at http://localhost:4848.

5. Default login credentials are **user name:** *admin*; **password:** *adminadmin*.

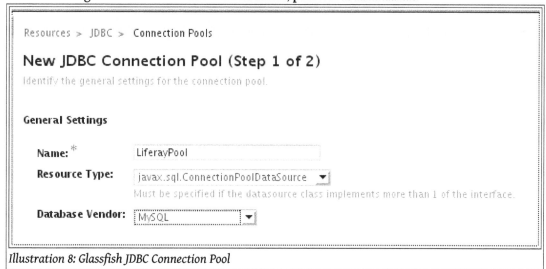

Illustration 8: Glassfish JDBC Connection Pool

6. Under *Other Tasks*, select *Create New JDBC Connection Pool*.

---

7. In the first screen, give it a name of *LiferayPool*, a Resource Type of *javax.sql.ConnectionPoolData-Source*, and select *MySQL* as the Database Vendor. Click *Next*.

8. On the next page, scroll down to the *Additional Properties* section. Find the property called *URL*, and set its value to:

```
jdbc:mysql://localhost/lportal?useUnicode=true&amp;characterEncoding=UTF-8&amp;emu-
lateLocators=true
```

   If your database is not on the same server as Glassfish, substitute your database server's host name for *localhost* above.

9. Click *Add Property*, and add a property called *user* with a value of the user name to connect to the database.

10. Click *Add Property* again, and add a property called *password* with a value of the password to connect to the database.

11. Click *Finish*.

12. You will now see a list of Connection Pools. To test your connection, click the *LiferayPool* and click the *Ping* button. If you get a **Ping Succeeded** message, everything has been set up correctly.

13. Click *JDBC Resources*. You will see a list of JDBC Resources by JNDI Name.

14. Click *New*.

15. Make the JNDI Name *jdbc/LiferayPool* and select the LiferayPool you created earlier.

16. Click *OK*.

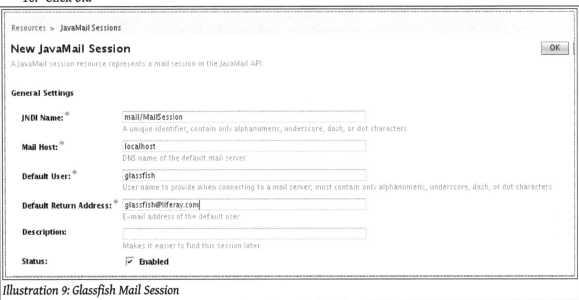

Illustration 9: Glassfish Mail Session

17. Under *Resources*, click *JavaMail Sessions*.

18. Click *New*.

19. Give the JavaMail Session a JNDI name of *mail/MailSession*, and fill out the rest of the form with the appropriate information for your mail server.

20. Click *OK*.

21. Click *Application Server* at the top of the tree hierarchy on the left.

22. Click *JVM Settings -> JVM Options*.

23. Click *Add JVM Option*, and enter the following:

```
-Dcom.sun.enterprise.server.ss.ASQuickStartup=false
```

24. Click *Save*.

25. Log out of the Administration Console and stop Glassfish.

26. Deploy Liferay by copying the liferay-portal-4.x.x.war file you downloaded in step 1 into the *$GLASSFISH_HOME/domains/domain1/autodeploy* directory.

27. Start Glassfish. When Liferay finishes starting, open http://localhost:8080 in your browser. You should see the default Liferay home page.

JETTY 5.1.1

1. Download and install Jetty 5.1.10-all.zip.

   Note: Only this version of Jetty is supported by Liferay. Others may work but will not be covered in this documentation. From now on the home directory where you installed Jetty will be called $JETTY_HOME.

2. Download liferay-portal-xxx.war.

3. Download Liferay's Portal Dependencies.

4. Create a *$JETTY_HOME/lib/ext* directory and copy unzip the dependencies in it.

5. Create a database for Liferay. For example:

```
create  database  lportal  character  set  utf8;
```

   Liferay will automatically create the tables and populate it the first time it starts.

6. Edit *$JETTY_HOME/extra/etc/start-plus.config*.

```
$(jetty.home)/lib/ext/
$(jetty.home)/lib/ext/*
```

7. Create a data source bound to *jdbc/LiferayPool* by editing *$JETTY_HOME/etc/jetty.xml*.

```
<Call name="addService">
        <Arg>
                <New  class="org.mortbay.jetty.plus.JotmService">
```

```
                        <Set   name="Name">TransactionMgr</Set>
                        <Call   name="addDataSource">
                                <Arg>jdbc/LiferayPool</Arg>
                                <Arg>
                                        <New   class="org.enhydra.jdbc.standard.Stand-
ardXADataSource">
                                                <Set   name="DriverName">com.mysql.jd-
bc.Driver</Set>
<Set name="Url">jdbc:mysql://localhost/lportal?
useUnicode=true&amp;characterEncoding=UTF-8</Set>
                                                <Set   name="User"></Set>
                                                <Set   name="Password"></Set>
                                        </New>
                                </Arg>
                                <Arg>
                                        <New   class="org.enhydra.jdbc.pool.Stand-
ardXAPoolDataSource">
                                                <Arg   type="Integer">4</Arg>
                                                <Set   name="MinSize">4</Set>
                                                <Set   name="MaxSize">15</Set>
                                        </New>
                                </Arg>
                        </Call>
                </New>
        </Arg>
</Call>
```

8. Download *mysql-connector-java-{$version}-bin.jar* and copy to to *$JETTY_HOME/lib/ext*. This is the JDBC driver for MySQL. If you are using a different database, copy the appropriate driver.

9. Create a mail session bound to *mail/MailSession* by editing *$JETTY_HOME/etc/jetty.xml*:

```
<Call name="addService">
<Arg>
<New   class="org.mortbay.jetty.plus.MailService">
<Set   name="Name">MailService</Set>
<Set   name="JNDI">mail/MailSession</Set>
<Put   name="mail.smtp.host">localhost</Put>
</New>
</Arg>
</Call>
```

10. Create *$JETTY_HOME/etc/jaas.config*.

```
PortalRealm {
com.liferay.portal.kernel.security.jaas.PortalLoginModule   required;
};
```

11. Create directory *$JETTY_HOME/webapps/root* and unpack *liferay-portal-4.3.x.war* into it.

12. To add support for accessing Liferay's services remotely and to access the document library using WebDAV follow these steps:

     1. Download *tunnel-web.war.*

     2. Create a directory called *$JETTY_HOME/webapps/tunnel* and unzip the WAR contents inside.

13. Repeat the previous step for *cms-web.war* to use the legacy Liferay CMS. If this is a new installation, you do not need to do this.

14. Go to *$JETTY_HOME/webapps/root/WEB-INF/lib* and delete *xercesImpl.jar* and *xml-apis.jar.*

15. Copy *$JETTY_HOME/webapps/root/WEB-INF/lib/commons-logging.jar* to *$JETTY_HOME/ext* (overwriting existing one).

16. Create batch file.

     1. Create a directory *$JETTY_HOME/bin.*

     2. Create *run.bat* (Note, this is for Windows platform. For other platforms, configure accordingly).

```
@echo off

if  ""  ==  "%JAVA_HOME%"  goto  errorJavaHome

%JAVA_HOME%/bin/java  -Xmx512m  -Dfile.encoding=UTF8  -Duser.timezone=GMT  -Djava.secur-
ity.auth.login.config=../etc/jaas.config  -DSTART=../extra/etc/start-plus.config
-jar  ../start.jar  ../etc/jetty.xml

goto  end

:errorJavaHome
echo  JAVA_HOME  not  defined.

goto  end

:end
```

Note: If you get a java.lang.OutOfMemoryError exception while starting up Jetty, give your JVM more memory by setting *-Xmx512m.*

Start Liferay by running *run.bat.* Open your browser to http://localhost:8080. You should see the default Liferay home page.

JBoss 4.03sp1 / 4.04 / 4.05 with Jetty 5.1.1

1. Download and install Jboss AS into your preferred directory. This directory will be referred to below as *$JBOSS_HOME.*

2. Download the latest version of the liferay-portal-4.3.x.war.

3. Create file $JBOSS_HOME/server/default/deploy/liferay-ds.xml with following content:

```
<?xml version="1.0"?>
```

```
<datasources>
      <local-tx-datasource>
            <jndi-name>jdbc/LiferayPool</jndi-name>
            <connection-url>
                  jdbc:mysql://localhost/lportal?useUnicode=true&amp;characterEncod-
ing=UTF-8
            </connection-url>
            <driver-class>com.mysql.jdbc.Driver</driver-class>
            <user-name></user-name>
            <password></password>
            <min-pool-size>0</min-pool-size>
      </local-tx-datasource>
</datasources>
```

4. Go to *$JBOSS_HOME/server/default/lib/*. Download mysql-connector-java-{$version}-bin.jar and copy to this directory. (This is the JDBC connector for MySQL, for other databases, go to appropriate website to download.)

5. Create a database for Liferay. For example:

```
create  database  lportal  character  set  utf8;
```

Liferay will automatically create the tables and populate it the first time it starts.

6. Download Liferay's Portal 4.3 Dependencies. Unzip to *$JBOSS_HOME/server/default/lib*.

7. Set mail properties by replacing the contents of *$JBOSS_HOME/server/default/deploy/mail-service.xml* with:

```
<?xml version="1.0"?>
<server>
<mbean  code="org.jboss.mail.MailService"  name="jboss:service=MailSession">
<attribute  name="JNDIName">mail/MailSession</attribute>
<attribute  name="User">nobody</attribute>
<attribute  name="Password">password</attribute>
<attribute  name="Configuration">
<configuration>
<property  name="mail.store.protocol"  value="imap"  />
<property  name="mail.transport.protocol"  value="smtp"  />
<property  name="mail.imap.host"  value="localhost"  />
<property  name="mail.pop3.host"  value="localhost"  />
<property  name="mail.smtp.host"  value="localhost"  />
</configuration>
</attribute>
</mbean>
</server>
```

8. Configure JAAS. Edit *$JBOSS_HOME/server/default/conf/login-config.xml* and comment out the entire XML for policy 'other' in lines 140-156.

```
<!--<application-policy name = "other">-->
      ...
```

```
        <!--<authentication>
                <login-module  code  =  "org.jboss.security.auth.spi.UsersRoles-
LoginModule"
                        flag  =  "required"  />
        </authentication>
    </application-policy>-->
```

9. Deploy liferay-portal-4.3.x.war.

   1. Create directory *$JBOSS_HOME/server/default/deploy/liferay-portal.war*.

   2. Unzip liferay-portal-4.3.x.war to directory.

   3. Go to *$JBOSS_HOME/server/default/deploy/liferay-portal.war/lib*.

   4. Move dom4j.jar, jaxen.jar to *$JBOSS_HOME/lib*.

   5. Move commons-collections.jar to *$JBOSS_HOME/server/default/lib*.

   6. Remove hibernate3.jar,jboss-hibernate.jar from *$JBOSS_HOME/server/default/lib*.

10. Edit *$JBOSS_HOME/server/default/deploy/jbossjca-service.xml*. Change Debug attribute in line 63 from true to false:

```
<attribute   name="Debug">false</attribute>
```

11. In *$JBOSS/server/default/deploy/jbossws14.sar/META-INF/jboss-service.xml*, comment out the deployer service for JSE and EJB2.1 endpoints (lines 36-40 and lines 45-49).

```
<!--<mbean name="jboss.ws:service=WebServiceDeployerEJB21" code="org.jboss.ws.server-
.WebServiceDeployerEJB21">
        <depends-list  optional-attribute-name="Interceptables">
            <depends-list-element>jboss.ejb:service=EJBDeployer</depends-list-
element>
        </depends-list>
    </mbean>-->
```

lines 72-75

```
<!--<mbean name="jboss.ws:service=WebServiceDeployerNestedJSE" code="or-
g.jboss.ws.server.WebServiceDeployerNestedJSE">
        <depends  optional-attribute-name="MainDeployer"  proxy-
type="attribute">jboss.system:service=MainDeployer</depends>
        <depends>jboss.ws:service=WebServiceDeployerJSE</depends>
    </mbean>-->
```

12. Edit *$JBOSS_HOME/server/default/deploy/jms/jbossmq-destinations-service.xml*. Clear out text between server tags:

```
<?xml version="1.0"?>
<server>
</server>
```

13. Start JBoss. Open your browser to http://localhost:8080. You should see the default Liferay home

page.

JBoss 4.03sp1 / 4.04 / 4.05 / 4.2 with Tomcat

1. Download and install JBoss AS into your preferred directory. From now on, the directory where you installed JBoss will be referred to as $JBOSS_HOME.

2. Download liferay-portal-4.3.x.war.

3. Edit *$JBOSS_HOME/server/default/deploy/jbossweb-tomcat55.sar/conf/web.xml*. Replace the default servlet (lines 79-91) :

```
<servlet>
        <servlet-name>default</servlet-name>
        <servlet-class>org.apache.catalina.servlets.DefaultServlet</servlet-
class>
        <init-param>
            <param-name>debug</param-name>
            <param-value>0</param-value>
        </init-param>
        <init-param>
            <param-name>listings</param-name>
            <param-value>true</param-value>
        </init-param>
        <load-on-startup>1</load-on-startup>
    </servlet>
```

with:

```
<servlet>
        <servlet-name>default</servlet-name>
        <servlet-class>org.apache.catalina.servlets.DefaultServlet</servlet-
class>
        <init-param>
            <param-name>debug</param-name>
            <param-value>0</param-value>
        </init-param>
        <init-param>
            <param-name>listings</param-name>
            <param-value>false</param-value>
        </init-param>
        <init-param>
            <param-name>input</param-name>
            <param-value>4096</param-value>
        </init-param>
        <init-param>
            <param-name>output</param-name>
            <param-value>4096</param-value>
        </init-param>
        <load-on-startup>1</load-on-startup>
```

```
        </servlet>
```

4. Create *$JBOSS_HOME/server/default/deploy/liferay-ds.xml* with following content:

```
<datasources>
        <local-tx-datasource>
            <jndi-name>jdbc/LiferayPool</jndi-name>
            <connection-url>
                    jdbc:mysql://localhost/lportal?useUnicode=true&amp;characterEncod-
ing=UTF-8
            </connection-url>
            <driver-class>com.mysql.jdbc.Driver</driver-class>
            <user-name></user-name>
            <password></password>
            <min-pool-size>0</min-pool-size>
        </local-tx-datasource>
</datasources>
```

5. Go to *$JBOSS_HOME/server/default/lib/*, download mysql-connector-java-{$version}-bin.jar and copy to this directory. This is the JDBC driver for MySQL. If you are using a different database, copy the appropriate driver.

6. Download Liferay's Portal Dependencies. Unzip the downloaded archive into *$JBOSS_HOME/server/default/lib*.

7. Set mail properties by replacing the contents of *$JBOSS_HOME/server/default/deploy/mail-service.xml* with:

```
<?xml version="1.0"?>
<server>
<mbean  code="org.jboss.mail.MailService"  name="jboss:service=MailSession">
<attribute   name="JNDIName">mail/MailSession</attribute>
<attribute   name="User">nobody</attribute>
<attribute   name="Password">password</attribute>
<attribute   name="Configuration">
<configuration>
<property  name="mail.store.protocol"  value="imap"  />
<property  name="mail.transport.protocol"  value="smtp"  />
<property  name="mail.imap.host"  value="localhost"  />
<property  name="mail.pop3.host"  value="localhost"  />
<property  name="mail.smtp.host"  value="localhost"  />
</configuration>
</attribute>
</mbean>
</server>
```

8. Configure JAAS. Edit *$JBOSS_HOME/server/default/conf/login-config.xml* and comment out the entire XML for policy other in lines 140-156.

```
<!--<application-policy name = "other">-->
        ...
```

```
              <!--<authentication>
                   <login-module  code = "org.jboss.security.auth.spi.UsersRoles-
      LoginModule"
                            flag = "required" />
              </authentication>
          </application-policy>-->
```

9. Deploy liferay-portal-xxx.war.

   ● Create new directory *$JBOSS_HOME/server/default/deploy/liferay-portal.war*.

   ● Unzip liferay-portal-4.3.war to directory.

   ● Go into *$JBOSS_HOME/server/default/deploy/liferay-portal.war/lib*.

      ● Move dom4j.jar, jaxen.jar to *$JBOSS_HOME/lib*.

      ● Move commons-collections.jar goes to *$JBOSS_HOME/server/default/lib*.

      ● remove hibernate3.jar, jboss-hibernate.jar from *$JBOSS_HOME/server/default/lib*.

10. Edit *$JBOSS_HOME/server/default/deploy/jbossjca-service.xml*. Change the Debug attribute in line 63 from true to false:

```
<attribute  name="Debug">false</attribute>
```

11. Edit *$JBOSS_HOME/server/default/deploy/jms/jbossmq-destinations-service.xml*. Clear out text between server tags:

```
<?xml version="1.0"?>
<server>
</server>
```

12. Start JBoss. Open your browser to http://localhost:8080. You should see the default Liferay home page.

ORACLE APPLICATION SERVER (OC4J)

These instructions assume you have an installed OC4J container in a folder that will be referred to as *$OC4J_HOME*.

Unzip the dependencies archive (which is downloadable from Liferay's web site) into *$OC4J_HOME/j2ee/home/applib*. If you're using a database other than Oracle, put your JDBC driver here as well.

Shared Libraries

You will first need to create a Shared Library within OC4J that includes Apache's XML parser, which Liferay requires. You may either download this from http://xerces.apache.org or you can retrieve the files *xercesImpl.jar and xml-apis.jar* from the Liferay .war file.

1. Start OC4J. Go to http://<server>:8888/em.

2. Login in with the administrative credentials you used when you installed OC4J (user ID: oc4jadmin, password of your choosing).

3. Click *Administration -> Shared Libraries*.

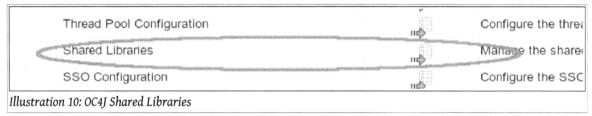

Illustration 10: OC4J Shared Libraries

4. Click the *Create* button. For Shared Library Name, enter *apache.xml* and for Shared Library Version, enter the version number of Xerces that you downloaded. Click *Next*.

5. You will add two archives to this Shared Library: *xercesImpl.jar* and *xml-apis.jar*. Click the *Add* button and browse to where you expanded your download of Xerces. First, add *xercesImpl.jar*, then click the *Add* button again and add *xml-apis.jar*. Click *Next*.

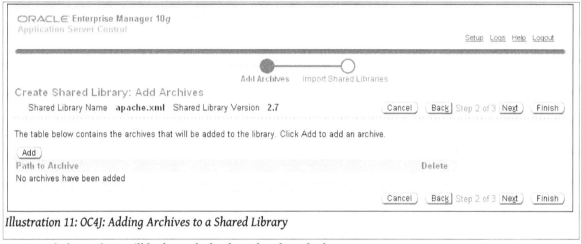

Illustration 11: OC4J: Adding Archives to a Shared Library

6. Click *Finish*. You'll be brought back to the Shared Library page.

7. Next, click the *OC4J: home* link in the top left of the page. This will bring you back to the home page of the OC4J console.

Database and Connection Pool

1. Click *Administration -> JDBC Resources*.

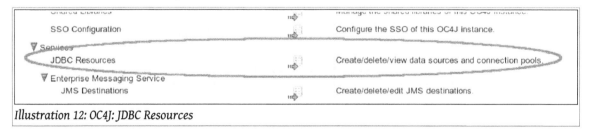

Illustration 12: OC4J: JDBC Resources

---

2. Under *Connection Pools*, click *Create*.

3. Select *New Connection Pool* and click *Continue*.

4. Give it a name, such as *LiferayPool*. If you are not using an Oracle database, you will have to specify the connection factory class manually. For example, the connection factory class for MySQL is *com.mysql.jdbc.jdbc2.optional.MysqlConnectionPoolDataSource*.

5. Fill out the JDBC URL to your database. You should have already configured your database and optionally run the Liferay create script.

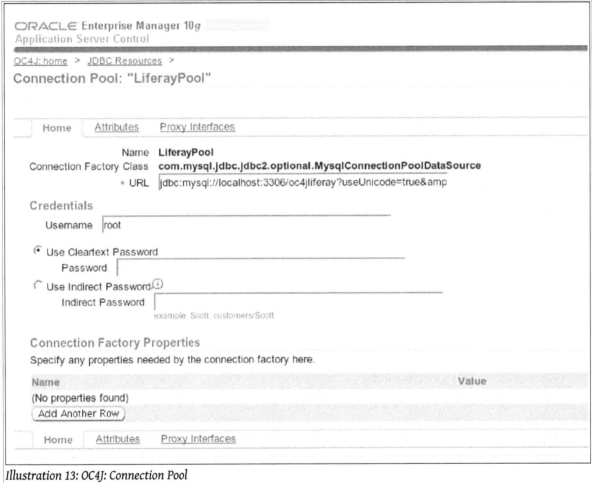

Illustration 13: OC4J: Connection Pool

6. Click *Finish*. Under *Data Sources*, click *Create*. Select *Managed Data Source* (default) and click *Continue*.

7. Give it a name (*LiferayDataSource*) and a JNDI location of *jdbc/LiferayPool*.

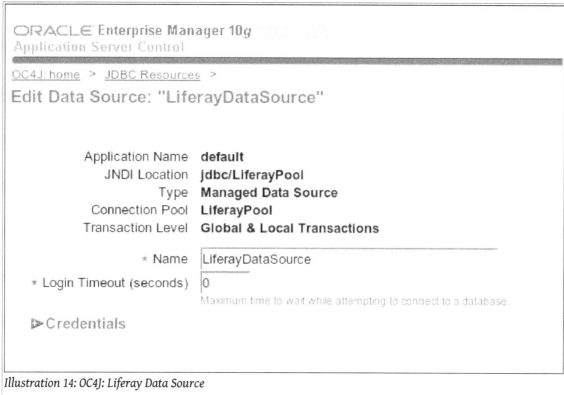

Illustration 14: OC4J: Liferay Data Source

8. Select the Connection Pool you created in the previous step and then click *Finish*.

9. Click the *Test Connection* icon. If you are not using an Oracle database, change the test SQL to something like *SELECT * from User_*, and then click Test. You should get a message saying *Connection to "LiferayDataSource" established successfully*. If not, go back and check your settings.

10. Click the *OC4J: home* link in the top left of the page.

Installing Liferay

1. Click *Applications*.

2. Click *Deploy*. Leave the default selected under Archive, and click the *Browse* button. Browse to where your Liferay .war file is.

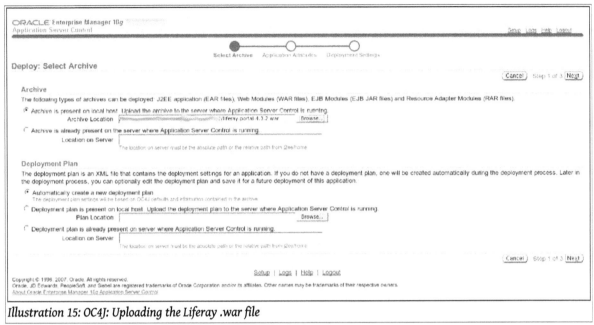

Illustration 15: OC4J: Uploading the Liferay .war file

3. With the location of the Liferay .war file in the Archive Location field, click *Next*. Wait a while while OC4J uploads the Liferay .war file.

4. The next screen allows you to give the application a name and set its context root. Use *Liferay* for the name and */portal* as the context root. Click *Next*.

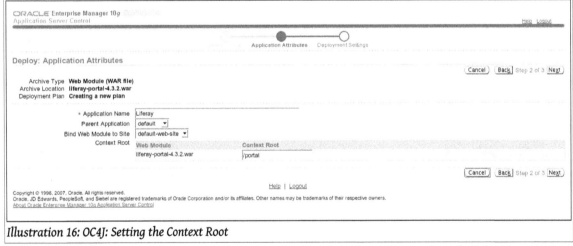

Illustration 16: OC4J: Setting the Context Root

5. On the next screen, click the *Configure Class Loading* Link. You will see a list of all the Shared Libraries currently defined in the server. On this first page, click the *apache.xml* Shared Library that you created previously.

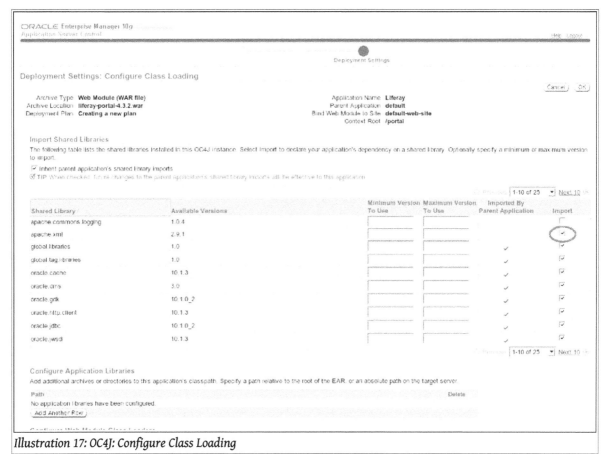

Illustration 17: OC4J: Configure Class Loading

6. Click the *Next 10* link at the bottom right of the page.

7. At the bottom of the next page, there may be an *oracle.xml* Shared Library. It also may appear on another page. If you don't see it, keep clicking the *Next 10* link until you find it. When you do find it, uncheck it.

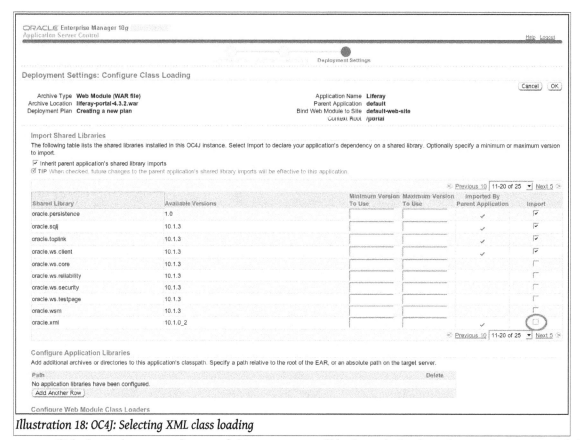

Illustration 18: OC4J: Selecting XML class loading

8. Click the *OK* button at the top of this page. You will be brought back to the previous screen. Click the *Deploy* button at the top right of the screen. OC4J will then deploy Liferay.

Illustration 19: OC4J: Deploying Liferay

9. Click the *Return* button at the top of the page.

10. Next, navigate to *$OC4J_HOME/j2ee/home/applications/Liferay/liferay-portal-<version>/WEB-INF/classes*. In this folder should be a file called *portal-ext.properties*. Open this file in a text editor. Add a directive for Portal Context, and give it a value of /portal, like so:

```
portal.ctx=/portal
```

11. Save this file.

12. Next, stop the OC4J instance to which you just installed Liferay. After it comes down, restart it. You should see Liferay start when the OC4J container starts.

13. You may see some messages stating that there are already some shared libraries on the class path, and that OC4J is going to use the ones it has rather than the ones that came with Liferay. You can remove these message either one of two ways:

    1. Go to *$OC4J_HOME/j2ee/home/applications/Liferay/liferay-portal-<version>/WEB-INF/lib* and remove the .jar files that are listed in the messages. Then shut down and restart OC4J.

    2. Create Shared Libraries for each one of the .jar files listed in the messages as you did above for the apache.xml .jars. Once you have done that, you will have to undeploy Liferay and then redeploy Liferay and select the Shared Libraries you have created for it during the deployment.

14. Once you have done one of the two steps above, OC4J should start normally without any messages other than the standard Liferay ones:

```
Starting OC4J from /usr/local/java/oc4j/j2ee/home ...
```

```
07/10/10 12:32:39 Loading code-source:/usr/local/java/oc4j/j2ee/home/applica-
tions/Liferay/liferay-portal-4.3.2/WEB-INF/lib/portal-impl.jar!/system.properties

07/10/10 12:32:40 Loading code-source:/usr/local/java/oc4j/j2ee/home/applica-
tions/Liferay/liferay-portal-4.3.2/WEB-INF/lib/portal-impl.jar!/portal.properties

07/10/10 12:32:40 Loading file:/usr/local/java/oc4j/j2ee/home/applications/Liferay/liferay-
portal-4.3.2/WEB-INF/classes/portal-ext.properties

07/10/10 12:32:49 Starting Liferay Enterprise Portal 4.3.2 (Owen / Build 4302 / September
18, 2007)

12:32:53,180 INFO  [com.liferay.portal.spring.hibernate.DynamicDialect] Determining dialect
for MySQL 5

12:32:53,191 INFO  [com.liferay.portal.spring.hibernate.DynamicDialect] Using dialect or-
g.hibernate.dialect.MySQLDialect

12:32:58,248 INFO  [com.liferay.portal.deploy.hot.PluginPackageHotDeployListener] Reading
plugin package for the root context

12:32:58,941 INFO  [com.liferay.portal.kernel.deploy.hot.HotDeployUtil] Initializing hot de-
ploy manager 11099528

12:32:59,322 INFO  [com.liferay.portal.kernel.util.ServerDetector] Detected server oc4j

12:32:59,616 INFO  [com.liferay.portal.kernel.deploy.auto.AutoDeployDir] Auto deploy scanner
started for /home/sezovr/liferay/deploy

07/10/10 12:33:02 Loading code-source:/usr/local/java/oc4j/j2ee/home/applica-
tions/Liferay/liferay-portal-4.3.2/WEB-INF/lib/portal-impl.jar!/portal.properties for 10092

07/10/10 12:33:02 Loading file:/usr/local/java/oc4j/j2ee/home/applications/Liferay/liferay-
portal-4.3.2/WEB-INF/classes/portal-ext.properties for 10092

07/10/10 12:33:03 Oracle Containers for J2EE 10g (10.1.3.3.0)  initialized
```

RESIN 3.0.X / 3.1.X

1. Download and install Resin into your preferred directory. From now on, the directory where you installed Resin will be referred to as *$RESIN_HOME*.

2. Edit *$RESIN_HOME/conf/resin.conf*. Replace lines 60-64 with:

```
<class-loader>
        <tree-loader  path="${resin.home}/lib"/>
        <tree-loader  path="${server.root}/lib"/>
        <compiling-loader  path="${server.rootDir}/common/classes"/>
        <library-loader  path="${server.rootDir}/common/lib"/>
    </class-loader>
```

And add the following:

```
<database>
<jndi-name>jdbc/LiferayPool</jndi-name>
<driver  type="com.mysql.jdbc.Driver">
<url>jdbc:mysql://localhost/lportal?useUnicode=true&amp;characterEncoding=UTF-8</url>
<user></user>
<password></password>
</driver>
<prepared-statement-cache-size>8</prepared-statement-cache-size>
<max-connections>20</max-connections>
<max-idle-time>30s</max-idle-time>
</database>
<resource  jndi-name="mail/MailSession"  type="javax.mail.Session">
```

```
<init>
<mail.store.protocol>imap</mail.store.protocol>
<mail.transport.protocol>smtp</mail.transport.protocol>
<mail.imap.host>localhost</mail.imap.host>
<mail.pop3.host>localhost</mail.pop3.host>
<mail.smtp.host>localhost</mail.smtp.host>
</init>
</resource>
<system-property
 javax.xml.parsers.DocumentBuilderFactory="org.apache.xerces.jaxp.DocumentBuilder-
FactoryImpl"
 />
<system-property javax.xml.parsers.SAXParserFactory="org.apache.xerces.jaxp.SAX-
ParserFactoryImpl" />
<system-property javax.xml.transform.TransformerFactory="org.apache.xalan.pro-
cessor.TransformerFactoryImpl" />
<system-property org.xml.sax.driver="org.apache.xerces.parsers.SAXParser" />
```

3. Go to *$RESIN_HOME* and create new directory *common/lib*. Download *mysql-connector-java-{$version}-bin.jar* and copy to this directory. (This is the JDBC connector for MySQL, for other databases, go to appropriate website to download.)

4. Create a database for Liferay. For example:

```
create database lportal character set utf8;
```

Liferay will automatically create the tables and populate it the first time it starts.

5. Download the Liferay Portal 4.3 Dependencies and unzip into *$RESIN_HOME/common/lib*.

6. Delete contents of *$RESIN_HOME/webapps/ROOT*.

7. Unzip liferay-portal-4.3.x.war to *$RESIN_HOME/webapps/ROOT*.

8. Download the sources of Liferay Portal and unzip them to a temporary directory:

    1. Go to *$LIFERAY_SOURCE/lib/development/* and copy activation.jar and mail.jar to *$RESIN_HOME/common/lib*. Copy saxpath.jar and xalan.jar to *$RESIN_HOME/lib*.

    2. Go to *$LIFERAY_SOURCE/lib/portal* and copy xercesImpl.jar and xml-apis.jar to *$RESIN_HOME/lib*.

9. To start the server, open a command prompt, navigate to the $RESIN_HOME and type:

```
java -jar lib/resin.jar start
```

10. Open your browser to http://localhost:8080. You should see the default Liferay home page.

TOMCAT 5.0.X / 5.5.X

1. Download and install Tomcat 5.5.X into your preferred directory. From now on, the directory where you installed Tomcat will be referred to as $TOMCAT_HOME.

Note: If you are using JDK 1.4, you must download and install the JDK 1.4 Compatibility Package at http://tomcat.apache.org. For JDK 1.4 users: delete *$TOMCAT_HOME/webapps/ROOT/WEB-INF/lib/xercesImpl.jar*. For JDK 5 users: move *$TOMCAT_HOME/webapps/ROOT/WEB-INF/lib/xercesImpl.jar* to *$TOMCAT_HOME/common/endorsed*.

2. Create and edit *$TOMCAT_HOME/conf/Catalina/localhost/ROOT.xml* to set up the portal web application.

```
<Context path="">
</Context>
```

3. Download liferay-portal-4.3.x.war.

4. Download Liferay's Portal 4.3 Dependencies. Create a *$TOMCAT_HOME/common/lib/ext* directory and unzip the dependencies ZIP in there. If the files do not extract to this directory, make sure they are in the correct directory by moving them there.

5. Edit $TOMCAT_HOME/conf/catalina.properties:

```
common.loader=
        ${catalina.home}/common/classes,\
        ...\
        ${catalina.home}/common/lib/ext/*.jar
```

6. Make sure your database server is installed and is working. If it's installed in a different machine, make sure that it's accessible from the one where Liferay is being installed.

7. Configure data sources for your database. Make sure the JDBC driver for your database is accessible by Tomcat. Obtain the JDBC driver for your version of the database server. In the case of MySQL use *mysql-connector-java-{$version}-bin.jar*. Next, copy the JAR file to *$TOMCAT_HOME/common/lib/ext*.

8. Edit *$TOMCAT_HOME/conf/Catalina/localhost/ROOT.xml*.

```
<Context...>
        <Resource
                name="jdbc/LiferayPool"
                auth="Container"
                type="javax.sql.DataSource"
                driverClassName="com.mysql.jdbc.Driver"
                url="jdbc:mysql://localhost/lportal?useUnicode=true&amp;characterEn-
coding=UTF-8"
                username=""
                password=""
                maxActive="100"
                maxIdle="30"
                maxWait="10000"
        />
</Context>
```

9. Create a database for Liferay. For example:

```
create database lportal character set utf8;
```

Liferay will automatically create the tables and populate it the first time it starts.

10. Create a mail session bound to *mail/MailSession*. Edit *$TOM-CAT_HOME/conf/Catalina/localhost/ROOT.xml* and configure a mail session.

```
<Context...>
<Resource
name="mail/MailSession"
auth="Container"
type="javax.mail.Session"
mail.transport.protocol="smtp"
mail.smtp.host="localhost"
mail.store.protocol="imap"
mail.imap.host="localhost"
/>
</Context>
```

11. Configure JAAS. Edit *$TOMCAT_HOME/conf/Catalina/localhost/ROOT.xml* and configure a security realm.

```
<Context...>
<Realm
className="org.apache.catalina.realm.JAASRealm"
appName="PortalRealm"
userClassNames="com.liferay.portal.security.jaas.PortalPrincipal"
roleClassNames="com.liferay.portal.security.jaas.PortalRole"
debug="99"
useContextClassLoader="false"
/>
</Context>
```

12. To add support for accessing Liferay's services remotely and to access the document library using WebDAV, follow these steps:

    1. Download *tunnel-web.war.*

    2. Create a directory called *$TOMCAT_HOME/webapps/tunnel-web* and unzip the WAR contents inside.

    3. Some versions of Tomcat require an extra step: make a copy of *ROOT.xml* in the same directory and name it *tunnel.xml.*

14. Repeat the previous step for cms-web.war to use the legacy Liferay CMS. If this is a new installation, ignore this step.

15. Create *$TOMCAT_HOME/conf/jaas.config.*

```
PortalRealm {
com.liferay.portal.kernel.security.jaas.PortalLoginModule  required;
};
```

16. Edit *$TOMCAT_HOME/bin/catalina.bat* (on Windows) or *$TOMCAT_HOME/bin/catalina.sh* (on Linux / Mac / Unix) so that Tomcat can reference the login module.

```
rem ----- Execute...
set JAVA_OPTS=-Xms128m  -Xmx512m  -Dfile.encoding=UTF8  -Duser.timezone=GMT
-Djava.security.auth.login.config=%CATALINA_HOME%/conf/jaas.config
```

17. Delete contents *$TOMCAT_HOME/webapps/ROOT* directory. This undeploys the default Tomcat home page.

18. Unpack liferay-portal-4.3.x.war to *$TOMCAT_HOME/webapps/ROOT*.

19. For supporting UTF-8 URI Encoding, edit *$TOMCAT_HOME/conf/server.xml*:

```
<!-- Define a non-SSL HTTP/1.1 Connector on port 8080 -->
    <Connector  port="8080"  maxHttpHeaderSize="8192"
                            maxThreads="150"  minSpareThreads="25"  max-
SpareThreads="75"
                            enableLookups="false"  redirectPort="8443"  ac-
ceptCount="100"
                            connectionTimeout="20000"  disableUploadTimeout="true"
                            URIEncoding="UTF-8"
    />
```

20. Run Tomcat, point browser to http://localhost:8080. You should see the default Liferay home page.

WebLogic 8 sp 5

Installation

1. Put the necessary global .jars on the server class path. You can do this by creating a lib folder in your domain folder (i.e., *bea/user_projects/domains/mydomain/lib*) and then copying the following .jars into this directory:

- portal-kernel.jar
- portal-service.jar
- portlet.jar
- database driver (i.e., MySQL) .jar
- xml-apis.jar and xercesImpl.jar (downloadable from http://xml.apache.org)

2. Inside your domain folder is a *startWebLogic.sh* (Unix) or *startWebLogic.cmd* (Windows) script. Open it and add the following (follow the syntax for your operating system):

```
# Set Liferay classpath
LIFERAY_WL_HOME="/<path to>/bea/user_projects/domains/mydomain/lib"
CLASSPATH="${WEBLOGIC_CLASSPATH}:${POINTBASE_CLASSPATH}:${JAVA_HOME}/jre/lib/rt.jar:$
{WL_HOME}/server/lib/webservices.jar:${LIFERAY_WL_HOME}/xercesImpl.jar:$
{LIFERAY_WL_HOME}/xml-apis.jar:${LIFERAY_WL_HOME}/portlet.jar:$
{LIFERAY_WL_HOME}/portal-kernel.jar:${LIFERAY_WL_HOME}/portal-service.jar:$
{LIFERAY_WL_HOME}/mysql-connector-java-5.0.5-bin.jar"
```

3. Start WebLogic.

4. Open the WebLogic Server Administration Console.

5. Under JDBC, click Connection Pools.

Illustration 20: Connecting to a database in WebLogic 8

6. Click *Configure a New Connection Pool.*

7. Select MySQL from the list. Select Other for Driver Type.

8. For the driver class name, use *com.mysql.jdbc.jdbc2.optional.MysqlConnectionPoolDataSource.*

9. For the database URL, use:

```
jdbc:mysql://<your server>/<your db name>?useUnicode=true&amp;characterEncoding=UTF-8
```

10. Use the user name and password you have set up for your database.

11. Click *Test Connection*, and after the connection is successful, click *Create and Deploy.*

12. Under JDBC, click Data Sources.

13. Click Configure a New JDBC Data Source.

14. Enter the name of the data source. The JNDI name should be *jdbc/LiferayPool.*

15. You will be presented with the Connect to Connection Pool screen. Select the Connection Pool you created earlier from the drop down, and click Continue.

16. Select the server to which you want to target this data source, and then click the Create button.

---

17. Under Deployments, click Web Application Modules.

18. Click Deploy a New Web Application Module.

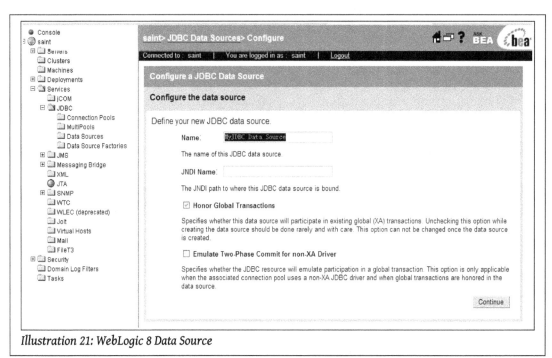

Illustration 21: WebLogic 8 Data Source

19. Select the *Upload Your File(s)* link.

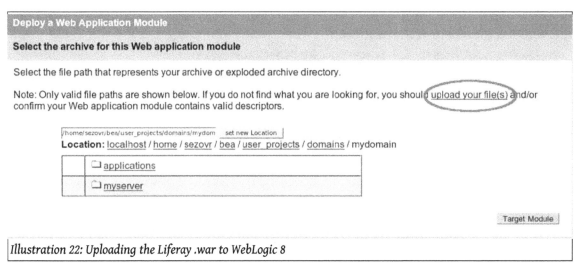

Illustration 22: Uploading the Liferay .war to WebLogic 8

20. Browse to where your Liferay .war file (for WebLogic 8.1, use the Servlet 2.3 .war) is and click the *Upload* button.

21. Select the Liferay .war you just uploaded and click the Target Module button.

22. Click Deploy.

23. Stop WebLogic and restart it. Point your browser to http://localhost:7001. You should see the default Liferay home page.

Troubleshooting

Weblogic 8 doesn't support JDK1.5 and servlet2.4. Make sure you have deployed the servlet 2.3 version of Liferay.

If a SocialBookmarkTag exception is thrown, add *util-taglib.jar* in your liferay-portal-4.x.x war to your domain's *lib* folder and reference it in the startup script you edited above.

If you can't see the home page, check your *weblogic.xml* for Liferay and make sure the following is set:

```
<context-root>/</context-root>
```

WebLogic 9 / 10

These instructions assume that you have already configured a domain and server, and that you have access to the WebLogic console.

Dependency Jars

1. Navigate to the folder which corresponds to the domain to which you will be installing Liferay. Inside this folder is a *lib* folder. Unzip the Liferay dependencies archive to this folder.

2. Copy the JDBC driver for your database to this folder as well.

3. You will also need the *xercesImpl.jar* or you will get SAX parsing errors after you deploy Liferay. You may download this from http://xerces.apache.org. Copy the *xercesImpl.jar* file into this directory.

Illustration 23: WebLogic: Data Sources

Installing Liferay

1. Browse to your WebLogic Console. Click the *Lock & Edit* button above the Domain Structure tree on the left side of the page.

2. From the Domain Structure tree on the left, select Data Sources. Then click the *New* button on the right side of the screen.

3. Give the Data Source a name, such as LiferayDataSource.

4. Define the JNDI name as jdbc/LiferayPool.

5. Select your Database Type and the Driver class, and then click the *Next* button.

---

6. Accept the defaults on the next screen by clicking *Next*.

7. On the next screen, put in your *Database Name, Host Name, Database User Name,* and *Password.* If you have been following the defaults we have been using so far, you would use *lportal, localhost, root,* and no password as the values. Click Next.

8. The next screen allows you to test your database configuration. Click the *Test Connection* button. If the test succeeds, you have configured your database correctly. Check off the server you want to deploy this Data Source to (AdminServer is the default). Click Finish.

9. Click the *Activate Changes* button on the left, above the Domain Structure tree.

10. In the Domain Structure tree, select *Mail Sessions.* Then click the *Lock & Edit* button again to enable modifying these settings.

11. Click the *New* button which is now enabled on the right side of the screen.

12. Give the Mail Session a name, such as LiferayMail.

13. Select your new LiferayMail session from the list by clicking on it.

14. On the screen that appears, define the JNDI name as *mail/MailSession.* Click the *Save* button.

15. Click the *Targets* tab. Check off the server you want to deploy this Data Source to (AdminServer is the default).

16. Click the *Activate Changes* button on the left side of the screen, above the Domain Structure tree.

17. Click the *Deployments* option in the Domain Structure tree on the left side of the screen.

Illustration 24: WebLogic: Mail Sessions

18. Click the *Lock & Edit* button above the Domain Structure tree.

19. Click the *Install* button on the right side of the screen.

20. Click the *Upload your file(s)* link.

21. Browse to where you have stored the Liferay .war file, select it, and then click *Next*.

22. Select the Liferay .war file from the list and click *Next*.

23. Leave *Install this deployment as an application* selected and click Next.

24. Give the application a name (the default name is fine). Leave the other defaults selected and then click Finish.

25. WebLogic will now deploy Liferay. When it is finished, a summary screen is displayed. Click the *Activate Changes* link on the left above the Domain Structure tree.

---

26. In the Deployments screen, select the Liferay application and click the *Start* button. Select *Servicing All Requests* in the pop up.

27. Click *Yes* to continue on the next screen.

Liferay will start. You will be able to get to it by browsing to http://<server name>:7001. If your browser is running on the same machine upon which you have installed Liferay, the URL is http://localhost:7001.

WEBSPHERE 6.0.X.X

Note: Throughout this installation and configuration process, WebSphere will prompt you to Click Save to apply changes to Master Configuration. Do so intermittently to save your changes.

Installation

1. Download Liferay Portal 4.3.x WAR , unzip and compile.

2. Download and extract these Liferay jars to *websphere/appserver/lib/ext*.

    o   Dependency libraries (Liferay Portal Dependencies)

    o   liferay-portal-jaas.jar (Liferay Portal Enterprise JAAS Libraries from Sourceforge)

    o   mysql-connector-java-5.x.x-bin.jar (MySQL)

Set Up Database Service

1. Start WebSphere.

2. Open Administrative Console and login.

3. Click *Resources*, click *JDBC Providers*.

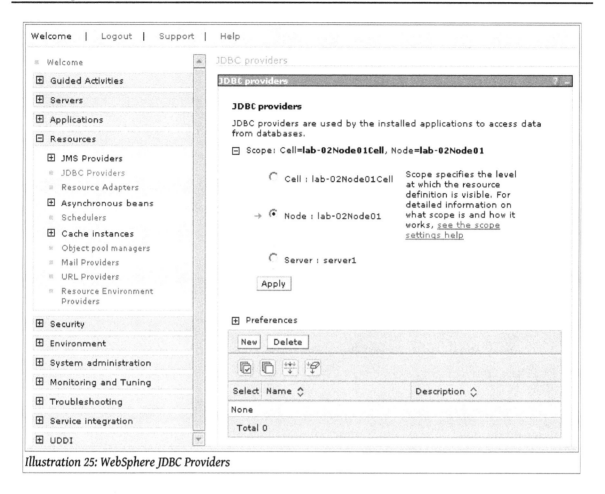

Illustration 25: WebSphere JDBC Providers

4. Click Next.

5. For name, enter name of JDBC provider, e.g. *liferayjdbc*.

6. Clear any text in class path.

7. For Implementation class name enter

```
com.mysql.jdbc.jdbc2.optional.MysqlConnectionPoolDataSource
```

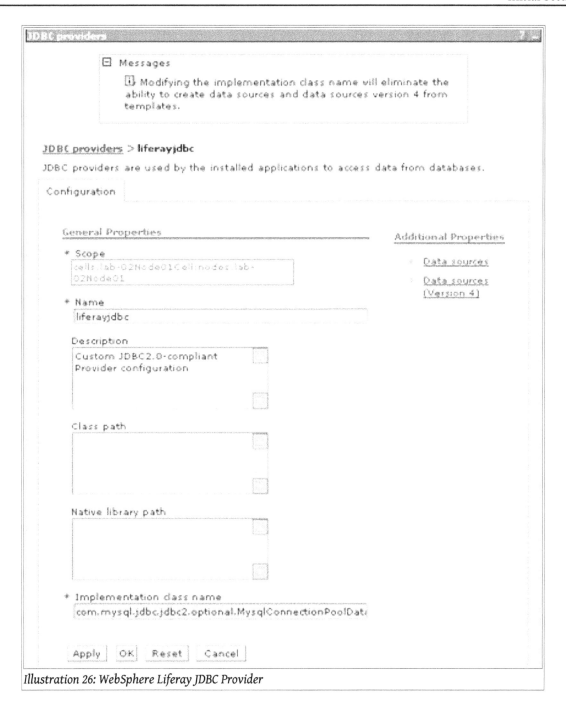

Illustration 26: WebSphere Liferay JDBC Provider

8. Click *OK*.

9. Click *Data sources* under *Additional Properties*.

10. Click *New*.

11. Enter a name: *liferaydatabasesource*.

12. Enter JNDI: *jdbc/LiferayPool*.

13. Everything else should stay default.

14. Click *OK*.

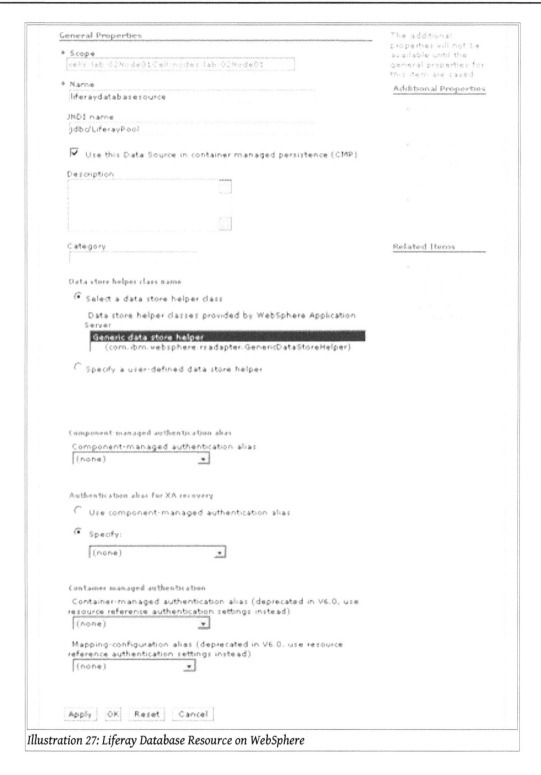

Illustration 27: Liferay Database Resource on WebSphere

15. Under *Additional Properties*, click *Custom properties*.

16. Click *New*.

17. Create three custom properties by entering Name, Value and clicking OK for each row in the following table:

Name	Value
1. user	root
2. serverName	localhost
3. databaseName	lportal

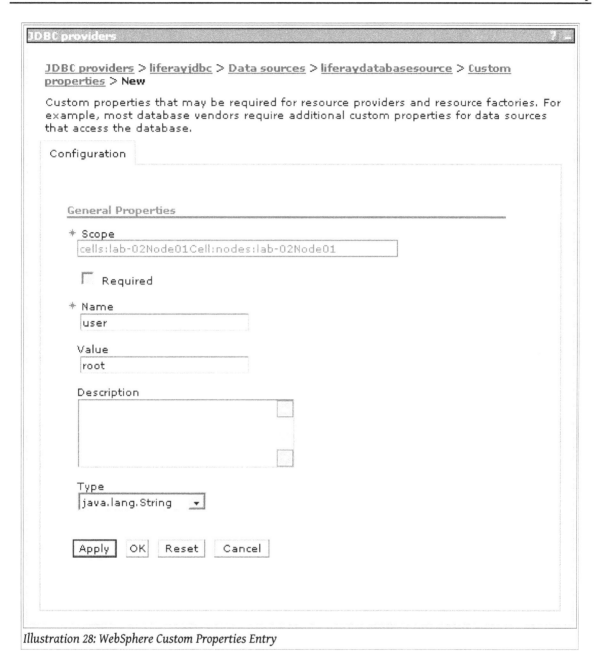

Illustration 28: WebSphere Custom Properties Entry

18. When done correctly, custom properties should look like this:

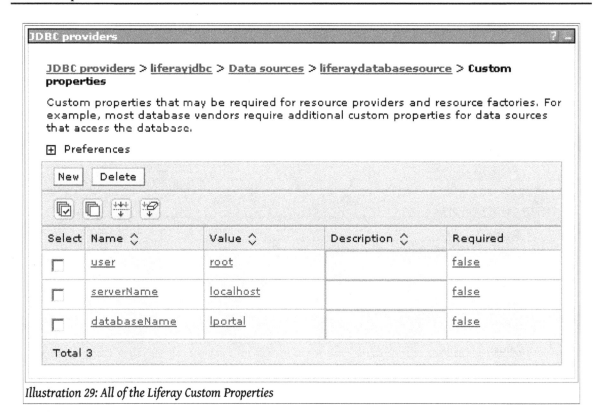

Illustration 29: All of the Liferay Custom Properties

19. Create a database for Liferay. For example:

```
create database lportal character set utf8;
```

Liferay will automatically create the tables and populate it the first time it starts.

20. Click Data Sources -> Test Connection to test.

Mail Configuration

1. Click *Resources -> Mail Providers*.

2. Click *Built-in Mail Provider*.

3. Click *Mail Sessions*.

4. Click *New*.

    1. **Name:** *liferaymail*

    2. **JNDI name:** *mail/MailSession*

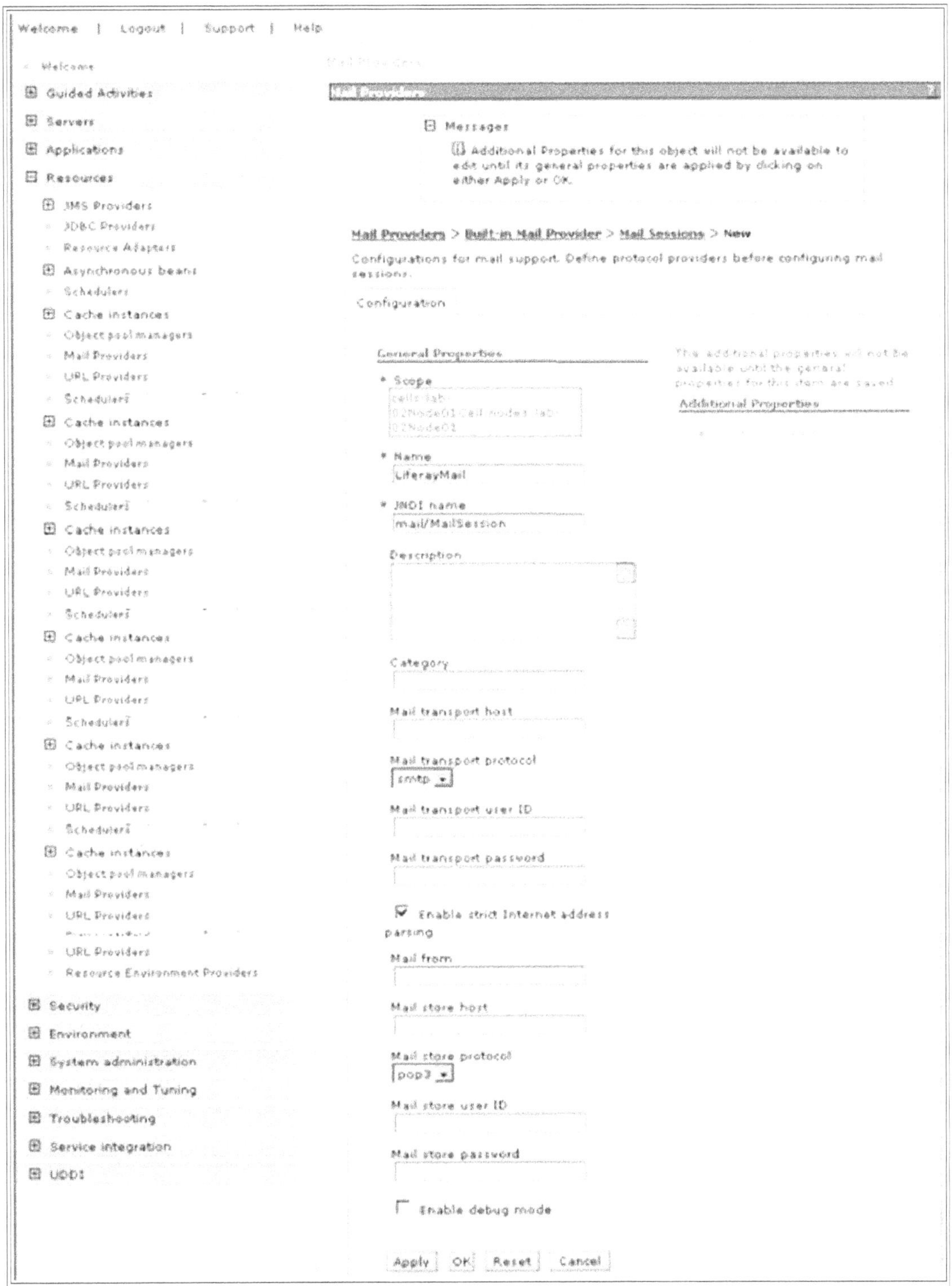

Illustration 30: Creating Mail Session on WebSphere

5. Click *OK*.

6. Click *Security*.

7. Click *Global Security*.

8. Select *Enable Global Security*.

9. Deselect *Enforce Java 2 Security*.

10. In *Active User Registry*, select *Custom User Registry*.

11. Click *Apply* to go to Custom user registry page.

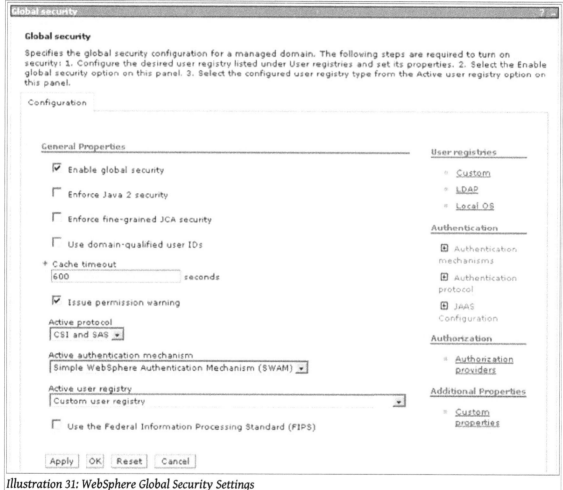

Illustration 31: WebSphere Global Security Settings

12. Enter *system* for server user ID.

13. Enter *password* for server user password.

14. Enter Custom registry class name *com.liferay.portal.security.jaas.ext.websphere.PortalUserRegistry.*

15. Click *Apply*.

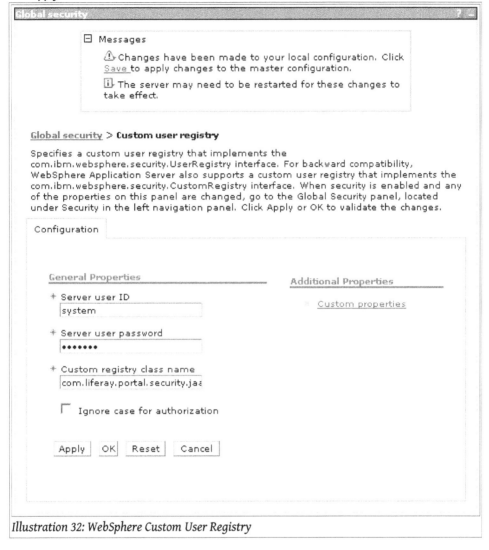

Illustration 32: WebSphere Custom User Registry

16. Insert user name/password into database:

    1. Open a MySQL console.

    2. Log in and select the Liferay database by typing *use lportal;*

    3. Enter the following SQL command:

```
Insert into User_ (companyId, userId, password_) values ('system', 'system',
'password');
```

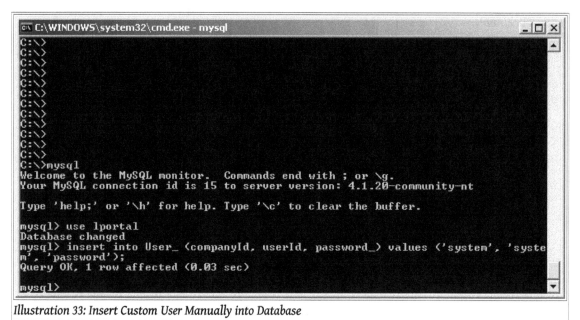

Illustration 33: Insert Custom User Manually into Database

Install Liferay

1. Click *Applications -> Install New Application.*

2. Browse for liferay-portal-4.3.x.war.

3. Enter context root /.

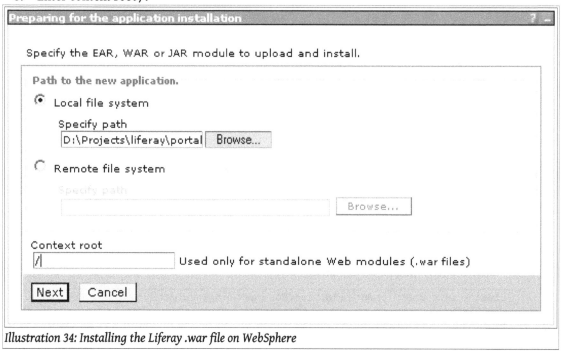

Illustration 34: Installing the Liferay .war file on WebSphere

---

4. Click *Next*

5. Select *Generate Default Bindings -> Override default bindings -> Use default virtual host name for web modules.*

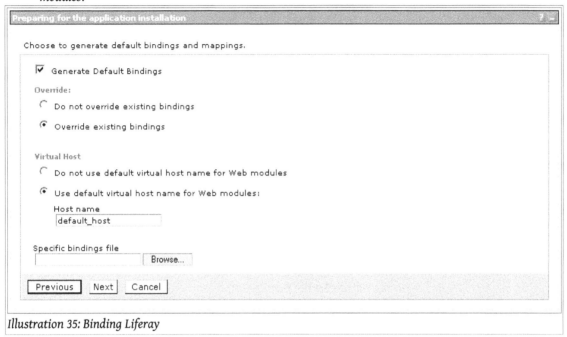

Illustration 35: Binding Liferay

6. Click *Next*. Click *Continue*. For Steps 1 to 4, click *Next* to apply defaults.

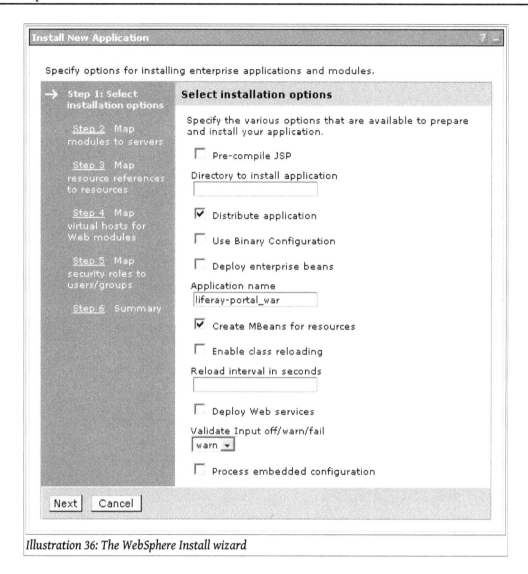

Illustration 36: The WebSphere Install wizard

7. In Step 5, check *all authenticated.*

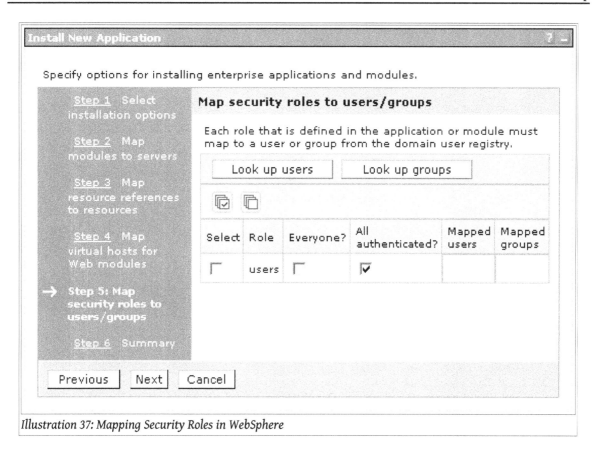

Illustration 37: Mapping Security Roles in WebSphere

8. Click *Next*.

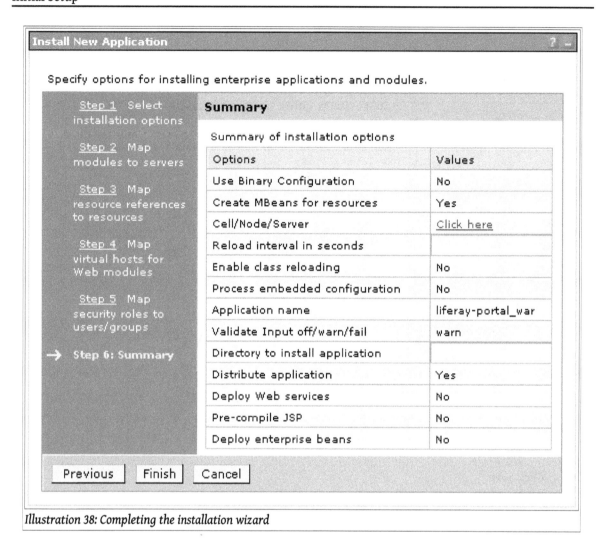

Illustration 38: Completing the installation wizard

9. Click *Finish*.

10. Wait for installation process.

Illustration 39: Liferay installed successfully on WebSphere

11. Save this configuration to master configuration by clicking on *System administration* and *Save Changes to Master Repository*.

Start Liferay Portal

1. Click *Applications*.

2. Click *Enterprise Applications*.

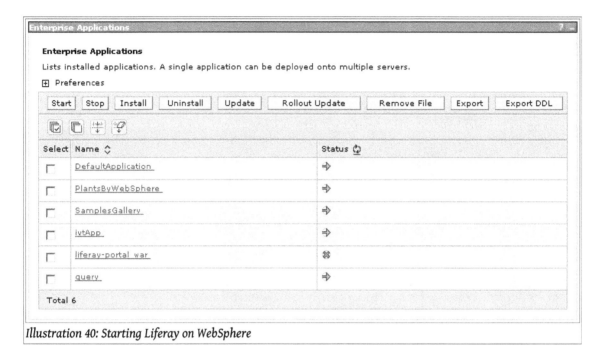

Illustration 40: Starting Liferay on WebSphere

3. Uninstall *DefaultApplication*, *PlantsByWebSphere* and *SamplesGallery*.

4. Select liferay-portal.war and click *Start*.

5. Open up browser and point to http://localhost:9080. You should see the default Liferay home page.

6. If you are running Windows, edit your Stop the Server shortcut to set the user id and password. If you don't do this, you will not be able to stop the server after you restart WebSphere:

```
"C:\Program Files\WebSphere\AppServer\bin\stopServer.bat" server1 -user system -pass-
word password
```

7. Stop WebSphere and restart it. Login on with *system* for user name and *password* for password.

WebSphere 6.1

Note: Throughout this installation and configuration process, Websphere will prompt you to Click Save to apply changes to Master Configuration. Do so intermittently to save your changes.

Installation

1. Download Liferay Portal 4.3.x WAR , unzip and compile.

2. Download and extract these Liferay jars to *websphere/appserver/lib/ext.*

   o Dependency libraries (Liferay Portal 4.3 Dependencies)

   o liferay-portal-jaas.jar (Liferay Portal Enterprise 4.3 JAAS Libraries from Sourceforge) o   mysql-connector-java-5.x.x-bin.jar (MySQL)

Set Up Database Service

1.   Start WebSphere.

2.   Open Administrative Console and login.

3.   Click *Resources*, click *JDBC Providers*.

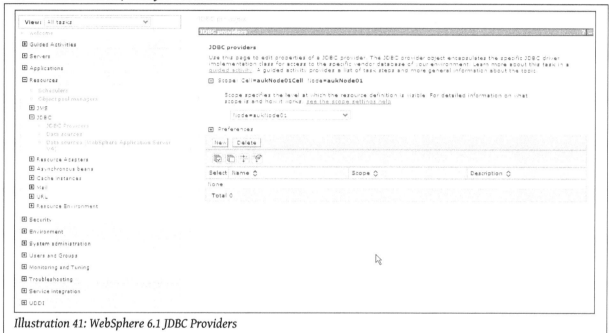

Illustration 41: WebSphere 6.1 JDBC Providers

4.   Click *New*.

5.   For name, enter name of JDBC provider, e.g. MySQL Jdbc Provider.

6.   For Implementation class name, enter:

```
com.mysql.jdbc.jdbc2.optional.MysqlConnectionPoolDataSource
```

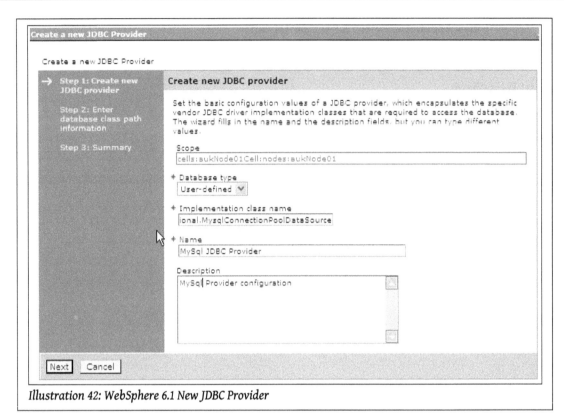

Illustration 42: WebSphere 6.1 New JDBC Provider

7.   Click *Next*.

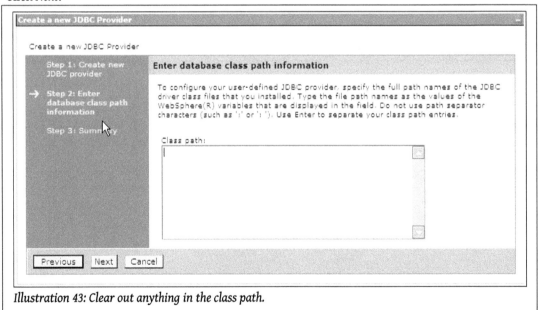

Illustration 43: Clear out anything in the class path.

8.   Clear any text in class path. You already copied the necessary .jars to a location on the server's class path.

9. Click *Next*.

Illustration 44: JDBC Provider summary screen

10. Click *Finish*.

11. Click *Data Sources* under *Additional Properties*.

12. Click *New*.

13. Enter a name: *liferaydatabasesource*.

14. Enter JNDI: *jdbc/LiferayPool*.

15. Everything else should stay default.

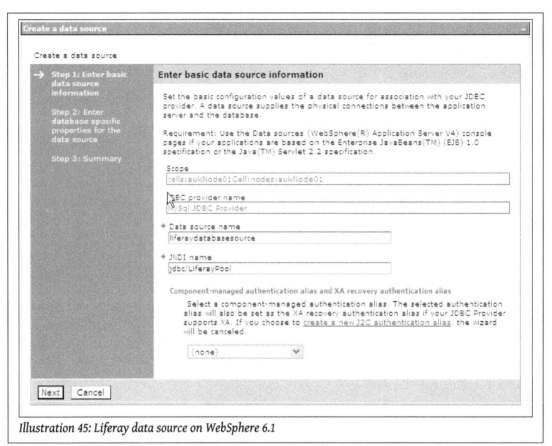

Illustration 45: Liferay data source on WebSphere 6.1

16. Click *Next*.

17. Under *Additional Properties*, click *Custom Properties*.

18. Click *New*.

19. Create three custom properties by entering Name, Value and clicking OK for each row in the following table.

Name	Value
1. user	root
2. serverName	localhost
3. databaseName	lportal

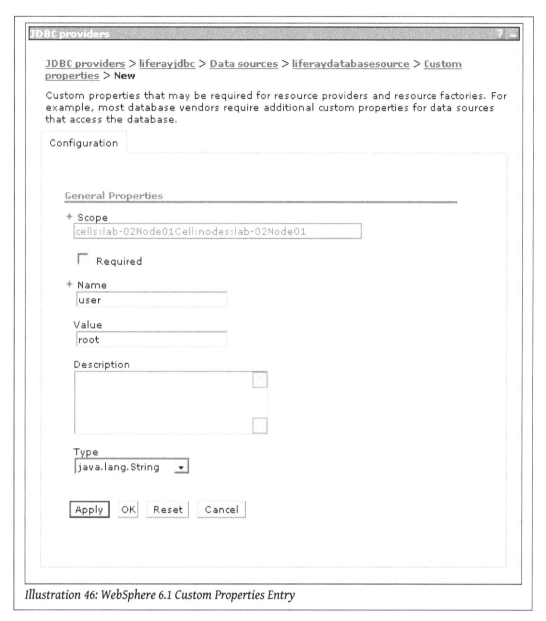

Illustration 46: WebSphere 6.1 Custom Properties Entry

20. When done correctly, custom properties should look like this:

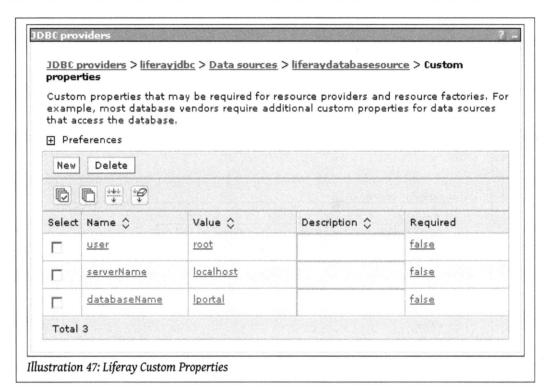

Illustration 47: Liferay Custom Properties

21. Click *Data Sources -> Test Connection* to test.

Mail Configuration

1. Click *Resources -> Mail Providers.*

2. Click *Built-in Mail Provider.*

3. Click *Mail Sessions.*

4. Click *New.*

   1. **Name:** *liferaymail*

   2. **JNDI Name:** *mail/MailSession*

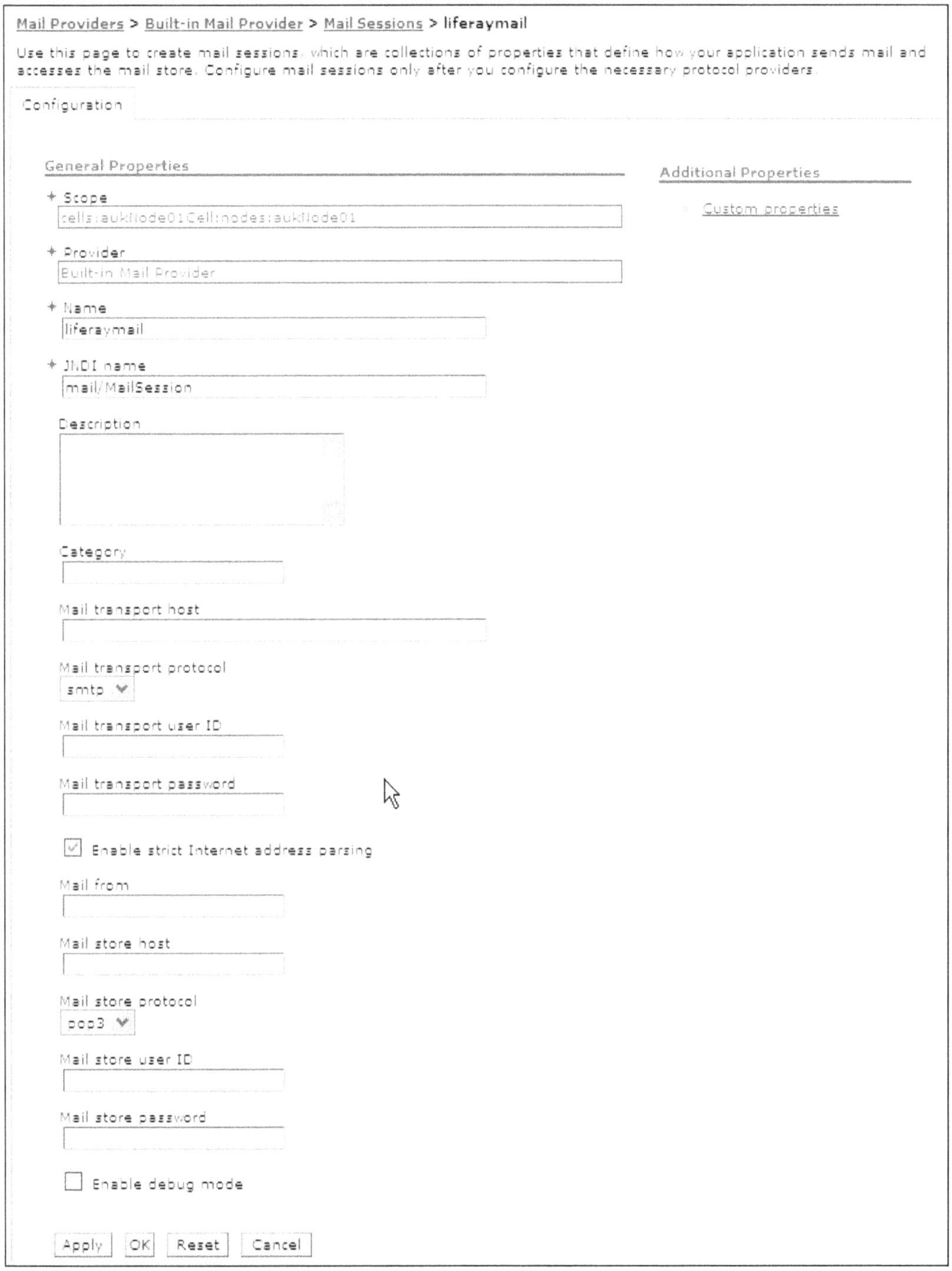

Illustration 48: Creating a Mail Session on WebSphere 6.1

5. Click *OK*.

6. Click *Security*.

7.   Click *Secure administration, applications, and infrastructure.*

8.   Select *Enable application security.*

9.   Deselect *Use Java 2 security to restrict application access to local resources.*

Install Liferay

1.   Click *Applications -> Install new applications.*

2.   Browse for liferay-portal-4.x.x.war.

Illustration 49: Installing the Liferay .war file on WebSphere 6.1

3.   Enter context root /.

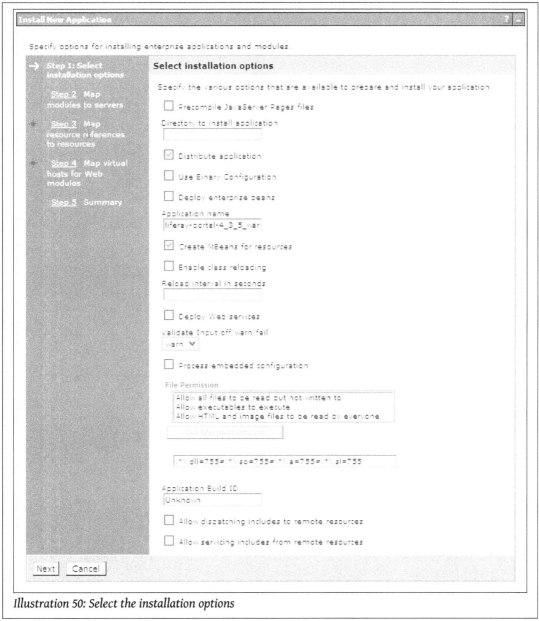

Illustration 50: Select the installation options

4.   Click *Next*. For Steps 1 to 3, click *Next* to apply defaults.

5.   Choose the Mail Session and Data Source, and then click *Next*

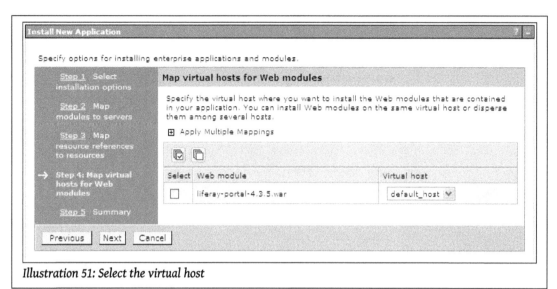

Illustration 51: Select the virtual host

6. Specify the virtual host upon which you want Liferay to run.

7. At the Summary Screen, click *Finish.*

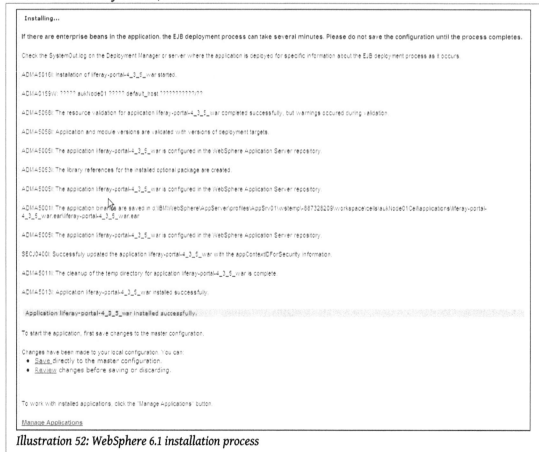

Illustration 52: WebSphere 6.1 installation process

8.   Wait for the installation process to complete.

9.   Save this configuration to master configuration by clicking on *System administration* and *Save Changes to Master Repository*.

Start Liferay Portal

1.   Applications.

2.   Click *Enterprise Applications*.

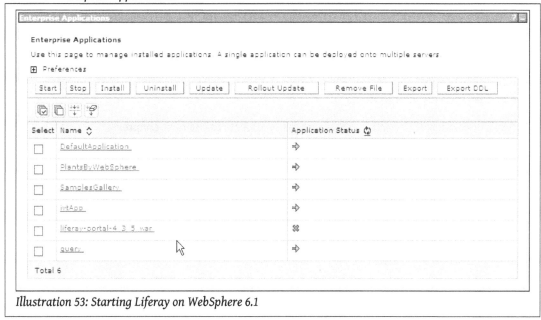

Illustration 53: Starting Liferay on WebSphere 6.1

3.   Uninstall *DefaultApplication*, *PlantsByWebSphere* and *SamplesGallery*.

4.   Select *liferay-portal.war*, click *Start*.

5.   Open up browser and point to http://localhost:9080. The default Liferay home page will be displayed.

Making Liferay Coexist with Other Java EE Applications

Liferay Portal by default is configured to sit at the root (i.e., /) of your application server. Dedicating your application server to running only Liferay Portal is a good practice, allowing for separation between your portal environment and your web application environment. If, however, you want Liferay to share space on an application server with other applications, there is no reason why you cannot do that. In this instance, you may not want to make Liferay the default application in the root context of the server.

There are two steps to modifying this behavior:

1.   Deploy Liferay in a context other than root (for example /portal).

2. Modify the *portal-ext.properties* file to tell Liferay the context to which it has been deployed.

The order in which you take these steps depends on your application server. If your application server deploys Liferay in such a manner that you can browse its directory structure and modify files, then you would make this change in the order above (i.e., *after* deploying Liferay, but *before* starting it). If your application server does not deploy Liferay in this way, then you will have to modify the *portal-ext.properties* file inside the Liferay .war itself. You would extract the file from the .war file, modify it, and then put it back in the .war file. Then deploy the modified Liferay .war file to the server in the proper context.

To change the file, open it in a text editor. The *portal.ctx* property will be at the top of the file:

```
portal.ctx=/
```

This default setting defines Liferay Portal as the application that sits at the root context. If you change it to something else, say */portal*, for example, you can then deploy Liferay in that context and it will live there instead of at the root context.

A full discussion of the *portal-ext.properties* file appears in the next chapter.

3. CONFIGURATION

Once Liferay is successfully installed, it will likely need further configuration, both to fit it to your environment and to fit it to your particular portal project. These activities generally need to be performed once you have Liferay installed, but before you start building out your Portal. They include customizing certain out-of-box defaults, security configuration, and plugin management. We will examine specifically these topics:

- *Advanced Liferay Configuration:* This includes the customization of the *portal-ext.properties* file.

- *Plugin Management:* You will learn how to install Plugins (portlets and themes) from Liferay's Official Repository and Liferay's Community Repository, as well as how to create your own plugin repository.

- *Liferay SOA:* Accessing Liferay services remotely, from outside the portal, will be discussed, as well as how to configure the security settings for these services.

Advanced Liferay Configuration

Liferay is configured by a combination of settings which are stored in the database (configured by the use of the various administration portlets) and settings which are stored in properties (text) files. These files can be modified to change Liferay's behavior in certain ways. There are a large number of configuration options that can be set, and so this section will have a wide-ranging set of topics. We will first go over the main configuration file, which is stored in *<Liferay Home>/WEB-INF/classes*, and is called *portal-ext.properties*.

The *portal-ext.properties* File

Liferay's properties files differ from the configuration files of most other products in that changing the default configuration file is discouraged. In fact, the file that contains all of the defaults is stored inside of a .jar file, making it more difficult to customize. Why is it set up this way? Because Liferay uses the concept of *overriding* the defaults in a separate file, rather than going in and customizing the default configuration file. You put just the settings you want to customize in your own configuration file, and then the configuration file for your portal is uncluttered and contains only the settings you need. This makes it far easier to determine whether a particular setting has been customized, and it makes the settings more portable across different instances of Liferay.

The default configuration file is called *portal.properties*, and it resides inside of the *portal-impl.jar* file. The file which is used to override the configuration is *portal-ext.properties*. This file is readily accessible inside of the *<Liferay Home>/WEB-INF/classes* folder. By default, it has very little information in it. What follows is a brief description of the options that can be placed there, thus overriding the defaults from the *portal.properties* file. These are presented in a logical order, not an alphabetical one, as many properties relate to other properties in the system.

Properties Override

This property specifies where to get the overridden properties. By default, it is *portal-ext.properties*. Updates should not be made on the original file (*portal.properties*) but on the overridden version of this file. Furthermore, each portal instance can have its own overridden property file following the convention portal-companyid.properties.

For example, one read order may be: portal.properties, then portal-ext.properties, then portal-liferay.com.properties.

Examples:

```
include-and-override=portal-ext.properties
include-and-override=portal-${easyconf:companyId}.properties
include-and-override=portal-test.properties
```

Portal Context

This specifies the path of the portal servlet context. This is needed because javax.servlet.ServletContext does not have access to the context path until Java EE 5.

Set this property if you deploy the portal to another path besides root.

Examples:

```
portal.ctx=/
portal.ctx=/portal
```

Resource Repositories Root

Specifies the default root path for various repository and resource paths. Under this path several directories will be created for the hot deploy feature, JCR, etc.

Examples:

```
resource.repositories.root=${user.home}/liferay
resource.repositories.root=/home/liferay
```

ERROR PROPERTIES

Set the following to true to log the error message.

```
error.message.log=true
```

Set the following to true to print the error message to the console.

```
error.message.print=false
```

Set the following to true to show the error message to the user.

```
error.message.show=true
```

Set the following to true to log the stack trace.

```
error.stack.trace.log=false
```

Set the following to true to print the stack trace to the console.

```
error.stack.trace.print=true
```

Set the following to true to show the stack trace to the user.

```
error.stack.trace.show=false
```

TECHNOLOGY COMPATIBILITY KIT

Set the following to true to enable programmatic configuration to let the Portlet TCK obtain a URL for each test. This should never be set to true unless you are running the TCK tests.

```
tck.url=false
```

SCHEMA

Set this to true to automatically create tables and populate with default data if the database is empty.

```
schema.run.enabled=true
```

Set this to to true to populate with the minimal amount of data. Set this to false to populate with a larger amount of sample data.

```
schema.run.minimal=true
```

UPGRADE

Input a list of comma delimited class names that implement com.liferay.portal.upgrade.Upgrade-Process. These classes will run on startup to upgrade older data to match with the latest version.

```
upgrade.processes=\
    com.liferay.portal.upgrade.UpgradeProcess_4_3_0,\
    com.liferay.portal.upgrade.UpgradeProcess_4_3_1,\
    com.liferay.portal.upgrade.UpgradeProcess_4_3_2,\
    com.liferay.portal.upgrade.UpgradeProcess_4_3_3,\
```

```
        com.liferay.portal.upgrade.UpgradeProcess_4_3_4,\
        com.liferay.portal.upgrade.UpgradeProcess_4_3_5
```

VERIFY

Input a list of comma delimited class names that implement com.liferay.portal.integrity.VerifyProcess. These classes will run on startup to verify and fix any integrity problems found in the database.

```
verify.processes=com.liferay.portal.verify.VerifyProcessSuite
```

Specify the frequency for verifying the integrity of the database.

Constants in VerifyProcess:

public static final int ALWAYS = -1;

public static final int NEVER = 0;

public static final int ONCE = 1;

```
verify.frequency=1
```

AUTO DEPLOY

Input a list of comma delimited class names that implement *com.liferay.portal.kernel.deploy.auto.AutoDeployListener*. These classes are used to process the auto deployment of WARs.

```
auto.deploy.listeners=\
  com.liferay.portal.deploy.auto.LayoutTemplateAutoDeployListener,\
  com.liferay.portal.deploy.auto.PortletAutoDeployListener,\
  com.liferay.portal.deploy.auto.ThemeAutoDeployListener,\
  com.liferay.portal.deploy.auto.exploded.tomcat.LayoutTemplateExplodedTomcatListener,\
  com.liferay.portal.deploy.auto.exploded.tomcat.PortletExplodedTomcatListener,\
  com.liferay.portal.deploy.auto.exploded.tomcat.ThemeExplodedTomcatListener
```

Set the following to true to enable auto deploy of layout templates, portlets, and themes.

```
auto.deploy.enabled=true
```

Set the directory to scan for layout templates, portlets, and themes to auto deploy.

```
auto.deploy.deploy.dir=${resource.repositories.root}/deploy
```

Set the directory where auto deployed WARs are copied to. The application server or servlet container must know to listen on that directory.

Different containers have different hot deploy paths. For example, Tomcat listens on *${catalina.base}/webapps* whereas JBoss listens on *${jboss.server.home.dir}/deploy*. Set a blank directory to automatically use the application server specific directory.

Examples:

```
auto.deploy.dest.dir=
auto.deploy.default.dest.dir=../webapps
```

```
auto.deploy.geronimo-tomcat.dest.dir=${org.apache.geronimo.base.dir}/deploy
auto.deploy.glassfish.dest.dir=${com.sun.aas.instanceRoot}/autodeploy
auto.deploy.jboss-jetty.dest.dir=${jboss.server.home.dir}/deploy
auto.deploy.jboss-tomcat.dest.dir=${jboss.server.home.dir}/deploy
auto.deploy.jetty.dest.dir=${jetty.home}/webapps
auto.deploy.jonas-jetty.dest.dir=${jonas.base}/webapps/autoload
auto.deploy.jonas-tomcat.dest.dir=${jonas.base}/webapps/autoload
auto.deploy.tomcat.dest.dir=${catalina.base}/webapps
auto.deploy.weblogic.dest.dir=${env.DOMAIN_HOME}/autodeploy
```

Set the interval in milliseconds on how often to scan the directory for changes.

```
auto.deploy.interval=10000
```

Set the number of attempts to deploy a file before blacklisting it.

```
auto.deploy.blacklist.threshold=10
```

Set the following to true if deployed WARs are unpacked. Set this to false if your application server has concurrency issues with deploying large WARs.

```
auto.deploy.unpack.war=true
```

Set the following to true if you want the deployer to rename portlet.xml to portlet-custom.xml. This is only needed when deploying the portal on WebSphere 6.1.x with a version before 6.1.0.7 because WebSphere's portlet container will try to process a portlet at the same time that Liferay is trying to process a portlet.

Note that according to IBM, on versions *after* 6.1.0.9, you need to add a context parameter to the web.xml descriptor in your portlet application called *com.ibm.websphere.portletcontainer.PortletDeploymentEnabled* and set it to *false*. This parameter causes WebSphere's built-in portlet container to ignore your portlet application when it is deployed, enabling Liferay to pick it up.

```
auto.deploy.custom.portlet.xml=false
```

Set this to 1 if you are using JBoss' PrefixDeploymentSorter. This will append a 1 in front of your WAR name. For example, if you are deploying a portlet called test-portlet.war, it will deploy it to 1test-portlet.war. JBoss now knows to load this portlet after the other WARs have loaded; however, it will remove the 1 from the context path.

Modify */server/default/conf/jboss-service.xml.*

See *org.jboss.deployment.scanner.PrefixDeploymentSorter.*

```
auto.deploy.jboss.prefix=1
```

Set the path to Tomcat's configuration directory. This property is used to auto deploy exploded WARs. Tomcat context XML files found in the auto deploy directory will be copied to Tomcat's configuration directory. The context XML file must have a docBase attribute that points to a valid WAR directory.

```
auto.deploy.tomcat.conf.dir=../conf/Catalina/localhost
```

Set the path to Tomcat's global class loader. This property is only used by Tomcat in a standalone environment.

```
auto.deploy.tomcat.lib.dir=../common/lib/ext
```

Set the URLs of Libraries that might be needed to download during the auto deploy process

```
library.download.url.quercus.jar=http://lportal.svn.sourceforge.net/viewvc/*checkout*/lporta
l/portal/trunk/lib/development/quercus.jar
library.download.url.resin-util.-
jar=http://lportal.svn.sourceforge.net/viewvc/*checkout*/lportal/portal/trunk/lib/develop-
ment/resin-util.jar
library.download.url.script-10.jar=http://lportal.svn.sourceforge.net/viewvc/*checkout*/lpor
tal/portal/trunk/lib/development/script-10.jar
```

HOT DEPLOY

Input a list of comma delimited class names that implement *com.liferay.portal.kernel.deploy.hot.HotDeployListener*. These classes are used to process the deployment and undeployment of WARs at runtime.

Note: PluginPackageHotDeployListener must always be first.

```
hot.deploy.listeners=\
    com.liferay.portal.deploy.hot.PluginPackageHotDeployListener,\
    com.liferay.portal.deploy.hot.LayoutTemplateHotDeployListener,\
    com.liferay.portal.deploy.hot.PortletHotDeployListener,\
    com.liferay.portal.deploy.hot.ThemeHotDeployListener,\
    com.liferay.portal.deploy.hot.ThemeLoaderHotDeployListener
```

PLUGIN

Input a list of comma delimited supported plugin types.

```
plugin.types=portlet,theme,layout-template
```

Input a list of Liferay plugin repositories separated by \n characters.

```
plugin.repositories.trusted=http://plugins.liferay.com/official
plugin.repositories.untrusted=http://plugins.liferay.com/community
```

Set this property to false to avoid receiving on screen notifications when there is a new version of an installed plugin.

```
plugin.notifications.enabled=true
```

Input a list of plugin packages ids separated by \n characters. Administrators won't be notified when a new version of these plugins are available. The ids are of the form groupId/artifactId. You can also end the id with an asterisk to match any id that start with the previous character.

```
plugin.notifications.packages.ignored=liferay/sample-jsp-portlet
```

PORTLET

Set this property to define the default virtual path for all hot deployed portlets. See liferay-portlet-app_4_3_0.dtd and the virtual-path element for more information.

```
portlet.virtual.path=
```

THEME

Set this property to true to load the theme's merged CSS files for faster loading for production. Set this property to false for easier debugging for development. You can also disable fast loading by setting the URL parameter *css_fast_load* to *0*.

```
theme.css.fast.load=false
```

Set this property to set the default virtual path for all hot deployed themes. See liferay-look-and-feel_4_3_0.dtd and the virtual-path element for more information.

```
theme.virtual.path=
```

Set this with an absolute path to specify where imported theme files from a LAR will be stored. This path will override the file-storage path specified in liferay-theme-loader.xml.

```
theme.loader.storage.path=
```

RESOURCE ACTIONS

Input a list of comma delimited resource action configurations that will be read from the class path.

```
resource.actions.configs=resource-actions/default.xml
```

MODEL HINTS

Input a list of comma delimited model hints configurations.

```
model.hints.configs=\
    META-INF/portal-model-hints.xml,\
    META-INF/workflow-model-hints.xml,\
    META-INF/ext-model-hints.xml,\
    META-INF/portlet-model-hints.xml
```

SPRING

Input a list of comma delimited Spring configurations.

```
spring.configs=\
    META-INF/activemq-spring-jms.xml,\
    META-INF/data-source-spring.xml,\
    META-INF/misc-spring.xml,\
    META-INF/counter-spring.xml,\
    META-INF/documentlibrary-spring.xml,\
    META-INF/documentlibrary-spring-jms.xml,\
    META-INF/lock-spring.xml,\
    META-INF/mail-spring.xml,\
    META-INF/mail-spring-jms.xml,\
```

```
    META-INF/portal-spring.xml,\
    META-INF/portal-spring-jcr.xml,\
    META-INF/portal-spring-jms.xml,\
    META-INF/ext-spring.xml
```

Set the bean name for the Liferay data source.

```
spring.hibernate.data.source=liferayDataSource
```

Set the bean name for the Liferay session factory.

```
spring.hibernate.session.factory=&liferaySessionFactory
```

HIBERNATE

Many of the following properties should only be customized if you have advanced knowledge of Hibernate. They map to various Hibernate configuration options which themselves have detailed documentation. Please see http://www.hibernate.org for more information.

Input a list of comma delimited Hibernate configurations.

```
hibernate.configs=\
    META-INF/counter-hbm.xml,\
    META-INF/mail-hbm.xml,\
    META-INF/portal-hbm.xml,\
    META-INF/ext-hbm.xml
```

Use the Liferay SQL dialect because it will automatically detect the proper SQL dialect based on your connection URL.

```
hibernate.dialect=com.liferay.portal.spring.hibernate.DynamicDialect
```

Set the Hibernate connection release mode. You should not modify this unless you know what you're doing. The default setting works best for Spring managed transactions. See the method buildSessionFactory in class *org.springframework.orm.hibernate3.LocalSessionFactoryBean* and search for the phrase "on_close" to understand how this works.

```
hibernate.connection.release_mode=on_close
```

Set the Hibernate cache provider. Ehcache is recommended in a clustered environment. See the property *net.sf.ehcache.configurationResourceName* for detailed configuration.

Examples:

```
hibernate.cache.provider_class=com.liferay.util.dao.hibernate.EhCacheProvider
hibernate.cache.provider_class=net.sf.hibernate.cache.HashtableCacheProvider
hibernate.cache.provider_class=com.liferay.portal.spring.hibernate.OSCacheProvider
```

This property is used if Hibernate is configured to use Ehcache's cache provider.

```
net.sf.ehcache.configurationResourceName=/ehcache/hibernate.xml
```

Use the following ehcache configuration in a clustered environment.

```
net.sf.ehcache.configurationResourceName=/ehcache/hibernate-clustered.xml
```

Set other Hibernate cache settings.

```
hibernate.cache.use_query_cache=true
hibernate.cache.use_second_level_cache=true
hibernate.cache.use_minimal_puts=true
hibernate.cache.use_structured_entries=false
```

Use these properties to disable Hibernate caching. This may be a performance hit; you may only want to use these properties for diagnostic purposes.

```
hibernate.cache.provider_class=org.hibernate.cache.NoCacheProvider
hibernate.cache.use_query_cache=false
hibernate.cache.use_second_level_cache=false
```

Set the JDBC batch size to improve performance. If you're using Oracle 9i, however, you must set the batch size to 0 as a workaround for a hanging bug in the Oracle driver. See http://support.liferay.com/browse/LEP-1234 for more information.

Examples:

```
hibernate.jdbc.batch_size=20
hibernate.jdbc.batch_size=0
```

Set other miscellaneous Hibernate properties.

```
hibernate.jdbc.use_scrollable_resultset=true
hibernate.bytecode.use_reflection_optimizer=true
hibernate.show_sql=false
```

Use the classic query factory until WebLogic and Hibernate 3 can get along. See http://www.hibernate.org/250.html#A23 for more information.

```
hibernate.query.factory_class=org.hibernate.hql.classic.ClassicQueryTranslatorFactory
```

Custom SQL

Input a list of comma delimited custom SQL configurations. Liferay Administrators should never need to customize this; this is more of an option for developers who are customizing Liferay's behavior.

```
custom.sql.configs=custom-sql/default.xml
```

Some databases do not recognize a NULL IS NULL check. Set the *custom.sql.function.isnull* and *custom.sql.function.isnotnull* properties for your specific database.

There is no need to manually set these properties because *com.liferay.portal.spring.hibernate.DynamicDialect* already sets it. These properties are set, however, so that you can see how you can override it for a database that DynamicDialect does not yet know how to auto configure.

DB2

```
custom.sql.function.isnull=CAST(? AS VARCHAR(32672)) IS NULL
custom.sql.function.isnotnull=CAST(? AS VARCHAR(32672)) IS NOT NULL
```

MySQL (for testing only)

```
custom.sql.function.isnull=IFNULL(?, '1') = '1'
custom.sql.function.isnotnull=IFNULL(?, '1') = '0'
```

Sybase

```
custom.sql.function.isnull=ISNULL(?, '1') = '1'
custom.sql.function.isnotnull=ISNULL(?, '1') = '0'
```

EHCACHE

Set the classpath to the location of the Ehcache config file for internal caches. Edit the file specified in the property *ehcache.multi-vm.config.location* to enable clustered cache.

```
ehcache.single.vm.config.location=/ehcache/liferay-single-vm.xml
ehcache.multi.vm.config.location=/ehcache/liferay-multi-vm.xml
```

Use the following in a clustered environment.

```
ehcache.multi.vm.config.location=/ehcache/liferay-multi-vm-clustered.xml
```

COMMONS POOL

Commons Pool is used to pool and recycle objects that are used very often. This can help lower memory usage. There is some debate over the synchronization issues related to Commons Pool. Set this to false to disable object pooling.

```
commons.pool.enabled=true
```

JAVASCRIPT

Set a list of JavaScript files that will be loaded programmatically in */html/common/themes/top_js.jsp*.

The ordering of the JavaScript files is important. Specifically, all JQuery scripts should go first.

The Liferay scripts are grouped in such a way that the first grouping denotes utility scripts that are used by the second and third groups. The second grouping denotes utility classes that rely on the first group, but does not rely on the second or third group. The third grouping denotes modules that rely on the first and second group.

```
javascript.files=\
    \
    #
    # JQuery scripts
    #
    \
    jquery/jquery.js,\
    jquery/cookie.js,\
    jquery/dimensions.js,\
```

```
jquery/hover_intent.js,\
jquery/interface.js,\
jquery/interface.patch.js,\
jquery/j2browse.js,\
jquery/jeditable.js,\
jquery/json.js,\
jquery/media.js,\
jquery/tabs.js,\
\
#
# Miscellaneous scripts
#
\
misc/class.js,\
misc/swfobject.js,\
\
#
# Liferay base utility scripts
#
\
liferay/liferay.js,\
liferay/browser.js,\
liferay/util.js,\
liferay/language.js,\
liferay/layout.js,\
\
#
# Liferay utility scripts
#
\
liferay/ajax.js,\
liferay/animate.js,\
liferay/coordinates.js,\
liferay/ldrag.js,\
#liferay/leditable.js,\
liferay/lresize.js,\
liferay/popup.js,\
liferay/portal.js,\
liferay/portlet.js,\
liferay/publisher.js,\
\
#
# Liferay modules
#
\
liferay/auto_fields.js,\
liferay/color_picker.js,\
liferay/columns.js,\
```

```
liferay/dock.js,\
liferay/dynamic_select.js,\
liferay/freeform.js,\
liferay/layout_configuration.js,\
liferay/menu.js,\
liferay/messaging.js,\
liferay/notice.js,\
liferay/navigation.js,\
liferay/session.js,\
liferay/tags_selector.js
```

Set this property to true to load the combined JavaScript files from the property *javascript.files* into one compacted file for faster loading for production. Set this property to false for easier debugging for development. You can also disable fast loading by setting the URL parameter *js_fast_load* to *0*.

```
javascript.fast.load=false
```

Set the following to true to enable the display of JavaScript logging.

```
javascript.log.enabled=false
```

COMPANY

This sets the default web id. Omni admin users must belong to the company with this web id.

```
company.default.web.id=liferay.com
```

The portal can authenticate users based on their email address, screen name, or user id.

```
company.security.auth.type=emailAddress
company.security.auth.type=screenName
company.security.auth.type=userId
```

Set this to true to ensure users login with https.

```
company.security.auth.requires.https=false
```

Set the following to true to allow users to select the *remember me* feature to automatically login to the portal.

```
company.security.auto.login=true
```

Set the following to the maximum age (in number of seconds) of the browser cookie that enables the *remember me* feature. A value of 31536000 signifies a lifespan of one year. A value of -1 signifies a lifespan of a browser session.

Rather than setting this to 0, set the property *company.security.auto.login* to false to disable the *remember me* feature.

```
company.security.auto.login.max.age=31536000
```

Set the following to true to allow users to ask the portal to send them their password.

```
company.security.send.password=true
```

Set the following to true to allow strangers to create accounts and register themselves on the portal.

```
company.security.strangers=true
```

Set the following to true if strangers can create accounts with email addresses that match the company mail suffix. This property is not used unless *company.security.strangers* is also set to true.

```
company.security.strangers.with.mx=true
```

Set the following to true if strangers who create accounts need to be verified via email.

```
company.security.strangers.verify=false
```

Set the following to true to allow community administrators to use their own logo instead of the enterprise logo.

```
company.security.community.logo=true
```

Users

Set the following to false if users cannot be deleted.

```
users.delete=true
```

Set the following to true to always autogenerate user screen names even if the user gives a specific user screen name.

```
users.screen.name.always.autogenerate=false
```

Input a class name that extends *com.liferay.portal.security.auth.ScreenNameGenerator*. This class will be called to generate user screen names.

```
users.screen.name.generator=com.liferay.portal.security.auth.ScreenNameGenerator
```

Input a class name that extends *com.liferay.portal.security.auth.ScreenNameValidator*. This class will be called to validate user ids.

Examples:

```
users.screen.name.validator=com.liferay.portal.security.auth.ScreenNameValidator
users.screen.name.validator=com.liferay.portal.security.auth.LiberalScreenNameValidator
```

Set the maximum file size for user portraits. A value of 0 for the maximum file size can be used to indicate unlimited file size. However, the maximum file size allowed by the system is set in property *com.liferay.util.servlet.UploadServletRequest.max.size* found in system.properties.

```
users.image.max.size=307200
```

Groups and Roles

Input a list of comma delimited system group names that will exist in addition to the standard system groups. When the server starts, the portal checks to ensure all system groups exist. Any missing system group will be created by the portal.

```
system.groups=
```

Input a list of comma delimited system role names that will exist in addition to the standard system roles. When the server starts, the portal checks to ensure all system roles exist. Any missing system role will be created by the portal.

```
system.roles=
```

Input a list of comma delimited system community role names that will exist in addition to the standard system community roles. When the server starts, the portal checks to ensure all system community roles exist. Any missing system community role will be created by the portal.

```
system.community.roles=
```

Omni admin users can administer the portal's core functionality: gc, shutdown, etc. Omni admin users must belong to the default company.

Multiple portal instances might be deployed on one application server, and not all of the administrators should have access to this core functionality. Input the ids of users who are omniadmin users.

Leave this field blank if users who belong to the right company and have the Administrator role are allowed to administer the portal's core functionality.

```
omniadmin.users=
```

Set the following to true if all users are required to agree to the terms of use.

```
terms.of.use.required=true
```

ORGANIZATIONS AND LOCATIONS

Set the following to true if users must belong to a parent organization.

```
organizations.parent.organization.required=false
```

Set the following to true if organizations must have an associated country.

```
organizations.country.required=true
```

Set the following to true if users must belong to a location. If location is required, then a parent organization is also required.

```
organizations.location.required=false
```

Set the following to false to disable location management from the portal. This setting simplifies the UI for cases in which locations are not necessary.

```
organizations.location.enabled=true
```

LANGUAGES AND TIME ZONES

Specify the available locales. Messages corresponding to a specific language are specified in properties files with file names matching that of *content/Language_*.properties*. These values can also be overridden in properties files with file names matching that of *content/Language-ext_*.properties*. Use a comma to separate each entry.

All locales must use UTF-8 encoding.

See the following links to specify language and country codes:

http://ftp.ics.uci.edu/pub/ietf/http/related/iso639.txt

http://userpage.chemie.fu-berlin.de/diverse/doc/ISO_3166.html

```
locales=ar_SA,ca_AD,ca_ES,zh_CN,zh_TW,cs_CZ,nl_NL,en_US,fi_FI,fr_FR,de_DE,el_GR,hu_HU,it_IT,
ja_JP,ko_KR,fa_IR,pt_BR,ru_RU,es_ES,sv_SE,tr_TR,vi_VN
```

Set the following to true if unauthenticated users get their preferred language from the Accept-Language header. Set the following to false if unauthenticated users get their preferred language from their company.

```
locale.default.request=false
```

Specify the available time zones. The specified ids must match those from the class *java.util.-TimeZone*.

```
time.zones=Pacific/Midway,Pacific/Honolulu,AST,PST,MST,CST,EST,PRT,CNT,BET,America/Noronha,A
tlantic/Azores,GMT,WET,CET,EET,Asia/Jerusalem,Asia/Baghdad,Iran,Asia/Dubai,Asia/Kabul,Asia/K
arachi,IST,Asia/Katmandu,Asia/Dhaka,Asia/Rangoon,VST,CTT,JST,ROK,ACT,AET,SST,NST,Pacific/En-
derbury,Pacific/Kiritimati
```

LOOK AND FEEL

Set the following to false if the system does not allow users to modify the look and feel.

```
look.and.feel.modifiable=true
```

Set the default theme id for regular themes.

```
default.regular.theme.id=classic
```

Set the default color scheme id for regular themes.

```
default.regular.color.scheme.id=01
```

Set the default theme id for wap themes.

```
default.wap.theme.id=mobile
```

Set the default color scheme id for wap themes.

```
default.wap.color.scheme.id=01
```

Set the following to true if you want a change in the theme selection of the public or private group to automatically be applied to the other (i.e. if public and private group themes should always be the same).

```
theme.sync.on.group=false
```

REQUEST

Portlets that have been configured to use private request attributes in *liferay-portlet.xml* may still want to share some request attributes. This property allows you to configure which request attributes will be shared.

Set a comma delimited list of attribute names that will be shared when the attribute name starts with one of the specified attribute names. For example, if you set the value to *hello_,world_*, then all attribute names that start with *hello_* or *world_* will be shared.

```
request.shared.attributes=LIFERAY_SHARED_
```

SESSION

Specify the number of minutes before a session expires. This value is always overridden by the value set in *web.xml*.

```
session.timeout=30
```

Specify the number of minutes before a warning is sent to the user informing the user of the session expiration. Specify 0 to disable any warnings.

```
session.timeout.warning=1
```

Set the auto-extend mode to true to avoid having to ask the user whether to extend the session or not. Instead it will be automatically extended. The purpose of this mode is to keep the session open as long as the user browser is open and with a portal page loaded. It is recommended to use this setting along with a smaller *session.timeout*, such as 5 minutes for better performance.

```
session.timeout.auto.extend=false
```

Portlets that have been configured to use private session attributes in *liferay-portlet.xml* may still want to share some session attributes. This property allows you to configure which session attributes will be shared. Set a comma delimited list of attribute names that will be shared when the attribute name starts with one of the specified attribute names. For example, if you set the value to *hello_,world_*, then all attribute names that start with *hello_* or *world_* will be shared.

Note that this property is used to specify the sharing of session attributes from the portal to the portlet. This is not used to specify session sharing between portlet WARs or from the portlet to the portal.

```
session.shared.attributes=org.apache.struts.action.LOCALE,COMPANY_,USER_,LIFERAY_SHARED_
```

Set this to false to disable all persistent cookies. Features like automatically logging in will not work.

```
session.enable.persistent.cookies=true
```

The login process sets several cookies if persistent cookies are enabled. Set this property to set the domain of those cookies.

```
session.cookie.domain=
```

Set the following to true to invalidate the session when a user logs into the portal. This helps prevents phishing. Set this to false if you need the guest user and the authenticated user to have the same session.

```
session.enable.phishing.protection=true
```

Set the following to true to test whether users have cookie support before allowing them to sign in. This test will always fail if *tck.url* is set to true because that property disables session cookies.

```
session.test.cookie.support=true
```

Set the following to true to disable sessions. Doing this will use cookies to remember the user across requests. This is useful if you want to scale very large sites where the user may be sent to a different server for each request. The drawback to this approach is that you must not rely on the API for sessions provided by the servlet and portlet specs.

This feature is only available for Tomcat and requires that you set Tomcat's Manager class to *com.liferay.support.tomcat.session.SessionLessManagerBase*.

```
session.disabled=false
```

Input a list of comma delimited class names that extend *com.liferay.portal.struts.SessionAction*. These classes will run at the specified event.

```
#
# Servlet session create event
#
servlet.session.create.events=com.liferay.portal.events.SessionCreateAction

#
# Servlet session destroy event
#
servlet.session.destroy.events=com.liferay.portal.events.SessionDestroyAction
```

Set the following to true to track user clicks in memory for the duration of a user's session. Setting this to true allows you to view all live sessions in the Admin portlet.

```
session.tracker.memory.enabled=true
```

Set the following to true to track user clicks in the database after a user's session is invalidated. Setting this to true allows you to generate usage reports from the database. Use this cautiously because this will store a lot of usage data.

```
session.tracker.persistence.enabled=false
```

Enter a list of comma delimited paths that should not be tracked.

```
session.tracker.ignore.paths=\
    /document_library/get_file,\
    /portal/ajax,\
    /portal/css_cached,\
    /portal/javascript_cached,\
    /portal/render_portlet
```

JAAS

Set the following to true if the portal will use *com.liferay.portal.security.jaas.PortalConfiguration* as the

JAAS master configuration.

```
portal.configuration=true
```

Set the following to false to disable JAAS security checks. Disabling JAAS speeds up login. JAAS must be disabled if administrators are to be able to impersonate other users.

```
portal.jaas.enable=false
```

By default, *com.liferay.portal.security.jaas.PortalLoginModule* loads the correct JAAS login module based on what application server or servlet container the portal is deployed on. Set a JAAS implementation class to override this behavior.

```
portal.jaas.impl=
```

The JAAS process may pass in an encrypted password and the authentication will only succeed if there is an exact match. Set this property to false to relax that behavior so the user can input an unencrypted password.

```
portal.jaas.strict.password=false
```

Set the following to true to enable administrators to impersonate other users. JAAS must also be disabled for this feature to work.

```
portal.impersonation.enable=true
```

LDAP

Set the values used to connect to a LDAP store.

```
ldap.factory.initial=com.sun.jndi.ldap.LdapCtxFactory
ldap.base.provider.url=ldap://localhost:10389
ldap.base.dn=dc=example,dc=com
ldap.security.principal=uid=admin,ou=system
ldap.security.credentials=secret
```

Settings for *com.liferay.portal.security.auth.LDAPAuth* can be configured from the Admin portlet. It provides out of the box support for Apache Directory Server, Microsoft Active Directory Server, Novell eDirectory, and OpenLDAP. The default settings are for Apache Directory Server.

The LDAPAuth class must be specified in the property *auth.pipeline.pre* to be executed.

Encryption is implemented by *com.liferay.util.Encryptor.provider.class* in *system.properties*.

```
ldap.auth.enabled=false
ldap.auth.required=false
```

Set either bind or password-compare for the LDAP authentication method. Bind is preferred by most vendors so that you don't have to worry about encryption strategies.

```
ldap.auth.method=bind
```

Active Directory stores information about the user account as a series of bit fields in the UserAccountControl attribute.

If you want to prevent disabled accounts from logging into the portal you need to use a search filter similiar to the following:

```
(&(objectclass=person)(userprincipalname=@email_address@)(!(UserAccountControl:
1.2.840.113556.1.4.803:=2)))
```

See the following links:

http://support.microsoft.com/kb/305144/

http://support.microsoft.com/?kbid=269181

```
ldap.auth.search.filter=(mail=@email_address@)
ldap.auth.password.encryption.algorithm=
ldap.auth.password.encryption.algorithm.types=MD5,SHA
```

The portal uses this DN value for two purposes. When searching for users to import, the portal will search for users under this DN. Also, when exporting a user, the portal will export the user to this DN.

```
ldap.users.dn=ou=users,dc=example,dc=com
```

You can write your own class that extends *com.liferay.portal.security.ldap.LDAPUser* to customize the behavior for exporting portal users to the LDAP store.

```
ldap.user.impl=com.liferay.portal.security.ldap.LDAPUser
```

When a user is exported to LDAP and the user does not exist, the user will be created with the following default object classes.

```
ldap.user.default.object.classes=top,person,inetOrgPerson,organizationalPerson
```

When importing and exporting users, the portal will use this mapping to connect LDAP user attributes and portal user variables.

```
ldap.user.mappings=screenName=cn\npassword=userPassword\nemailAddress=mail\nfirstName=given-
Name\nlastName=sn\njobTitle=title\ngroup=groupMembership
```

The portal uses this DN value for two purposes. When searching for groups to import, the portal will search for groups under this DN. Also, when exporting a group, the portal will export the group to this DN.

```
ldap.groups.dn=ou=groups,dc=example,dc=com
```

When importing groups, the portal will use this mapping to connect LDAP group attributes and portal user group variables.

```
ldap.group.mappings=groupName=cn\ndescription=description\nuser=uniqueMember
```

Settings for importing users and groups from LDAP to the portal.

```
ldap.import.enabled=false
ldap.import.on.startup=false
ldap.import.interval=10
ldap.import.user.search.filter=(objectClass=inetOrgPerson)
ldap.import.group.search.filter=(objectClass=groupOfUniqueNames)
```

Set either user or group for import method. If set to user, portal will import all users and the groups associated with those users. If set to group, the portal import all groups and the users associated those groups.

This value should be set based on how your LDAP server stores group membership information.

```
ldap.import.method=user
ldap.import.method=group
```

Settings for exporting users from the portal to LDAP. This allows a user to modify his first name, last name, etc. in the portal and have that change get pushed to the LDAP server. This will only be active if the property *ldap.auth.enabled* is also set to true.

```
ldap.export.enabled=true
```

Set this to true to use the LDAP's password policy instead of the portal password policy.

```
ldap.password.policy.enabled=false
```

Set these values to be a portion of the error message returned by the appropriate directory server to allow the portal to recognize messages from the LDAP server. The default values will work for Fedora DS.

```
ldap.error.password.age=age
ldap.error.password.expired=expired
ldap.error.password.history=history
ldap.error.password.not.changeable=not allowed to change
ldap.error.password.syntax=syntax
ldap.error.password.trivial=trivial
ldap.error.user.lockout=retry limit
```

CAS

Set this to true to enable CAS single sign on. NTLM will work only if LDAP authentication is also enabled and the authentication is made by screen name. If set to true, then the property *auto.login.hooks* must contain a reference to the class *com.liferay.portal.security.auth.CASAutoLogin* and the filter *com.liferay.portal.servlet.filters.sso.cas.CASFilter* must be referenced in web.xml.

```
cas.auth.enabled=false
```

A user may be authenticated from CAS and not yet exist in the portal. Set this to true to automatically import users from LDAP if they do not exist in the portal.

```
cas.import.from.ldap=false
```

Set the default values for the required CAS URLs. Set either *cas.server.name* or *cas.service.url*. Setting *cas.server.name* allows deep linking. See LEP-4423.

```
cas.login.url=https://localhost:8443/cas-web/login
cas.logout.url=https://localhost:8443/cas-web/logout
cas.server.name=localhost:8080
cas.service.url=
#cas.service.url=http://localhost:8080/c/portal/login
```

```
cas.service.url=http://localhost:8080/c/portal/login
cas.validate.url=https://localhost:8443/cas-web/proxyValidate
```

NTLM

Set this to true to enable NTLM single sign on. NTLM will work only if LDAP authentication is also enabled and the authentication is made by screen name. If set to true, then the property "auto.login.hooks" must contain a reference to the class *com.liferay.portal.security.auth.NtlmAutoLogin* and the filter *com.liferay.portal.servlet.filters.sso.ntlm.NtlmFilter* must be referenced in web.xml.

```
ntlm.auth.enabled=false
ntlm.auth.domain.controller=127.0.0.1
ntlm.auth.domain=EXAMPLE
```

OpenID

Set this to true to enable OpenId authentication. If set to true, then the property *auto.login.hooks* must contain a reference to the class *com.liferay.portal.security.auth.OpenIdAutoLogin*.

```
open.id.auth.enabled=true
```

OpenSSO

These properties control Liferay's integration with OpenSSO.

Set this to true to enable OpenSSO authentication.

```
open.sso.auth.enabled=false
```

Set the log in URL and log out URL. The first URL is the link to your OpenSSO server (which can be the same server as the one running Liferay); the second URL is the link to your Liferay Portal.

```
open.sso.login.url=http://localhost:8080/opensso/UI/Login?goto=http://localhost:8080/
open.sso.logout.url=http://localhost:8080/opensso/UI/Logout?goto=http://localhost:8080/
```

Set the URL to the OpenSSO service.

```
open.sso.service.url=http://localhost:8080/opensso/identity
```

Set the name of the OpenSSO cookie. This is the default.

```
open.sso.subject.cookie.name=iPlanetDirectoryPro
```

AUTHENTICATION PIPELINE

Input a list of comma delimited class names that implement *com.liferay.portal.security.auth.Authenticator*. These classes will run before or after the portal authentication begins.

The Authenticator class defines the constant values that should be used as return codes from the classes implementing the interface. If# authentication is successful, return SUCCESS; if the user exists but the passwords do not match, return FAILURE; and if the user does not exist on the system, return DNE.

Constants in Authenticator:

```
public static final int SUCCESS = 1;
public static final int FAILURE = -1;
public static final int DNE = 0;
```

In case you have several classes in the authentication pipeline, all of them have to return SUCCESS if you want the user to be able to login. If one of the authenticators returns FAILURE or DNE, the login fails.

Under certain circumstances, you might want to keep the information in the portal database in sync with an external database or an LDAP server. This can easily be achieved by implementing a class via LDAPAuth that updates the information stored in the portal user database whenever a user signs in.

Each portal instance can be configured at run time to either authenticate based on user ids or email addresses. See the Admin portlet for more information.

Available authenticators are:

com.liferay.portal.security.auth.LDAPAuth

See the LDAP properties to configure the behavior of the LDAPAuth class.

```
auth.pipeline.pre=com.liferay.portal.security.auth.LDAPAuth
auth.pipeline.post=
```

Set this to true to enable password checking by the internal portal authentication. If set to false, you're essentially delegating password checking is delegated to the authenticators configured in *auth.pipeline.pre* and *auth.pipeline.post* settings.

```
auth.pipeline.enable.liferay.check=true
```

Input a list of comma delimited class names that implement *com.liferay.portal.security.auth.AuthFailure*. These classes will run when a user has a failed login or when a user has reached the maximum number of failed logins.

```
auth.failure=com.liferay.portal.security.auth.LoginFailure
auth.max.failures=com.liferay.portal.security.auth.LoginMaxFailures
auth.max.failures.limit=5
```

Set the following to true if users are allowed to have simultaneous logins from different sessions.

```
auth.simultaneous.logins=true
```

Set the following to true if users are forwarded to the last visited path upon successful login. If set to false, users will be forwarded to their default layout page.

```
auth.forward.by.last.path=true
```

The login page reads a redirect by a parameter named *redirect*. If this property is set to true, then users will be redirected to the given redirect path upon successful login. If the user does not have permission to view that page, then the rule set by the property *auth.forward.by.last.path* will apply.

You can set the redirect manually from another application, by appending the *redirect* parameter in a url that looks like this: */c/portal/login?redirect=%2Fgroup%2Femployees%2Fcalendar*. This url will redirect the user to the path */group/employees/calendar* upon successful login.

```
auth.forward.by.redirect=true
```

Enter a list of comma delimited paths that can be considered part of the last visited path.

```
auth.forward.last.paths=/document_library/get_file
```

Enter a list of comma delimited paths that do not require authentication.

```
auth.public.paths=\
    /blogs/find_entry,\
    /blogs/rss,\
    \
    /bookmarks/open_entry,\
    \
    /document_library/get_file,\
    \
    /journal/get_article,\
    /journal/get_articles,\
    /journal/get_latest_article_content,\
    /journal/get_structure,\
    /journal/get_template,\
    /journal/view_article_content,\
    /journal_articles/view_article_content,\
    \
    /message_boards/find_category,\
    /message_boards/find_message,\
    /message_boards/find_thread,\
    /message_boards/get_message_attachment,\
    /message_boards/rss,\
    \
    /messaging/action,\
    \
    /polls/view_chart,\
    \
    /portal/expire_session,\
    /portal/extend_session,\
    /portal/extend_session_confirm,\
    /portal/json_service,\
    /portal/logout,\
    /portal/open_id_request,\
    /portal/open_id_response,\
    /portal/session_click,\
    /portal/session_tree_js_click,\
    \
    /search/open_search,\
    /search/open_search_description.xml,\
    \
```

```
/shopping/notify
```

Auto Login

Input a list of comma delimited class names that implement *com.liferay.portal.security.auth.AutoLogin*. These classes will run in consecutive order for all unauthenticated users until one of them return a valid user id and password combination. If no valid combination is returned, then the request continues to process normally. If a valid combination is returned, then the portal will automatically login that user with the returned user id and password combination.

For example, *com.liferay.portal.security.auth.RememberMeAutoLogin* reads from a cookie to automatically log in a user who previously logged in while checking the *Remember Me* box.

This interface allows deployers to easily configure the portal to work with other SSO servers. See *com.liferay.portal.security.auth.CASAutoLogin* for an example of how to configure the portal with Yale's SSO server.

```
auto.login.hooks=com.liferay.portal.security.auth.CASAutoLogin,com.liferay.portal.secur-
ity.auth.NtlmAutoLogin,com.liferay.portal.security.auth.OpenIdAutoLogin,com.liferay.-
portal.security.auth.OpenSSOAutoLogin,com.liferay.portal.security.auth.RememberMeAutoLogin
```

SSO with MAC (Message Authentication Code)

To use SSO with MAC, post to an URL like:

http://localhost:8080/c/portal/login?cmd=already-registered&login=<userId| emailAddress>&password=<MAC>

Pass the MAC in the password field. Make sure the MAC gets URL encoded because it might contain characters not allowed in a URL.

SSO with MAC also requires that you set the following property in system.properties:

```
com.liferay.util.servlet.SessionParameters=false
```

See the following links:

http://support.liferay.com/browse/LEP-1288

http://en.wikipedia.org/wiki/Message_authentication_code

Set the following to true to enable SSO with MAC.

```
auth.mac.allow=false
```

Set the algorithm to use for MAC encryption.

```
auth.mac.algorithm=MD5
```

Set the shared key used to generate the MAC.

```
auth.mac.shared.key=
```

Passwords

Set the following encryption algorithm to encrypt passwords. The default algorithm is SHA (SHA-1). If set to NONE, passwords are stored in the database as plain text. The SHA-512 algorithm is currently unsupported.

Examples:

```
passwords.encryption.algorithm=CRYPT
passwords.encryption.algorithm=MD2
passwords.encryption.algorithm=MD5
passwords.encryption.algorithm=NONE
passwords.encryption.algorithm=SHA
passwords.encryption.algorithm=SHA-256
passwords.encryption.algorithm=SHA-384
passwords.encryption.algorithm=SSHA
```

Input a class name that extends *com.liferay.portal.security.pwd.BasicToolkit*. This class will be called to generate and validate passwords.

Examples:

```
passwords.toolkit=com.liferay.portal.security.pwd.PasswordPolicyToolkit
passwords.toolkit=com.liferay.portal.security.pwd.RegExpToolkit
```

If you choose to use *com.liferay.portal.security.pwd.PasswordPolicyToolkit* as your password toolkit, you can choose either static or dynamic password generation. Static is set through the property *passwords.-passwordpolicytoolkit.static* and dynamic uses the class *com.liferay.util.PwdGenerator* to generate the password. If you are using LDAP password syntax checking, you will also have to use the static generator so that you can guarantee that passwords obey its rules.

Examples:

```
passwords.passwordpolicytoolkit.generator=static
passwords.passwordpolicytoolkit.generator=dynamic
passwords.passwordpolicytoolkit.static=iheartliferay
```

If you choose to use *com.liferay.portal.security.pwd.RegExpToolkit* as your password toolkit, set the regular expression pattern that will be used to generate and validate passwords.

Note that \ is replaced with \\ to work in Java.

The first pattern ensures that passwords must have at least 4 valid characters consisting of digits or letters.

The second pattern ensures that passwords must have at least 8 valid characters consisting of digits or letters.

Examples:

```
passwords.regexptoolkit.pattern=(?=.{4})(?:[a-zA-Z0-9]*)
passwords.regexptoolkit.pattern=(?=.{8})(?:[a-zA-Z0-9]*)
```

Set the length and key for generating passwords.

Examples:

```
passwords.regexptoolkit.charset=0123456789
passwords.regexptoolkit.charset=0123456789ABCDEFGHIJKLMNOPQRSTUVWXYZabcdefghijklmnopqr-
stuvwxyz
```

Examples:

```
passwords.regexptoolkit.length=4
passwords.regexptoolkit.length=8
```

Set the name of the default password policy.

```
passwords.default.policy.name=Default Password Policy
```

PERMISSIONS

Set the default permission checker class used by *com.liferay.portal.security.permission.PermissionCheckerFactory* to check permissions for actions on objects. These classes can be overridden with custom classes that extend *com.liferay.portal.security.permission.PermissionCheckerImpl*.

```
permissions.checker=com.liferay.portal.security.permission.PermissionCheckerImpl
```

Set the algorithm used to check permissions for a user. This is useful so that you can optimize the search for different databases. See *com.liferay.portal.service.impl.PermissionLocalServiceImpl*. The default is method two.

The first algorithm uses several *if* statements to query the database for these five things in order. If it finds any one of them, it returns *true:*

- Is the user connected to one of the permissions via group or organization roles?
- Is the user associated with groups or organizations that are directly connected to one of the permissions?
- Is the user connected to one of the permissions via user roles?
- Is the user connected to one of the permissions via user group roles?
- Is the user directly connected to one of the permissions?

```
permissions.user.check.algorithm=1
```

The second algorithm (the default) does a database join and checks the permissions in one step, by calling *countByGroupsRoles*, *countByGroupsPermissions*, *countByUsersRoles*, *countByUserGroupRole*, and *countByUsersPermissions* in one method.

```
permissions.user.check.algorithm=2
```

The third algorithm checks the permissions by checking for three things. It combines the role check into one step. If it finds any of the following items, it returns *true:*

- Is the user associated with groups or organizations that are directly connected to one of the permissions?

- Is the user associated with a role that is directly connected to one of the permissions?

- Is the user directly connected to one of the permissions?

```
permissions.user.check.algorithm=3
```

The fourth algorithm does a database join and checks the permissions that algorithm three checks in one step, by calling *countByGroupsPermissions*, *countByRolesPermissions*, and *countByUsersPermissions* in one method.

```
permissions.user.check.algorithm=4
```

CAPTCHA

Set the maximum number of captcha checks per portlet session. Set this value to 0 to always check. Set this value to a number less than 0 to never check. Unauthenticated users will always be checked on every request if captcha checks is enabled.

```
captcha.max.challenges=1
```

STARTUP EVENTS

Input a list of comma delimited class names that extend *com.liferay.portal.struts.SimpleAction*. These classes will run at the specified event.

The following is a global startup event that runs once when the portal initializes.

```
global.startup.events=com.liferay.portal.events.GlobalStartupAction
```

The following is an application startup event that runs once for every web site instance of the portal that initializes.

```
application.startup.events=com.liferay.portal.events.AppStartupAction
```

SHUTDOWN EVENTS

Input a list of comma delimited class names that extend *com.liferay.portal.struts.SimpleAction*. These classes will run at the specified event.

Global shutdown event that runs once when the portal shuts down.

```
global.shutdown.events=com.liferay.portal.events.GlobalShutdownAction
```

Application shutdown event that runs once for every web site instance of the portal that shuts down.

```
application.shutdown.events=com.liferay.portal.events.AppShutdownAction
```

Programmatically kill the Java process on shutdown. This is a workaround for a bug in Tomcat and Linux where the process hangs on forever.

See http://support.liferay.com/browse/LEP-2048 for more information.

```
shutdown.programmatically.exit=false
```

PORTAL EVENTS

Input a list of comma delimited class names that extend *com.liferay.portal.struts.Action*. These classes will run before or after the specified event.

Servlet service event: the pre-service events have an associated error page and will forward to that page if an exception is thrown during excecution of the events. The pre-service events process before Struts processes the request.

Examples:

```
servlet.service.events.pre=com.liferay.portal.events.ServicePreAction
servlet.service.events.pre=com.liferay.portal.events.LogMemoryUsageAction,com.liferay.-
portal.events.LogThreadCountAction,com.liferay.portal.events.ServicePreAction
servlet.service.events.pre=com.liferay.portal.events.LogSessionIdAction,com.liferay.-
portal.events.ServicePreAction
servlet.service.events.pre=com.liferay.portal.events.ServicePreAction,com.liferay.-
portal.events.RandomLayoutAction
servlet.service.events.pre=com.liferay.portal.events.ServicePreAction,com.liferay.-
portal.events.RandomLookAndFeelAction
```

Use the following to define the error page.

```
servlet.service.events.pre.error.page=/common/error.jsp
```

The post-service events process after Struts processes the request.

```
servlet.service.events.post=com.liferay.portal.events.ServicePostAction
```

LOGIN EVENT

Define events that can occur pre-login and post-login.

```
login.events.pre=com.liferay.portal.events.LoginPreAction
login.events.post=com.liferay.portal.events.LoginPostAction,com.liferay.portal.events.De-
faultLandingPageAction
```

LOGOUT EVENT

Similarly, events can be defined for the log out event.

```
logout.events.pre=com.liferay.portal.events.LogoutPreAction
```

Example post events:

```
logout.events.post=com.liferay.portal.events.LogoutPostAction
logout.events.post=com.liferay.portal.events.LogoutPostAction,com.liferay.portal.event-
s.GarbageCollectorAction
```

DEFAULT LANDING PAGE

Set the default landing page path for logged in users relative to the server path. For example, if you want the default landing page to be http://localhost:8080/web/guest/home, set this to /web/guest/home. To activate this feature, set auth.forward.by.last.path to true. To customize the behavior, see *com.liferay.portal.events.DefaultLandingPageAction* in the *login.events.post* property above.

```
default.landing.page.path=/web/guest/home
```

DEFAULT GUEST

The Guest group at least one public page. The settings for the initial public page are specified in the following properties. For more complex behavior, override the *addDefaultLayouts* method in *com.liferay.portal.service.impl.GroupLocalServiceImpl*.

Set the layout name.

```
default.guest.layout.name=Welcome
```

Set the layout template id that matches an existing TPL.

Examples:

```
default.guest.layout.template.id=1_2_1_columns
default.guest.layout.template.id=1_column
default.guest.layout.template.id=2_2_columns
default.guest.layout.template.id=2_columns_i
default.guest.layout.template.id=2_columns_ii
default.guest.layout.template.id=2_columns_iii
default.guest.layout.template.id=3_columns
```

Set the layout ids for the column specified in the layout template.

```
default.guest.layout.column-1=58,
default.guest.layout.column-2=47,
default.guest.layout.column-3=
default.guest.layout.column-4=
```

Set the friendly url. This will only have an effect if the Guest group also has a friendly URL set.

```
default.guest.friendly.url=/home
```

DEFAULT USER

Users who have the Power User role must have at least one private personal page. The settings for the initial private page are specified in the following properties. For more complex behavior, override the *addDefaultLayouts* method in *com.liferay.portal.events.ServicePreAction*.

Set the layout name.

```
default.user.layout.name=Home
```

Set the layout template id that matches an existing TPL.

Examples:

```
default.user.layout.template.id=1_2_1_columns
default.user.layout.template.id=1_column
default.user.layout.template.id=2_2_columns
default.user.layout.template.id=2_columns_i
default.user.layout.template.id=2_columns_ii
default.user.layout.template.id=2_columns_iii
default.user.layout.template.id=3_columns
```

Set the layout ids for the column specified in the layout template.

```
default.user.layout.column-1=71_INSTANCE_OYOd,82,23,61,65,
default.user.layout.column-2=11,29,8,19
default.user.layout.column-3=
default.user.layout.column-4=
```

DEFAULT ADMIN

Set the default admin password.

```
default.admin.password=test
```

Set the default admin screen name prefix.

```
default.admin.screen.name=test
```

Set the default admin email address prefix.

```
default.admin.email.address.prefix=test
```

Set the default admin first name.

```
default.admin.first.name=Test
```

Set the default admin middle name.

```
default.admin.middle.name=
```

Set the default admin last name.

```
default.admin.last.name=Test
```

LAYOUTS

Set the list of layout types. The display text of each of the layout types is set in *content/Language.-properties* and prefixed with *layout.types*. You can create new layout types and specify custom settings for each layout type. End users input dynamic values as designed in the edit page. End users see the layout as designed in the view page. The generated URL can reference properties set in the edit page. Parentable layouts can contain child layouts.

```
layout.types=portlet,embedded,article,url,link_to_layout
```

Default settings layouts.

```
layout.edit.page=/portal/layout/edit/portlet.jsp
layout.view.page=/portal/layout/view/portlet.jsp
```

```
layout.url=${liferay:mainPath}/portal/layout?p_l_id=${liferay:plid}
layout.url.friendliable=true
layout.parentable=true
layout.sitemapable=true
```

Settings for portlet layouts are inherited from the default settings.

```
layout.edit.page[portlet]=/portal/layout/edit/portlet.jsp
layout.view.page[portlet]=/portal/layout/view/portlet.jsp
layout.url[portlet]=${liferay:mainPath}/portal/layout?p_l_id=${liferay:plid}
layout.url.friendliable[portlet]=true
layout.parentable[portlet]=true
```

Settings for embedded layouts.

```
layout.edit.page[embedded]=/portal/layout/edit/embedded.jsp
layout.view.page[embedded]=/portal/layout/view/embedded.jsp
layout.url[embedded]=${liferay:mainPath}/portal/layout?p_l_id=${liferay:plid}
layout.url.friendliable[embedded]=true
layout.parentable[embedded]=false
layout.sitemapable[embedded]=true
```

Settings for article layouts.

```
layout.edit.page[article]=/portal/layout/edit/article.jsp
layout.view.page[article]=/portal/layout/view/article.jsp
layout.url.friendliable[article]=true
layout.url[article]=${liferay:mainPath}/portal/layout?p_l_id=${liferay:plid}
layout.parentable[article]=false
layout.sitemapable[article]=true
```

Settings for URL layouts.

```
layout.edit.page[url]=/portal/layout/edit/url.jsp
layout.view.page[url]=
layout.url[url]=${url}
layout.url.friendliable[url]=true
layout.parentable[url]=false
layout.sitemapable[url]=false
```

Settings for page layouts.

```
layout.edit.page[link_to_layout]=/portal/layout/edit/link_to_layout.jsp
layout.view.page[link_to_layout]=
layout.url[link_to_layout]=${liferay:mainPath}/portal/layout?p_l_id=${linkToPlid}
layout.url.friendliable[link_to_layout]=true
layout.parentable[link_to_layout]=true
layout.sitemapable[link_to_layout]=false
```

Specify static portlets that cannot be moved and will always appear on every layout. Static portlets will take precedence over portlets that may have been dynamically configured for the layout.

For example, if you want the Hello World portlet to always appear at the start of the iteration of the first column for user layouts, set the property *layout.static.portlets.start.column-1[user]* to *47*. If you want the Hello World portlet to always appear at the end of the second column for user layouts, set the property *layout.static.portlets.end.column-2[user]* to *47*. You can input a list of comma delimited portlet ids to specify more than one portlet. If the portlet is instanceable, add the suffix *_INSTANCE_abcd* to the portlet id, where *abcd* is any random alphanumeric string.

The static portlets are fetched based on the properties controlled by custom filters using EasyConf. By default, the available filters are user, community, and organization.

```
layout.static.portlets.start.column-1[user]=3,6
layout.static.portlets.end.column-1[user]=14
layout.static.portlets.start.column-2[user]=71_INSTANCE_abcd,7
layout.static.portlets.end.column-2[user]=34,70
layout.static.portlets.start.column-3[user]=
layout.static.portlets.end.column-3[user]=
```

It is also possible to add a static portlet which only shows in the first layout of a user or community.

```
layout.static.portlets.start.column-1[user][firstLayout]=3,6
layout.static.portlets.end.column-2[community][firstLayout]=14
```

Set the static layouts for community layouts.

```
layout.static.portlets.start.column-1[community]=
layout.static.portlets.end.column-1[community]=
layout.static.portlets.start.column-2[community]=
layout.static.portlets.end.column-2[community]=
layout.static.portlets.start.column-3[community]=
layout.static.portlets.end.column-3[community]=
```

Set the static layouts for organization layouts.

```
layout.static.portlets.start.column-1[organization]=
layout.static.portlets.end.column-1[organization]=
layout.static.portlets.start.column-2[organization]=
layout.static.portlets.end.column-2[organization]=
layout.static.portlets.start.column-3[organization]=
layout.static.portlets.end.column-3[organization]=
```

Set the private group, private user, and public servlet mapping for *com.liferay.portal.servlet.Friendly-URLServlet*. This value must match the servlet mapping set in web.xml.

For example, if the private group pages are mapped to */group* and the group's friendly URL is set to */guest* and the layout's friendly URL is set to */company/community*, then the friendly URL for the page will be *http://www.liferay.com/group/guest/company/community*. Private group pages map to a community's private pages and are only available to authenticated users with the proper permissions.

For example, if the public pages are mapped to */web* and the group or user's friendly URL is set to */guest* and the layout's friendly URL is set to */company/community*, then the friendly URL for the page will be *http://www.liferay.com/web/guest/company/community*. Public pages are available to unauthenticated users.

The friendly URLs for users, groups, and layouts can be set during runtime.

```
layout.friendly.url.private.group.servlet.mapping=/group
layout.friendly.url.private.user.servlet.mapping=/user
layout.friendly.url.public.servlet.mapping=/web
```

Redirect to this resource if the user requested a friendly URL that does not exist. Leave it blank to display nothing.

```
layout.friendly.url.page.not.found=/html/portal/404.html
```

Set the reserved keywords that cannot be used in a friendly URL.

```
layout.friendly.url.keywords=c,group,web,image,wsrp,page,public,private,blogs,calendar,docu-
ment_library,image_gallery,journal,message_boards,podcast,rss,tags,wiki
```

Set the following to true if users are allowed to add portlets from the layout page.

```
layout.add.portlets=true
```

Set the maximum length to display a layout name.

```
layout.name.max.length=10
```

Set the maximum number of tabs per row.

```
layout.tabs.per.row=7
```

Set the following to true if layouts should remember (across sessions) that a window state was set to maximized.

```
layout.remember.session.window.state.maximized=false
```

Set the following to true if layouts should remember (across requests) that a window state was set to maximized.

```
layout.remember.request.window.state.maximized=false
```

Set the following to true if guest users should see the maximize window icon.

```
layout.guest.show.max.icon=false
```

Set the following to true if guest users should see the minimize window icon.

```
layout.guest.show.min.icon=false
```

Set the following to true if users are shown that they do not have access to a portlet. The portlet init parameter *show-portlet-access-denied* will override this setting.

```
layout.show.portlet.access.denied=true
```

Set the following to true if users are shown that a portlet is inactive. The portlet init parameter *show-portlet-inactive* will override this setting.

```
layout.show.portlet.inactive=true
```

Set the default layout template id used when creating layouts.

```
layout.default.template.id=2_columns_ii
```

Set the following to false to disable parallel rendering. You can also disable it on a per request basis by setting the attribute key *com.liferay.portal.util.WebKeys.PORTLET_PARALLEL_RENDER* to the *Boolean.FALSE* in a pre service event or by setting the URL parameter *p_p_parallel* to *0*.

```
layout.parallel.render.enable=true
```

Set the name of a class that implements *com.liferay.portal.util.LayoutClone*. This class is used to remember maximized and minimized states on shared pages. The default implementation persists the state in the browser session.

```
layout.clone.impl=com.liferay.portal.util.SessionLayoutClone
```

Set the following to true to cache the content of layout templates. This is recommended because it improves performance for production servers. Setting it to false is useful during development if you need to make a lot of changes.

```
layout.template.cache.enabled=true
```

Set the default value for the *p_l_reset* parameter. If set to true, then render parameters are cleared when different pages are hit. This is not the behavior promoted by the portlet specification, but is the one that most end users seem to prefer.

```
layout.default.p_l_reset=true
```

Portlet URL

Set the following to true if calling setParameter on a portlet URL appends the parameter value versus replacing it. There is some disagreement in the interpretation of the JSR 168 spec among portlet developers over this specific behavior. Liferay Portal successfully passes the portlet TCK tests whether this value is set to true or false.

See http://support.liferay.com/browse/LEP-426 for more information.

```
portlet.url.append.parameters=false
```

Set the following to true to allow portlet URLs to generate with an anchor tag.

```
portlet.url.anchor.enable=false
```

Preferences

Set the following to true to validate portlet preferences on startup.

```
preference.validate.on.startup=false
```

Struts

Input the custom Struts request processor that will be used by Struts based portlets. The custom class must extend *com.liferay.portal.struts.PortletRequestProcessor* and have the same constructor.

```
struts.portlet.request.processor=com.liferay.portal.struts.PortletRequestProcessor
```

IMAGES

Set the location of the default spacer image that is used for missing images. This image must be found in the class path.

```
image.default.spacer=com/liferay/portal/dependencies/spacer.gif
```

Set the location of the default company logo image that is used for missing company logo images. This image must be found in the class path.

```
image.default.company.logo=com/liferay/portal/dependencies/company_logo.png
```

Set the location of the default user portrait image that is used for missing user portrait images. This image must be found in the class path.

```
image.default.user.portrait=com/liferay/portal/dependencies/user_portrait.gif
```

EDITORS

You can configure individual JSP pages to use a specific implementation of the available WYSIWYG editors: liferay, fckeditor, simple, tinymce, or tinymcesimple.

```
editor.wysiwyg.default=fckeditor
editor.wysiwyg.portal-web.docroot.html.portlet.blogs.edit_entry.jsp=fckeditor
editor.wysiwyg.portal-web.docroot.html.portlet.calendar.edit_configuration.jsp=fckeditor
editor.wysiwyg.portal-web.docroot.html.portlet.enterprise_admin.view.jsp=fckeditor
editor.wysiwyg.portal-web.docroot.html.portlet.invitation.edit_configuration.jsp=fckeditor
editor.wysiwyg.portal-web.docroot.html.portlet.journal.edit_article_content.jsp=fckeditor
editor.wysiwyg.portal-web.docroot.html.portlet.journal.edit_article_content_xsd_el.jsp=fckeditor
editor.wysiwyg.portal-web.docroot.html.portlet.journal.edit_configuration.jsp=fckeditor
editor.wysiwyg.portal-web.docroot.html.portlet.mail.edit.jsp=fckeditor
editor.wysiwyg.portal-web.docroot.html.portlet.mail.edit_message.jsp=fckeditor
editor.wysiwyg.portal-web.docroot.html.portlet.message_boards.edit_configuration.jsp=fckeditor
editor.wysiwyg.portal-web.docroot.html.portlet.shopping.edit_configuration.jsp=fckeditor
editor.wysiwyg.portal-web.docroot.html.portlet.wiki.edit_page.jsp=fckeditor
```

FIELDS

Set the following fields to false so users cannot see them. Some company policies require gender and birthday information to always be hidden.

```
field.enable.com.liferay.portal.model.Contact.male=true
field.enable.com.liferay.portal.model.Contact.birthday=true
```

MIME TYPES

Input a list of comma delimited mime types that are not available by default from *javax.activation.-MimetypesFileTypeMap.*

```
mime.types=\
```

```
application/pdf pdf,\
application/vnd.ms-excel xls,\
application/vnd.ms-powerpoint ppt,\
application/msword doc
```

AMAZON LICENSE KEYS

Enter a list of valid Amazon license keys. Configure additional keys by incrementing the last number. The keys are used following a Round-Robin algorithm. This is made available only for personal use. Please see the Amazon license at http://www.amazon.com for more information.

```
amazon.license.0=
amazon.license.1=
amazon.license.2=
amazon.license.3=
```

INSTANT MESSENGER

Set the AIM login and password which the system will use to communicate with users.

```
aim.login=
aim.password=
```

Due to a bug in JOscarLib 0.3b1, you must set the full path to the ICQ jar.

See the following posts:

http://sourceforge.net/forum/message.php?msg_id=1972697

http://sourceforge.net/forum/message.php?msg_id=1990487

```
icq.jar=C:/Java/orion-2.0.7/lib/icq.jar
```

Set the ICQ login and password which the system will use to communicate with users.

```
icq.login=
icq.password=
```

Set the MSN login and password which the system will use to communicate with users.

```
msn.login=
msn.password=
```

Set the YM login and password which the system will use to communicate with users.

```
ym.login=
ym.password=
```

LUCENE SEARCH

Set the following to true if you want to index your entire library of files on startup.

```
index.on.startup=false
```

Set the following to true if you want the indexing on startup to be executed on a separate thread to speed up execution.

```
index.with.thread=true
```

Designate whether Lucene stores indexes in a database via JDBC, file system, or in RAM.

Examples:

```
lucene.store.type=jdbc
lucene.store.type=file
lucene.store.type=ram
```

Lucene's storage of indexes via JDBC has a bug where temp files are not removed. This can eat up disk space over time. Set the following property to true to automatically clean up the temporary files once a day. See LEP-2180.

```
lucene.store.jdbc.auto.clean.up=true
```

Set the JDBC dialect that Lucene uses to store indexes in the database. This is only referenced if Lucene stores indexes in the database. Liferay will attempt to load the proper dialect based on the URL of the JDBC connection. For example, the property *lucene.store.jdbc.dialect.mysql* is read for the JDBC connection URL *jdbc:mysql://localhost/lportal.*

```
lucene.store.jdbc.dialect.db2=org.apache.lucene.store.jdbc.dialect.DB2Dialect
lucene.store.jdbc.dialect.derby=org.apache.lucene.store.jdbc.dialect.DerbyDialect
lucene.store.jdbc.dialect.hsqldb=org.apache.lucene.store.jdbc.dialect.HSQLDialect
lucene.store.jdbc.dialect.jtds=org.apache.lucene.store.jdbc.dialect.SQLServerDialect
lucene.store.jdbc.dialect.microsoft=org.apache.lucene.store.jdbc.dialect.SQLServerDialect
lucene.store.jdbc.dialect.mysql=org.apache.lucene.store.jdbc.dialect.MySQLDialect
#lucene.store.jdbc.dialect.mysql=org.apache.lucene.store.jdbc.dialect.MySQLInnoDBDialect
#lucene.store.jdbc.dialect.mysql=org.apache.lucene.store.jdbc.dialect.MySQLMyISAMDialect
lucene.store.jdbc.dialect.oracle=org.apache.lucene.store.jdbc.dialect.OracleDialect
lucene.store.jdbc.dialect.postgresql=org.apache.lucene.store.jdbc.dialect.PostgreSQLDialect
```

Set the directory where Lucene indexes are stored. This is only referenced if Lucene stores indexes in the file system.

```
lucene.dir=${resource.repositories.root}/lucene/
```

Input a class name that extends *com.liferay.portal.lucene.LuceneFileExtractor.* This class is called by Lucene to extract text from complex files so that they can be properly indexed.

```
lucene.file.extractor=com.liferay.portal.lucene.LuceneFileExtractor
```

The file extractor can sometimes return text that is not valid for Lucene. This property expects a regular expression. Any character that does not match the regular expression will be replaced with a blank space. Set an empty regular expression to disable this feature.

Examples:

```
lucene.file.extractor.regexp.strip=
lucene.file.extractor.regexp.strip=[\\d\\w]
```

Set the default analyzer used for indexing and retrieval.

Examples:

```
lucene.analyzer=org.apache.lucene.analysis.br.BrazilianAnalyzer
lucene.analyzer=org.apache.lucene.analysis.cn.ChineseAnalyzer
lucene.analyzer=org.apache.lucene.analysis.cjk.CJKAnalyzer
lucene.analyzer=org.apache.lucene.analysis.cz.CzechAnalyzer
lucene.analyzer=org.apache.lucene.analysis.nl.DutchAnalyzer
lucene.analyzer=org.apache.lucene.analysis.fr.FrenchAnalyzer
lucene.analyzer=org.apache.lucene.analysis.de.GermanAnalyzer
lucene.analyzer=org.apache.lucene.analysis.KeywordAnalyzer
lucene.analyzer=org.apache.lucene.index.memory.PatternAnalyzer
lucene.analyzer=org.apache.lucene.analysis.PerFieldAnalyzerWrapper
lucene.analyzer=org.apache.lucene.analysis.ru.RussianAnalyzer
lucene.analyzer=org.apache.lucene.analysis.SimpleAnalyzer
lucene.analyzer=org.apache.lucene.analysis.snowball.SnowballAnalyzer
lucene.analyzer=org.apache.lucene.analysis.standard.StandardAnalyzer
lucene.analyzer=org.apache.lucene.analysis.StopAnalyzer
lucene.analyzer=org.apache.lucene.analysis.WhitespaceAnalyzer
```

Set Lucene's merge factor. Higher numbers mean indexing goes faster but uses more memory. The default value from Lucene is 10. This should never be set to a number lower than 2.

```
lucene.merge.factor=10
```

Set how often to run Lucene's optimize method. Optimization speeds up searching but slows down writing. Set this property to 0 to always optimize. Set this property to an integer greater than 0 to optimize every X writes.

```
lucene.optimize.interval=1
```

VALUE OBJECT

You can add a listener for a specific class by setting the property *value.object.listener* plus the class name to a class that implements *com.liferay.portal.model.ModelListener*.

```
value.object.listener.com.liferay.portal.model.Contact=com.liferay.portal.model.ContactL-
istener
value.object.listener.com.liferay.portal.model.Layout=com.liferay.portal.model.LayoutListen-
er
value.object.listener.com.liferay.portal.model.LayoutSet=com.liferay.portal.model.LayoutSet-
Listener
value.object.listener.com.liferay.portal.model.PortletPreferences=com.liferay.portal.model.-
PortletPreferencesListener
value.object.listener.com.liferay.portal.model.User=com.liferay.portal.model.UserListener
value.object.listener.com.liferay.portlet.journal.model.JournalArticle=com.liferay.portlet.-
journal.model.JournalArticleListener
value.object.listener.com.liferay.portlet.journal.model.JournalTemplate=com.liferay.portlet.-
journal.model.JournalTemplateListener
```

Value objects are cached by default. You can disable caching for all objects or per object.

For mapping tables, the key is the mapping table itself.

```
value.object.finder.cache.enabled=true
value.object.finder.cache.enabled.com.liferay.portal.model.Layout=true
value.object.finder.cache.enabled.com.liferay.portal.model.User=true
value.object.finder.cache.enabled.Users_Roles=true
```

LAST MODIFIED

Set the following to true to check last modified date on server side CSS and JavaScript.

```
last.modified.check=true
```

Enter a list of comma delimited paths that will only be executed when newer than the last modified date. These paths must extend *com.liferay.portal.lastmodified.LastModifiedAction.*

```
last.modified.paths=\
    /portal/css_cached,\
    /portal/javascript_cached
```

XSS (CROSS SITE SCRIPTING)

Set the following to false to ensure that all persisted data is stripped of XSS hacks.

```
xss.allow=false
```

You can override the *xss.allow* setting for a specific class by setting the property *xss.allow* plus the class name.

```
xss.allow.com.liferay.portal.model.Portlet=true
xss.allow.com.liferay.portal.model.PortletPreferences=true
```

You can override the *xss.allow* setting for a specific field in a class by setting the property *xss.allow* plus the class and field name.

```
xss.allow.com.liferay.portlet.journal.model.JournalArticle.content=true
xss.allow.com.liferay.portlet.journal.model.JournalStructure.xsd=true
xss.allow.com.liferay.portlet.journal.model.JournalTemplate.xsl=true
```

COMMUNICATION LINK

Set the JGroups properties used by the portal to communicate with other instances of the portal. This is only needed if the portal is running in a clustered environment. The JGroups settings provide a mechanism for the portal to broadcast messages to the other instances of the portal. The specified multicast address should be unique for internal portal messaging only. You will still need to set the Hibernate and OSCache settings for database clustering.

```
comm.link.properties=UDP(bind_addr=127.0.0.1;mcast_addr=231.12.21.102;mcast_port=45566;ip_tt
l=32;mcast_send_buf_size=150000;mcast_recv_buf_size=80000):PING(timeout=2000;num_initial_mem
bers=3):MERGE2(min_interval=5000;max_interval=10000):FD_SOCK:VERIFY_SUSPECT(timeout=1500):pb-
cast.NAKACK(gc_lag=50;retransmit_timeout=300,600,1200,2400,4800;max_xmit_size=8192):UNICAST(
timeout=300,600,1200,2400):pbcast.STABLE(desired_avg_gossip=20000):FRAG(frag_size=8096;down_
thread=false;up_thread=false):pbcast.GMS(join_timeout=5000;join_retry_timeout=2000;shun=fals
```

```
e;print_local_addr=true)
```

CONTENT DELIVERY NETWORK

Set the hostname that will be used to serve static content via a CDN. This property can be overridden dynamically at runtime by setting the HTTP parameter *cdn_host*.

```
cdn.host=
```

COUNTER

Set the number of increments between database updates to the Counter table. Set this value to a higher number for better performance.

```
counter.increment=100
```

LOCK

Set the lock expiration time for each class.

Example: 1 Day

```
lock.expiration.time.com.liferay.portlet.documentlibrary.model.DLFileEntryModel=86400000
```

Example: 20 Minutes

```
lock.expiration.time.com.liferay.portlet.wiki.model.WikiPageModel=1200000
```

JABBER

```
jabber.xmpp.server.enabled=false
jabber.xmpp.server.address=localhost
jabber.xmpp.server.name=localhost
jabber.xmpp.server.port=5222
jabber.xmpp.user.password=L1f3RayJabb3r
```

JBI

Connect to either Mule or ServiceMix as your ESB.

Examples:

```
jbi.workflow.url=http://localhost:8080/mule-web/workflow
jbi.workflow.url=http://localhost:8080/servicemix-web/workflow
```

JCR

Liferay includes Jackrabbit (http://jackrabbit.apache.org) by default as its JSR-170 Java Content Repository.

```
jcr.initialize.on.startup=false
jcr.workspace.name=liferay
```

```
jcr.node.documentlibrary=documentlibrary
jcr.jackrabbit.repository.root=${resource.repositories.root}/jackrabbit
jcr.jackrabbit.config.file.path=${jcr.jackrabbit.repository.root}/repository.xml
jcr.jackrabbit.repository.home=${jcr.jackrabbit.repository.root}/home
jcr.jackrabbit.credentials.username=none
jcr.jackrabbit.credentials.password=none
```

REVERSE AJAX

```
reverse.ajax.enabled=false
reverse.ajax.heartbeat=180000
```

SCHEDULER

Set this to false to disable all scheduler classes defined in *liferay-portlet.xml*.

```
scheduler.enabled=true
```

SMTP

```
smtp.server.enabled=false
smtp.server.port=48625
smtp.server.subdomain=events
```

SOCIAL BOOKMARKS

The Blogs portlet allows for the posting of entries to various popular social bookmarking sites. The example ones are the defaults; to configure more, just add the site in the format below.

```
social.bookmark.types=blinklist,delicious,digg,furl,newsvine,reddit,technorati
social.bookmark.post.url[blinklist]=http://blinklist.com/index.php?Action=Blink/ad-
dblink.php&url=${liferay:social-bookmark:url}&Title=${liferay:social-bookmark:title}
social.bookmark.post.url[delicious]=http://del.icio.us/post?url=${liferay:social-
bookmark:url}&title=${liferay:social-bookmark:title}
social.bookmark.post.url[digg]=http://digg.com/submit?phase=2&url=${liferay:social-
bookmark:url}
social.bookmark.post.url[furl]=http://furl.net/storeIt.jsp?u=${liferay:social-
bookmark:url}&t=${liferay:social-bookmark:title}
social.bookmark.post.url[newsvine]=http://www.newsvine.com/_tools/seed&save?u=${liferay:so-
cial-bookmark:url}&h=${liferay:social-bookmark:title}
social.bookmark.post.url[reddit]=http://reddit.com/submit?url=${liferay:social-
bookmark:url}&title=${liferay:social-bookmark:title}
social.bookmark.post.url[technorati]=http://technorati.com/cosmos/search.html?url=$
{liferay:social-bookmark:url}
```

VELOCITY ENGINE

Input a list of comma delimited class names that extend *com.liferay.util.velocity.VelocityResourceListener*. These classes will run in sequence to allow you to find the applicable ResourceLoader to load a Velocity template.

```
velocity.engine.resource.listeners=com.liferay.portal.velocity.ServletVelocityResourceL-
istener,com.liferay.portal.velocity.JournalTemplateVelocityResourceListener,com.liferay.-
portal.velocity.ThemeLoaderVelocityResourceListener,com.liferay.portal.velocity.ClassLoad-
erVelocityResourceListener
```

Set the Velocity resource managers. We extend the Velocity's default resource managers for better scalability.

```
velocity.engine.resource.manager=com.liferay.portal.velocity.LiferayResourceManager
velocity.engine.resource.manager.cache=com.liferay.portal.velocity.LiferayResourceCache
velocity.engine.resource.manager.cache.enabled=false
```

Input a list of comma delimited macros that will be loaded. These files must exist in the class path.

```
velocity.engine.velocimacro.library=VM_global_library.vm,VM_liferay.vm
```

Set the Velocity logging configuration.

```
velocity.engine.logger=org.apache.velocity.runtime.log.SimpleLog4JLogSystem
velocity.engine.logger.category=org.apache.velocity
```

VIRTUAL HOSTS

Set the hosts that will be ignored for virtual hosts.

```
    virtual.hosts.ignore.hosts=\
        127.0.0.1,\
        localhost
```

Set the paths that will be ignored for virtual hosts.

```
virtual.hosts.ignore.paths=\
        /c,\
        \
        /c/portal/change_password,\
        /c/portal/css_cached,\
        /c/portal/extend_session,\
        /c/portal/extend_session_confirm,\
        /c/portal/javascript_cached,\
        /c/portal/json_service,\
        /c/portal/layout,\
        /c/portal/login,\
        /c/portal/logout,\
        /c/portal/render_portlet,\
        /c/portal/reverse_ajax,\
        /c/portal/session_tree_js_click,\
        /c/portal/update_layout,\
        /c/portal/update_terms_of_use,\
        /c/portal/upload_progress_poller,\
        \
        /c/chat/roster,\
        \
        /c/layout_configuration/templates,\
```

```
   /c/layout_management/update_page,\
   \
   /c/messaging/action
```

WEB SERVER

Set the HTTP and HTTPs ports when running the portal in a J2EE server that is sitting behind another web server like Apache. Set the values to -1 if the portal is not running behind another web server like Apache.

```
web.server.http.port=-1
web.server.https.port=-1
```

Set the hostname that will be used when the portlet generates URLs. Leaving this blank will mean the host is derived from the servlet container.

```
web.server.host=
```

Set the preferred protocol.

```
web.server.protocol=https
```

MAIN SERVLET

Servlets can be protected by *com.liferay.filters.secure.SecureFilter*.

Input a list of comma delimited IPs that can access this servlet. Input a blank list to allow any IP to access this servlet. SERVER_IP will be replaced with the IP of the host server.

```
main.servlet.hosts.allowed=
```

Set the following to true if this servlet can only be accessed via https.

```
main.servlet.https.required=false
```

AXIS SERVLET

See Main Servlet on how to protect this servlet.

```
axis.servlet.hosts.allowed=127.0.0.1,SERVER_IP
axis.servlet.https.required=false
```

JSON TUNNEL SERVLET

See Main Servlet on how to protect this servlet.

```
json.servlet.hosts.allowed=
json.servlet.https.required=false
```

LIFERAY TUNNEL SERVLET

See Main Servlet on how to protect this servlet.

```
tunnel.servlet.hosts.allowed=127.0.0.1,SERVER_IP
tunnel.servlet.https.required=false
```

Spring Remoting Servlet

See Main Servlet on how to protect this servlet.

```
spring.remoting.servlet.hosts.allowed=127.0.0.1,SERVER_IP
spring.remoting.servlet.https.required=false
```

WebDAV Servlet

See Main Servlet on how to protect this servlet.

```
webdav.servlet.hosts.allowed=
webdav.servlet.https.required=false
```

Admin Portlet

You can set some administrative defaults by using these properties. The first time you bring up your portal, these values will then already be set in the Admin portlet.

Set up default group names.

```
admin.default.group.names=
```

Set up default role names.

```
admin.default.role.names=Power User\nUser
```

Set up default user group names.

```
admin.default.user.group.names=
```

The rest of these properties map to their values in the Admin portlet.

```
admin.mail.host.names=
admin.reserved.screen.names=
admin.reserved.email.addresses=
admin.email.from.name=Joe Bloggs
admin.email.from.address=test@liferay.com
admin.email.user.added.enabled=true
admin.email.user.added.subject=com/liferay/portlet/admin/dependencies/email_user_added_sub-
ject.tmpl
admin.email.user.added.body=com/liferay/portlet/admin/dependencies/email_user_added_body.tm-
pl
admin.email.password.sent.enabled=true
admin.email.password.sent.subject=com/liferay/portlet/admin/dependencies/email_password_sent
_subject.tmpl
admin.email.password.sent.body=com/liferay/portlet/admin/dependencies/email_password_sent_bo
dy.tmpl
```

BLOGS PORTLET

The following properties affect the Blogs portlet.

```
blogs.email.comments.added.enabled=true
blogs.email.comments.added.subject=com/liferay/portlet/blogs/dependencies/email_comments_ad-
ded_subject.tmpl
blogs.email.comments.added.body=com/liferay/portlet/blogs/dependencies/email_comments_added_
body.tmpl
```

CALENDAR PORTLET

Set the list of event types. The display text of each of the event types is set in *content/Language.-properties.*

```
calendar.event.types=anniversary,appointment,bill-
payment,birthday,breakfast,call,chat,class,club-event,concert,dinner,event,graduation,happy-
hour,holiday,interview,lunch,meeting,movie,net-event,other,party,performance,press-
release,reunion,sports-event,travel,tv-show,vacation,wedding
calendar.email.from.name=Joe Bloggs
calendar.email.from.address=test@liferay.com
calendar.email.event.reminder.enabled=true
calendar.email.event.reminder.subject=com/liferay/portlet/calendar/dependencies/email_event_
reminder_subject.tmpl
calendar.email.event.reminder.body=com/liferay/portlet/calendar/dependencies/email_event_re-
minder_body.tmpl
```

DOCUMENT LIBRARY PORTLET

Set the name of a class that implements *com.liferay.documentlibrary.util.Hook.* The document library server will use this to persist documents.

Available hooks are:

- com.liferay.documentlibrary.util.FileSystemHook

- com.liferay.documentlibrary.util.JCRHook

- com.liferay.documentlibrary.util.S3Hook

Examples:

```
dl.hook.impl=com.liferay.documentlibrary.util.FileSystemHook
dl.hook.impl=com.liferay.documentlibrary.util.JCRHook
dl.hook.impl=com.liferay.documentlibrary.util.S3Hook
```

FileSystemHook

```
dl.hook.file.system.root.dir=${resource.repositories.root}/document_library
```

S3Hook

```
dl.hook.s3.access.key=
dl.hook.s3.secret.key=
```

```
dl.hook.s3.bucket.name=
```

Set the maximum file size and valid file extensions for documents. A value of 0 for the maximum file size can be used to indicate unlimited file size. However, the maximum file size allowed by the system is set in property *com.liferay.util.servlet.UploadServletRequest.max.size* found in *system.properties*. A file extension of * will permit all file extensions.

You can map a GIF for the extension by adding the image to the theme's image display and document library folder. The wildcard extension of * will be ignored. For example, the default image for the DOC extension would be found in: */html/themes/classic/images/document_library/doc.gif*.

Examples:

```
dl.file.max.size=307200
dl.file.max.size=1024000
dl.file.max.size=3072000
```

Example File Extensions:

```
dl.file.extensions=.bmp,.css,.doc,.dot,.gif,.gz,.htm,.html,.jpg,.js,.odb,.odf,.odg,.odp,.ods
,.odt,.pdf,.png,.ppt,.rtf,.swf,.sxc,.sxi,.sxw,.tar,.tiff,.tgz,.txt,.vsd,.xls,.xml,.zip
```

Set folder names that will be used to synchronize with a community's set of private and public layouts. This will allow users to manage layouts using the Document Library portlet, and ultimately, via Web-DAV. This feature is experimental.

```
dl.layouts.sync.enabled=false
dl.layouts.sync.private.folder=Pages - Private
dl.layouts.sync.public.folder=Pages - Public
```

IMAGE GALLERY PORTLET

Set the maximum file size and valid file extensions for images. A value of 0 for the maximum file size can be used to indicate unlimited file size. However, the maximum file size allowed by the system is set in property *com.liferay.util.servlet.UploadServletRequest.max.size* found in *system.properties*. A file extension of * will permit all file extensions.

Set the maximum thumbnail height or width to 0 to ignore that dimension.

```
ig.image.max.size=307200
ig.image.extensions=.bmp,.gif,.jpeg,.jpg,.png,.tif,.tiff
ig.image.thumbnail.max.height=50
ig.image.thumbnail.max.width=50
```

INVITATION PORTLET

```
invitation.email.max.recipients=20
invitation.email.message.body=com/liferay/portlet/invitation/dependencies/email_message_body
.tmpl
invitation.email.message.subject=com/liferay/portlet/invitation/dependencies/email_message_s
ubject.tmpl
```

JOURNAL PORTLET

Set this to true if article ids should always be autogenerated.

```
journal.article.force.autogenerate.id=true
```

Set this to true so that only the latest version of an article that is also not approved can be saved without incrementing version.

```
journal.article.force.increment.version=false
```

Set the list of article types. The display text of each of the article types is set in content/Language.-properties.

```
journal.article.types=announcements,blogs,general,news,press-release,test
```

Set the interval on which the CheckArticleJob will run. The value is set in one minute increments.

```
journal.article.check.interval=15
```

Set this to true if structure ids should always be autogenerated.

```
journal.structure.force.autogenerate.id=false
```

Set this to true if template ids should always be autogenerated.

```
journal.template.force.autogenerate.id=false
```

Set the maximum file size and valid file extensions for images. A value of 0 for the maximum file size can be used to indicate unlimited file size. However, the maximum file size allowed by the system is set in property *com.liferay.util.servlet.UploadServletRequest.max.size* found in *system.properties*. A file extension of * will permit all file extensions.

```
journal.image.small.max.size=51200
journal.image.extensions=.gif,.jpeg,.jpg,.png
```

Input a list of comma delimited class names that extend *com.liferay.portlet.journal.util.TransformerListener*. These classes will run in sequence to allow you to modify the XML and XSL before it's transformed and allow you to modify the final output.

```
journal.transformer.listener=\
    com.liferay.portlet.journal.util.TokensTransformerListener,\
    #com.liferay.portlet.journal.util.PropertiesTransformerListener,\
    com.liferay.portlet.journal.util.ContentTransformerListener,\
    com.liferay.portlet.journal.util.LocaleTransformerListener
```

Set whether to synchronize content searches when server starts.

```
journal.sync.content.search.on.startup=false
```

Other Settings

```
journal.email.from.name=Joe Bloggs
journal.email.from.address=test@liferay.com
journal.email.article.approval.denied.enabled=false
journal.email.article.approval.denied.subject=com/liferay/portlet/journal/dependencies/email
```

```
_article_approval_denied_subject.tmpl
journal.email.article.approval.denied.body=com/liferay/portlet/journal/dependencies/email_ar
ticle_approval_denied_body.tmpl
journal.email.article.approval.granted.enabled=false
journal.email.article.approval.granted.subject=com/liferay/portlet/journal/dependencies/emai
l_article_approval_granted_subject.tmpl
journal.email.article.approval.granted.body=com/liferay/portlet/journal/dependencies/email_a
rticle_approval_granted_body.tmpl
journal.email.article.approval.requested.enabled=false
journal.email.article.approval.requested.subject=com/liferay/portlet/journal/dependencies/em
ail_article_approval_requested_subject.tmpl
journal.email.article.approval.requested.body=com/liferay/portlet/journal/dependencies/email
_article_approval_requested_body.tmpl
journal.email.article.review.enabled=false
journal.email.article.review.subject=com/liferay/portlet/journal/dependencies/email_article_
review_subject.tmpl
journal.email.article.review.body=com/liferay/portlet/journal/dependencies/email_article_re-
view_body.tmpl
```

Specify the strategy used when Journal content is imported using the LAR system.

```
journal.lar.creation.strategy=com.liferay.portlet.journal.lar.JournalCreationStrategyImpl
```

JOURNAL ARTICLES PORTLET

Set the available values for the number of articles to display per page.

```
journal.articles.page.delta.values=5,10,25,50,100
```

MAIL PORTLET

Set the following to false if administrator should not be allowed to change the mail domain via the Admin portlet.

```
mail.mx.update=true
```

Set the name of a class that implements *com.liferay.mail.util.Hook*. The mail server will use this class to ensure that the mail and portal servers are synchronized on user information. The portal will not know how to add, update, or delete users from the mail server except through this hook.

Available hooks are:

- com.liferay.mail.util.CyrusHook

- com.liferay.mail.util.DummyHook

- com.liferay.mail.util.FuseMailHook

- com.liferay.mail.util.SendmailHook

- com.liferay.mail.util.ShellHook

Example:

```
mail.hook.impl=com.liferay.mail.util.DummyHook
```

CyrusHook

Set the commands for adding, updating, and deleting a user where %1% is the user id. Replace the password with the password for the cyrus user.

Add Examples:

```
mail.hook.cyrus.add.user=cyrusadmin password create %1%
mail.hook.cyrus.add.user=cyrus_adduser password %1%
```

Delete Examples:

```
mail.hook.cyrus.delete.user=cyrusadmin password delete %1%
mail.hook.cyrus.delete.user=cyrus_userdel password %1%
```

Other properties:

```
mail.hook.cyrus.home=/home/cyrus
```

FuseMailHook

See http://www.fusemail.com/support/api.html for more information. You must also update the *mail.account.finder* property.

```
mail.hook.fusemail.url=https://www.fusemail.com/api/request.html
mail.hook.fusemail.username=
mail.hook.fusemail.password=
mail.hook.fusemail.account.type=group_subaccount
mail.hook.fusemail.group.parent=
```

SendmailHook

Set the commands for adding, updating, and deleting a user where %1% is the user id and %2% is the password. Set the home and virtual user table information.

```
mail.hook.sendmail.add.user=adduser %1% -s /bin/false
mail.hook.sendmail.change.password=autopasswd %1% %2%
mail.hook.sendmail.delete.user=userdel -r %1%
mail.hook.sendmail.home=/home
mail.hook.sendmail.virtusertable=/etc/mail/virtusertable
mail.hook.sendmail.virtusertable.refresh=bash -c "makemap hash /etc/mail/virtusertable
< /etc/mail/virtusertable"
```

ShellHook

Set the location of the shell script that will interface with any mail server.

```
mail.hook.shell.script=/usr/sbin/mailadmin.ksh
```

Set the mail box style that your IMAP server uses. Washington IMAP uses "mail/" whereas Courier IMAP and Cyrus IMAP use "INBOX." as their mail box styles. The mail box style is an IMAP implementation

---

specific namespace that is used in referencing folders.

Examples:

```
mail.box.style=mail/
mail.box.style=INBOX.
```

Set the name of the Inbox folder. Most IMAP servers use *INBOX* as the folder name. Domino requires *Inbox* as the folder name.

Examples:

```
mail.inbox.name=INBOX
mail.inbox.name=Inbox
```

Set other default folder names.

```
mail.spam.name=Spam
mail.sent.name=Sent
mail.drafts.name=Drafts
mail.trash.name=Trash
```

The user will be warned once per session to empty their spam if their spam folder exceeds this size. Set the size to 0 to disable any warnings.

```
mail.spam.warning.size=5120000
```

The user will be warned once per session to empty their trash if their trash folder exceeds this size. Set the size to 0 to disable any warnings.

```
mail.trash.warning.size=5120000
```

Set to true to enable SMTP debugging.

```
mail.smtp.debug=false
```

Input a list of comma delimited email addresses that will receive a BCC of every email sent through the mail server.

```
mail.audit.trail=
```

Set the maximum file size for attachments. However, the maximum file size allowed by the system is set in property *com.liferay.util.servlet.UploadServletRequest.max.size* found in system.properties.

```
mail.attachments.max.size=3072000
```

Specify a class name that implements *com.liferay.portlet.mail.util.multiaccount.AccountFinder*. Another implementation could allow the Mail portlet to access multiple accounts.

Examples:

```
mail.account.finder=com.liferay.portlet.mail.util.multiaccount.EmailAddressAccountFinder
mail.account.finder=com.liferay.portlet.mail.util.multiaccount.FuseMailAccountFinder
mail.account.finder=com.liferay.portlet.mail.util.multiaccount.ScreenNameAccountFinder
mail.account.finder=com.liferay.portlet.mail.util.multiaccount.UserIdAccountFinder
```

The password lookup algorithm for account finders first checks the session and then the User_ table for the passsword. Sometimes it's helpful for testing purposes to be able to manually set a password for all users. This can also useful if the IMAP mail server is secure behind a firewall and you don't want to deal with synchronizing passwords between systems.

```
mail.account.finder.password=
```

Input a list of comma delimited class names that implement *com.liferay.portlet.mail.util.recipient.RecipientFinder*. These classes will be used to find available recipients for the mail portlet.

```
mail.recipient.finder=com.liferay.portlet.mail.util.recipient.DirectoryRecipientFinder
```

MESSAGE BOARDS PORTLET

Miscellaneous properties.

```
message.boards.email.from.name=Joe Bloggs
message.boards.email.from.address=test@liferay.com
message.boards.email.message.added.enabled=true
message.boards.email.message.added.subject.prefix=com/liferay/portlet/messageboards/depend-
encies/email_message_added_subject_prefix.tmpl
message.boards.email.message.added.body=com/liferay/portlet/messageboards/dependencies/email
_message_added_body.tmpl
message.boards.email.message.added.signature=com/liferay/portlet/messageboards/dependencies/
email_message_added_signature.tmpl
message.boards.email.message.updated.enabled=true
message.boards.email.message.updated.subject.prefix=com/liferay/portlet/messageboards/de-
pendencies/email_message_updated_subject_prefix.tmpl
message.boards.email.message.updated.body=com/liferay/portlet/messageboards/dependencies/ema
il_message_updated_body.tmpl
message.boards.email.message.updated.signature=com/liferay/portlet/messageboards/dependen-
cies/email_message_updated_signature.tmpl
```

Enter time in minutes on how often this job is run. If a user's ban is set to expire at 12:05 PM and the job runs at 2 PM, the expire will occur during the 2 PM run.

```
message.boards.expire.ban.job.interval=120
```

Enter time in days to automatically expire bans on users. Set to 0 to disable auto expire.

Examples:

```
message.boards.expire.ban.interval=10
message.boards.expire.ban.interval=0
```

Enter rss feed content length. This value limits what goes in the RSS feed from the beginning of the message board post. The default is the first 80 characters.

```
message.boards.rss.content.length=80
```

Set the user attribute to signify the user name.

Examples:

```
message.boards.user.name.attribute=user.name.nickName
message.boards.user.name.attribute=user.name.full
```

My Places Portlet

Set this to true to show user public sites with no layouts.

```
my.places.show.user.public.sites.with.no.layouts=true
```

Set this to true to show user private sites with no layouts.

```
my.places.show.user.private.sites.with.no.layouts=true
```

Set this to true to show organization public sites with no layouts.

```
my.places.show.organization.public.sites.with.no.layouts=true
```

Set this to true to show organization private sites with no layouts.

```
my.places.show.organization.private.sites.with.no.layouts=true
```

Set this to true to show community public sites with no layouts.

```
my.places.show.community.public.sites.with.no.layouts=true
```

Set this to true to show community private sites with no layouts.

```
my.places.show.community.private.sites.with.no.layouts=true
```

Navigation Portlet

Specify the options that will be provided to the user in the edit configuration mode of the portlet.

```
navigation.display.style.options=1,2,3,4,5,6
```

Define each mode with 4 comma delimited strings that represent the form: headerType, rootLayoutType, rootLayoutLevel, and includedLayouts.

```
navigation.display.style[1]=breadcrumb,relative,0,auto
navigation.display.style[2]=root-layout,absolute,2,auto
navigation.display.style[3]=root-layout,absolute,1,auto
navigation.display.style[4]=none,absolute,1,auto
navigation.display.style[5]=none,absolute,1,all
navigation.display.style[6]=none,absolute,0,auto
```

Portlet CSS Portlet

Set this to true to enable the ability to modify portlet CSS at runtime via the Look and Feel icon. Disabling it can speed up performance.

```
portlet.css.enabled=true
```

Shopping Portlet

Set the following to true if cart quantities must be a multiple of the item's minimum quantity.

```
shopping.cart.min.qty.multiple=true
```

Set the following to true to forward to the cart page when adding an item from the category page.

The item must not have dynamic fields. All items with dynamic fields will forward to the item's details page regardless of the following setting.

```
shopping.category.forward.to.cart=false
```

Set the following to true to show special items when browsing a category.

```
shopping.category.show.special.items=false
```

Set the following to true to show availability when viewing an item.

```
shopping.item.show.availability=true
```

Set the maximum file size and valid file extensions for images. A value of 0 for the maximum file size can be used to indicate unlimited file size. However, the maximum file size allowed by the system is set in property *com.liferay.util.servlet.UploadServletRequest.max.size* found in *system.properties*. A file extension of * will permit all file extensions.

```
shopping.image.small.max.size=51200
shopping.image.medium.max.size=153600
shopping.image.large.max.size=307200
shopping.image.extensions=.gif,.jpeg,.jpg,.png
shopping.email.from.name=Joe Bloggs
shopping.email.from.address=test@liferay.com
shopping.email.order.confirmation.enabled=true
shopping.email.order.confirmation.subject=com/liferay/portlet/shopping/dependencies/email_or
der_confirmation_subject.tmpl
shopping.email.order.confirmation.body=com/liferay/portlet/shopping/dependencies/email_or-
der_confirmation_body.tmpl
shopping.email.order.shipping.enabled=true
shopping.email.order.shipping.subject=com/liferay/portlet/shopping/dependencies/email_order_
shipping_subject.tmpl
shopping.email.order.shipping.body=com/liferay/portlet/shopping/dependencies/email_order_shi
pping_body.tmpl
```

SOFTWARE CATALOG PORTLET

Set the maximum file size and max file dimensions for thumbnnails. A value of 0 for the maximum file size can be used to indicate unlimited file size. However, the maximum file size allowed by the system is set in property *com.liferay.util.servlet.UploadServletRequest.max.size* found in *system.properties*.

```
sc.image.max.size=307200
sc.image.thumbnail.max.height=200
sc.image.thumbnail.max.width=160
```

TAGS COMPILER PORTLET

Set this to true to enable the ability to compile tags from the URL. Disabling it can speed up performance.

```
tags.compiler.enabled=true
```

Tags Portlet

Input a class name that extends *com.liferay.portlet.tags.util.TagsAssetValidator*. This class will be called to validate assets. The TagsAssetValidator class is just an empty class that doesn't actually do any validation. The BasicTagsAssetValidator requires all assets to have at least one tag entry.

Examples:

```
tags.asset.validator=com.liferay.portlet.tags.util.TagsAssetValidator
tags.asset.validator=com.liferay.portlet.tags.util.BasicTagsAssetValidator
```

Translator Portlet

Set the default languages to translate a given text.

```
translator.default.languages=en_es
```

Web Form Portlet

Set the maximum number of dynamic fields to process.

```
web.form.portlet.max.fields=50
```

Wiki Portlet

Set the URL of a page that contains more information about the classic syntax of the wiki. It will be shown to the user when editing a page.

```
wiki.classic.syntax.help.url=http://wiki.liferay.com/index.php/Wiki_Portlet
```

Set the name of the default page for a wiki node. The name for the default page must be a valid wiki word. A wiki word follows the format of having an upper case letter followed by a series of lower case letters followed by another upper case letter and another series of lower case letters. See http://www.use-mod.com/cgi-bin/wiki.pl?WhatIsaWiki for more information on wiki naming conventions.

```
wiki.front.page.name=FrontPage
```

Set the name of the default node that will be automatically created when the Wiki portlet is first used in a community.

```
wiki.initial.node.name=Main
```

Plugin Management

One of the primary ways of extending the functionality of Liferay Portal is by the use of *plugins*. Plugins are an umbrella term for installable *portlet* and *theme* Java EE .war files. Though Liferay comes bundled with a number of functional portlets and themes, plugins provide a means of extending Liferay to be able to do almost anything.

Portlets

Portlets are small web applications that run in a portion of a web page. The heart of any portal implementation is its portlets, because all of the functionality of a portal resides in its portlets. Liferay's core is a portlet container. The container's job is to manage the portal's pages and to aggregate the set of portlets that are to appear on any particular page. This means that all of the features and functionality of a portal application must be in its portlets.

Portlet applications, like servlet applications, have become a Java standard which various portal server vendors have implemented. The JSR-168 standard defines the portlet specification. A JSR-168 standard portlet should be deployable on any JSR-168 portlet container. Portlets are placed on the page in a certain order by the end user and are served up dynamically by the portal server. This means that certain "givens" that apply to servlet-based projects, such as control over URLs or access to the HttpServletRequest object, don't apply in portlet projects, because the portal server generates these objects dynamically.

Portal applications come generally in two flavors: 1) portlets can be written to provide small amounts of functionality and then aggregated by the portal server into a larger application, or 2) whole applications can be written to reside in only one or a few portlet windows. The choice is up to those designing the application. The developer only has to worry about what happens inside of the portlet itself; the portal server handles building out the page as it is presented to the user.

Most developers nowadays like to use certain frameworks to develop their applications, because those frameworks provide both functionality and structure to a project. For example, Struts enforces the Model-View-Controller design pattern and provides lots of functionality—such as custom tags and form validation—that make it easier for a developer to implement certain standard features. With Liferay, developers are free to use all of the leading frameworks in the Java EE space, including Struts, Spring, and Java Server Faces. This allows developers familiar with those frameworks to more easily implement portlets, and also facilitates the quick porting of an application using those frameworks over to a portlet implementation.

Does your organization make use of any Enterprise Planning (ERP) software that exposes its data via web services? You could write a portlet plugin for Liferay that can consume that data and display it as part of a dashboard page for your users. Do you subscribe to a stock service? You could pull stock quotes from that service and display them on your page, instead of using Liferay's built-in Stocks portlet. Do you have a need to combine the functionality of two or more servlet-based applications on one page? You could make them into portlet plugins and have Liferay display them in whatever layout you want. Do you have existing Struts, Spring MVC, or JSF applications that you want to integrate with your portal? It is a straightforward task to migrate these applications into Liferay, and then they can take advantage of the layout, security, and administration infrastructure that Liferay provides.

Themes

Themes are hot deployable plugins which can completely transform the look and feel of the portal. Most organizations have their own look and feel standards which go across all of the web sites and web applications in the infrastructure. Liferay makes it possible for a site designer to create a theme plugin which can then be installed, allowing for the complete transformation of the portal to whatever look and feel is needed. There are lots of available theme plugins on Liferay's web site, and more are being added every day. This makes it easier for those who wish to develop themes for Liferay, as you can now choose a theme which most closely resembles what you want to do and then customize it. This is much easier than starting a theme from scratch. There is more about theme development in the *Liferay Developer's Guide*.

Installing Plugins from Liferay's Official and Community Repositories

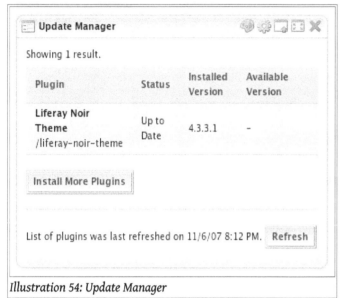

Illustration 54: Update Manager

Liferay Portal comes with two portlets which can handle plugin installation: the **Plugin Installer** and the **Update Manager**. Both portlets have similar functionality; the only difference between them is that the Update Manager can go out to the repositories and determine if you are running the most recent version of a plugin. For this reason, we will use the Update Manager portlet to install plugins.

From an appropriate private page on either a personal or public community, go up to the Dock and select *Add Content*. From the *Admin* category, click the *Add* button next to *Update Manager*. Then close the Add Content window.

You should now see the Update Manager on your page. Move it to an appropriate area of the page.

The default look of the Update Manager shows which plugins are already installed on the system, what their version numbers are, and whether an update is available.

If you would like to see what plugins are available, you can do so by clicking the *Install More Plugins* button. Please note that the machine upon which Liferay is running must have access to the Internet in order to be able to read the Official and Community repositories. If the machine does not have access to the Internet, you will need to download the plugins from the site and install them manually. We will discuss how to do this later in this chapter.

From the initial page you can also refresh the list of plugins. This causes the portlet to access the repository on the Internet and update the list of plugins that are available. When the refresh is complete, a status message is displayed which shows whether the refresh was successful.

After the *Install More Plugins* button is clicked, a new view of the portlet appears. This view has multiple tabs, and by default, displays the *Portlet Plugins* tab. Note that the list displayed is a list of all of the plugins that are available across all of the repositories to which the server is subscribed. Above this is a search mechanism which allows you to search for plugins by their name, by whether they are installed, by tag, or by which repository they are in.

To install a plugin, choose the plugin by clicking on its name. For example, if your web site is for an organization to which visitors are likely to travel, you might want to install the Google Maps plugin. This plugin provides a handy interface to Google Maps from inside of Liferay, and therefore from inside of your web site.

Find the Google Maps plugin in the list by searching for it or browsing to it. Once you have found it, click on its name. Another page will be displayed which describes the portlet plugin in more detail. Below the description is an *Install* button. Click this button to install your plugin.

Illustration 55: Google Maps portlet installation

The plugin chosen will be automatically downloaded and installed on your instance of Liferay. If you have the Liferay console open, you can view the deployment as it happens. When it is finished, you should be able to go back to the Add Content window and add your new plugin to a page in your portal.

The same procedure is used for installing new Liferay Themes. Instead of the *Portlet Plugins* tab, you would use the *Theme Plugins* tab of the Plugin Installer to view the themes. Convenient thumbnails (plus a larger version when you click on the details of a particular theme) are shown in the list.

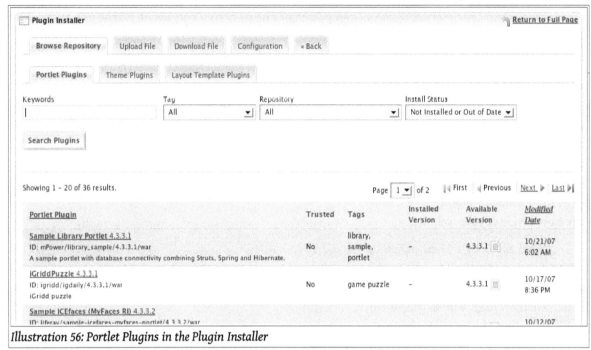

Illustration 56: Portlet Plugins in the Plugin Installer

After clicking on the *Install* button for a theme, the theme becomes available on the *Look and Feel* tab of any page.

Installing Plugins Manually

Installing plugins manually is almost as easy as installing plugins via the Plugin Installer. There are several scenarios in which you would need to install plugins manually rather than from Liferay's repositories:

● Your server is firewalled without access to the Internet. This makes it impossible for your instance of Liferay to connect to the plugin repositories.

● You are installing portlets which you have either purchased from a vendor, downloaded separately, or developed yourself.

● For security reasons, you do not want to allow portal administrators to install plugins from the Internet before they are evaluated.

You can still use the Update Manager / Plugin Installer portlets to install plugins that are not available from the on line repositories. This is by far the easiest way to install plugins.

If your server is firewalled, you will not see any plugins displayed in the *Portlet Plugins* tab or in the *Theme Plugins* tab. Instead, you will need to click the *Upload File* tab. This gives you a simple interface for uploading a .war file containing a portlet or a theme to your Liferay Portal.

Click the *Browse* button and navigate your file system to find the portlet or theme .war you have downloaded. The other field on the page is optional: you can specify your own context for deployment. If you leave this field blank, the default context defined in the plugin (or the .war file name itself) will be used.

That's all the information the Plugin Installer needs in order to deploy your portlet or theme. Click the *Install* button, and your plugin will be uploaded to the server and deployed. If it is a portlet, you should see it in the *Add Content* window. If it is a theme, it will be available on the *Look and Feel* tab in the page definition.

If you do not wish to use the Update Manager or Plugin Installer to deploy plugins, you can also deploy them at the operating system level. The first time Liferay starts, it creates a hot deploy folder which is by default created inside the home folder of the user who launched Liferay. For example, say that on a Linux system, the user *lportal* was created in order to run Liferay. The first time Liferay is launched, it will create a folder structure in */home/lportal/liferay* to house various configuration and administrative data. One of the folders it creates is called *deploy*. If you copy a portlet or theme plugin into this folder, Liferay will deploy it and make it available for use just as though you'd installed it via the Update Manager or Plugin Installer. In fact, this is what the Update Manager and Plugin Installer portlets are doing behind the scenes.

You can change the defaults for this directory structure so that it is stored anywhere you like by modifying the appropriate properties in your *portal-ext.properties* file. Please see the above section called **Advanced Liferay Configuration** for more information.

To have Liferay hot deploy a portlet or theme plugin, copy the plugin into your hot deploy folder, which by default is in *<User Home>/liferay/deploy*. If you are watching the Liferay console, you should see messages like the following:

```
17:44:16,811 INFO  [AutoDeployDir:76] Processing sample-struts-liferay-portlet-4.3.4.1.war
17:44:16,812 INFO  [PortletAutoDeployListener:77] Copying portlets
for /home/rsezov/liferay/deploy/sample-struts-liferay-portlet-4.3.4.1.war
17:44:16,819 INFO  [BaseDeployer:487] Deploying sample-struts-liferay-portlet-4.3.4.1.war
  Expanding: /home/rsezov/liferay/deploy/sample-struts-liferay-portlet-4.3.4.1.war
into /java/liferay/liferay-portal-tomcat5-4.3.4/temp/20071107174416905
  Copying 1 file to /java/liferay/liferay-portal-tomcat5-4.3.4/temp/20071107174416905/WEB-
INF
  Copying 1 file to /java/liferay/liferay-portal-tomcat5-4.3.4/temp/20071107174416905/WEB-
INF
17:44:19,016 INFO  [BaseDeployer:1074] Modifying Geronimo /java/liferay/liferay-portal-tomc-
at5-4.3.4/temp/20071107174416905/WEB-INF/geronimo-web.xml
17:44:19,049 INFO  [BaseDeployer:1120] Modifying Servlet 2.3 /java/liferay/liferay-portal-
tomcat5-4.3.4/temp/20071107174416905/WEB-INF/web.xml
  Copying 10 files to /java/liferay/liferay-portal-tomcat5-4.3.4/bin/../webapps/sample-
struts-liferay-portlet
  Copying 1 file to /java/liferay/liferay-portal-tomcat5-4.3.4/bin/../webapps/sample-struts-
liferay-portlet
  Deleting directory /java/liferay/liferay-portal-tomcat5-4.3.4/temp/20071107174416905
17:44:19,220 INFO  [PortletAutoDeployListener:87] Portlets
for /home/rsezov/liferay/deploy/sample-struts-liferay-portlet-4.3.4.1.war copied success-
fully
```

```
Nov 7, 2007 5:44:23 PM org.apache.catalina.startup.HostConfig checkResources
INFO: Reloading context [/sample-struts-liferay-portlet]
17:44:23,496 INFO  [PluginPackageHotDeployListener:74] Reading plugin package for sample-
struts-liferay-portlet
17:44:23,503 INFO  [PluginPackageHotDeployListener:221] Plugin package liferay/sample-
struts-liferay-portlet/4.3.4.1/war unregistered successfully
17:44:23,504 INFO  [PortletHotDeployListener:420] Unregistering portlets for sample-struts-
liferay-portlet
17:44:23,515 INFO  [PortletHotDeployListener:454] Portlets for sample-struts-liferay-portlet
unregistered successfully
17:44:24,185 INFO  [PluginPackageHotDeployListener:74] Reading plugin package for sample-
struts-liferay-portlet
17:44:24,243 INFO  [PluginPackageHotDeployListener:187] Plugin package liferay/sample-
struts-liferay-portlet/4.3.4.1/war registered successfully
17:44:24,244 INFO  [PortletHotDeployListener:129] Registering portlets for sample-struts-
liferay-portlet
17:44:24,261 INFO  [PortletHotDeployListener:383] Portlets for sample-struts-liferay-portlet
registered successfully
```

As long as you see the *registered successfully* message, your plugin was installed correctly, and will be available for use in the portal.

Plugin Troubleshooting

Sometimes for various reasons plugins fail to install. There are different reasons for this based on several factors, including

- Liferay configuration

- The container upon which Liferay is running

- Changing the configuration options in multiple places

- How Liferay is being launched

You will often be able to tell if you have a plugin deployment problem by looking at the Liferay server console. If you see the plugin get recognized by the hot deploy listener, you will see a *plugin copied successfully* message. If this message is not followed up by a *plugin registered successfully* message, you have an issue with your plugin deployment configuration, and it is likely one of the factors above.

We will look at each of these factors.

LIFERAY CONFIGURATION ISSUES

Liferay by default comes as a bundle or as a .war file. Though every effort has been made to make the .war file as generic as possible, sometimes the default settings are inappropriate for the container upon which Liferay is running. Most of these problems have been resolved in Liferay 4.3.5 with the addition of code that allows Liferay to determine which application server it is running on and adjust the way it deploys plugins as a result.

In versions of Liferay prior to 4.3.5, there is a property called *auto.deploy.dest.dir* that defines the folder where plugins are deployed after the hot deploy utilities have finished preparing them. This folder maps to a folder that the container defines as an auto-deploy or a hot deploy folder. By default, this property is set to *../webapps*. This default value works for Tomcat containers (if Tomcat has been launched from its *bin* folder), but will not work for other containers that define their hot deploy folders in a different place.

For example, Glassfish defines the hot deploy folder as a folder called *autodeploy* inside of the domain folder in which your server is running. By default, this is in *<Glassfish Home>/domains/domain1/autodeploy*. JBoss defines the hot deploy folder as a root folder inside of the particular server configuration you are using. By default, this is in *<JBoss Home>/server/default/deploy*. WebLogic defines this folder inside of the domain directory. By default, this is in *<Bea Home>/user_projects/domains/<domain name>/autodeploy*.

You will first need to determine where the hot deploy folder is for the container you are running. Consult your product documentation for this. Once you have this value, there are two places in which you can set it: the *portal-ext.properties* file and in the Plugin Installer portlet.

To change this setting in the *portal-ext.properties* file, browse to where Liferay was deployed in your application server. Inside of this folder should be a *WEB-INF/classes* folder. Here you will find the *portal-ext.properties* file. Open this file in a text editor and look for the property *auto.deploy.dest.dir*. If it does not appear in the file, you can add it. The safest way to set this property—as we will see later—is to define the property using an absolute path from the root of your file system to your application server's hot deploy folder. For example, if you are using Glassfish, and you have the server installed in */java/glassfish*, your *auto.deploy.dest.dir* property would look like the following:

```
auto.deploy.dest.dir=/java/glassfish/domains/domain1/autodeploy
```

Remember, if you are on a Windows system, use forward slashes instead of back slashes, like so:

```
auto.deploy.dest.dir=C:/java/glassfish/domains/domain1/autodeploy
```

Save the file and then restart your container. Now plugins should install correctly.

If you would rather change this setting via the Plugin Installer portlet (because you do not wish to restart your container), you can do that by clicking on the *Configuration* tab. On this page are a number of settings you can change, including the default folders for hot deploy, where Liferay should look for plugin repositories, and so on.

Destination Directory	../webapps

Illustration 57: Changing the hot deploy destination directory

The setting to change is the field marked *Destination Directory*. Change this to the full path to your container's auto deploy folder from the root of your file system. When you are finished, click the *Save* button at the bottom of the form. The setting will now take effect without your having to restart your container.

Note that the setting in the portlet overrides the setting in the properties file.

If you are having hot deploy trouble in Liferay versions 4.3.5 and greater, it is possible that the administrator of your application server has changed the default folder for auto deploy in your application server. In this case, you would want to set *auto.deploy.dest.dir* to the customized folder location as you would with older versions of Liferay. In Liferay 4.3.5 and greater, this setting still exists, but is blank. Add the property to your *portal-ext.properties* file and set its value to the fully qualified path to the auto deploy folder configured in your application server.

THE CONTAINER UPON WHICH LIFERAY IS RUNNING

There are some containers, such as Oracle Application Server and WebSphere®, which do not have a hot deploy feature. Unfortunately, these containers do not work with Liferay's hot deploy system. But this does not mean that you cannot install plugins on these containers. Some users have had success deploying plugins manually using the application server's deployment tools. On some containers, Liferay is able to pick up the portlet plugins once they get deployed to the container manually, especially if you add it to the same Enterprise Application project that was created for Liferay.

CHANGING THE CONFIGURATION OPTIONS IN MULTIPLE PLACES

Sometimes, especially during development when several people have administrative access to the server at the same time, the auto deploy folder location can get customized in both the *portal-ext.properties* file and in the Plugin Installer portlet. If this happens, the value in the Plugin Installer takes precedence over the value in the properties file. If you go into the Plugin Installer and change the value to the correct setting, plugin deployment will start working again.

HOW LIFERAY IS BEING LAUNCHED

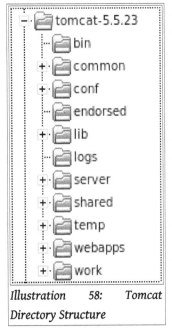

Illustration 58: Tomcat Directory Structure

In versions of Liferay prior to 4.3.5, the default value of the hot deploy destination directory is a relative path (e.g., *../webapps* or *../server/default/deploy*). This path is relative to the folder from which the application server is normally launched. For example, Tomcat has the pictured directory structure.

The start up and shut down scripts are in the *bin* folder. So to start Tomcat, you would normally go into the *bin* folder to run the startup script which starts Liferay running in Tomcat.

Tomcat's hot deploy folder is the *webapps* folder. This folder is on the same level the *bin* folder is on. If you are at the command prompt inside of the *bin* folder (where you started Tomcat), to get to a file in the hot deploy folder you would reference it by using two dots to go back up one folder, and then the path separator (/), and then the name of the folder (*webapps*). So in the default configuration, the hot deploy destination directory is relative to the folder from which the application server was launched.

If you are launching your application server from another script—perhaps as part of a cron job—and your script does not enter the folder the application server's startup scripts are in (in this case, *<Tomcat Home>/bin*), the relative path that is set by default will not work. Instead, the path will be relative to the path from which you launched the startup script. This will cause Liferay to create—in the Tomcat example —a *webapps* folder one folder up from where the startup script was launched. Since this is not the correct hot deploy folder for your application server, you will see the *copied successfully* message in the server console, but you will never see the *registered successfully* message.

To fix this, you can do one of two things: 1) Change the relative path to an absolute path as recommended above; or 2) Change the way you launch Liferay by making sure you go into the folder where the application server's startup scripts are before you launch them. Either one of these methods should fix your hot deploy problem and will result in the successful deployment of portlet and theme plugins.

Creating Your Own Plugin Repository

As your enterprise builds its own library of portlets for internal use, you can create your own plugin repository. This will allow different departments who may be running different instances of Liferay to share portlets and install them as needed. If you are a software development house, you may wish to create a plugin repository for your own products. Liferay makes it easy for you to create your own plugin repository and make it available to others.

You can create your plugin repository in two ways:

1. Add the Software Catalog portlet to an instance of Liferay and create the repository by using its graphical interface and an HTTP server.

2. Create an XML file using the Liferay Plugin Repository DTD (http://www.liferay.com/dtd/liferay-plugin-repository_4_3_0.dtd) and an HTTP server.

Both methods have their benefits. The first method allows users to upload their plugins to an HTTP server to which they have access. They can then register their plugins with the repository by adding a link to it via the portlet's graphical user interface. Liferay will then generate the XML necessary to connect the repository to a Plugin Installer portlet running another instance of Liferay. This XML file can then be placed on an HTTP server, and the URL to it can be added to the Plugin Installer, making the portlets in this repository available to the server running Liferay.

The second method does not require an instance of Liferay to be running. You can upload plugins to an HTTP server of your choice, and then create an XML file called *liferay-plugin-repository.xml* manually. If you make this file available on an HTTP server (it can be the same one upon which the plugins are stored, or a different one altogether), you can connect the repository to a Plugin Installer portlet running on an instance of Liferay.

We will first look at creating a plugin repository using the Software Catalog portlet.

THE SOFTWARE CATALOG PORTLET

You will want to use the Software Catalog portlet if you will have multiple users submitting portlets into the repository, and if you don't want to worry about creating the liferay-plugin-repository.xml file yourself.

The Software Catalog portlet is not an *instanceable* portlet, which means that each community can have only one instance of the portlet. If you add the portlet to another page in the community, it will hold the same data as the portlet that was first added. Different communities, however, can have different software repositories, so you can host several software repositories on the same instance of Liferay if you wish —they just have to be in different communities.

Choose the community that will host the plugin repository and add the Software Catalog portlet to the appropriate page in that community. You can do this by navigating to the page, selecting *Add Content*

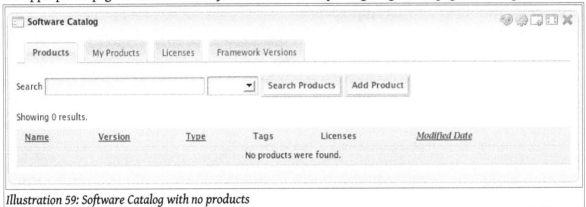

Illustration 59: Software Catalog with no products

from the Dock, expanding the *Admin* category, and clicking the *Add* button next to the Software Catalog. Close the *Add Content* window and then drag the Software Catalog portlet to a wide column and drop it there.

The Software Catalog portlet has several tabs. The first tab is labeled *Products*. The default view of the portlet, when populated with software, displays what plugins are available for install or download. This can be seen in the version on Liferay's home page.

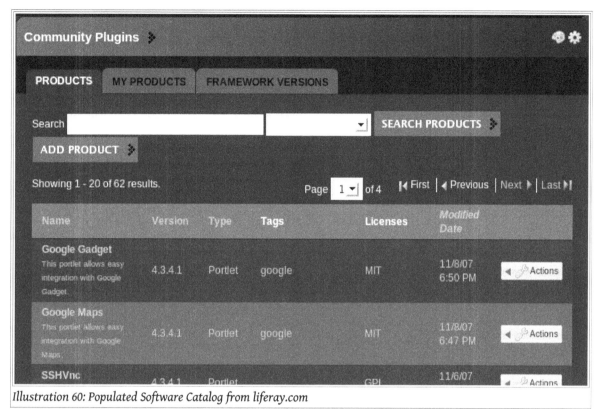

Illustration 60: Populated Software Catalog from liferay.com

We will use an example community in order to better illustrate how to use the Software Catalog portlet. Assume you, as the portal administrator, have created a community called *Old Computers*. This community will be a web site for users to collaborate on setting up and using old computers with obsolete hardware and operating systems. Users who participate in the site will eventually get upgraded to Power User status and get their own blog page. To implement this, you have created a My Summary portlet (we will use the My Summary portlet from Liferay's plugin repository as the example) which displays the user's name, picture, and description from his or her user profile. Because this portlet is generic enough that it could be useful to anyone using Liferay, you have decided to make it available in your own software catalog.

In your *Old Computers* community, you have created a page called *Software*. This is where you have added your Software Catalog portlet.

The first step in adding a plugin to your software repository is to add a *license* for your product. A license communicates to users the terms upon which you are allowing them to download and use your software. Click the *Licenses* tab and then click the *Add License* button that appears. You will then see a form which allows you to enter the title of your license, a URL pointing to the actual license document, and check boxes denoting whether the license is open source, active, or recommended.

When you have finished filling out the form, click the *Save* button. Your license will be saved. Once you have at least one license in the system, you can begin adding software products to your software catalog. Click the *Products* tab, and then click the *Add Product* button.

Your next step will be to create the product record in the software catalog portlet. This will register the product in the software catalog and allow you to start adding versions of your software for users to download and / or install directly from their instances of Liferay. You will first want to have put the .war file containing your software on a web server that is accessible without authentication to the users who will be installing your software. In the example above, the *Old Computers* site is on the Internet, so you would place the file on a web server that is accessible to anyone on the Internet. If you are creating a software catalog for an internal Intranet, you would place the file on a web server that is available to anyone inside of your organization's firewall.

To create the product record in the Software Catalog portlet, click the *Products* tab, and then click the *Add Product* button. Fill out the form with information about your product.

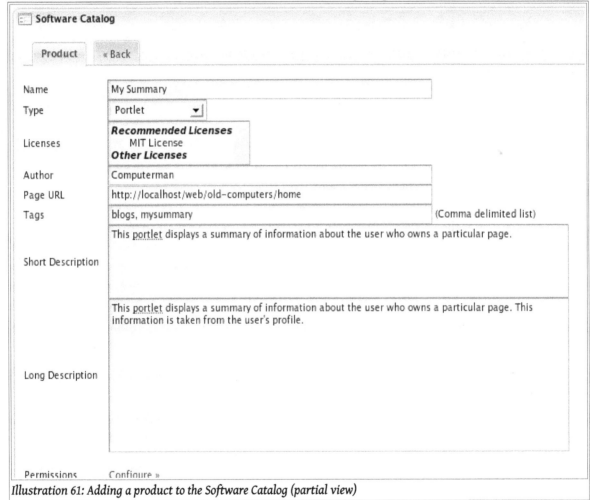

Illustration 61: Adding a product to the Software Catalog (partial view)

Name: The name of your software product.

Type: Select whether this is a portlet or a theme plugin.

Licenses: Select the license(s) under which you are releasing this software.

Author: Enter the name of the author of the software.

Page URL: If the software has a home page, enter its url here.

Tags: Enter any tags you would like added to this software.

Short Description: Enter a short description. This will be displayed in the summary table of your software catalog.

Long Description: Enter a longer description. This will be displayed on the details page for this software product.

Permissions: Click the *Configure* link to set permissions for this software product.

Group ID: Enter a group ID. A group ID is a name space which usually identifies the company or organization that made the software. For our example, we will use *old-computers*.

Artifact ID: Enter an Artifact ID. The artifact ID is a unique name within the name space for your product. For our example, we will use *my-summary-portlet*.

Screenshot: Click the *Add Screenshot* button to add a screen shot of your product for users to view.

When you have finished filling out the form, click the *Save* button. You will be brought back to the product summary page, and you will see that your product has been added to the repository.

Illustration 62: Product has been added to the Software Catalog

Notice that in the version column, *N/A* is being displayed. This is because there are not yet any released *versions* of your product. To make your product downloadable, you need to create a version of your product and point it to the file you uploaded to your HTTP server earlier.

Before you do that, however, you need to add a *Framework Version* to your software catalog. A Framework version denotes what version of Liferay your plugin is designed for and works on. You cannot add a version of your product without linking it to a version of the framework for which it is designed. So click the *Framework Versions* tab and then click the *Add Framework Version* button.

Give the framework a name, a URL, and leave the *Active* check box checked. For our example, we have entered *4.3.4* for the name and http://www.liferay.com for the URL. Click *Save.*

Now go back to the Products tab and click on your product. You will notice that a message is displayed stating that the product does not have any released versions. Click the *Add Product Version* button.

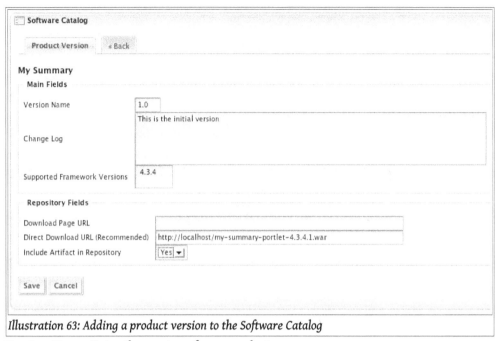

Illustration 63: Adding a product version to the Software Catalog

Version Name: Enter the version of your product.

Change Log: Enter some comments regarding what changed between this version and any previous versions.

Supported Framework Versions: Select the framework version for which your software product is intended.

Download Page URL: If your product has a descriptive web page, enter its URL here.

Direct Download URL (Recommended): Enter a direct download link to your software product here. The Plugin Installer portlet will follow this link in order to download your software product.

Include Artifact in Repository: To enable others to use the Plugin Installer portlet to connect to your repository and download your plugin, select *yes* here.

When you are finished filling out the form, click the *Save* button. Your product version will be saved, and your product will now be available in the software repository.

Generating The Software Catalog

The Software Catalog works by generating an XML document which the Plugin Installer reads. Using the data from this XML document, the Plugin Installer knows where it can download the plugins from, what version of Liferay the plugins are designed for, and all other data about the plugins that have been entered into the Software Catalog portlet.

In order to get your Software Catalog to generate this XML data, you will first need to know the Group ID of the community in which your Software Catalog portlet resides. You can do this by accessing the Liferay database and looking at the table called *Group_*. Find the group with your community's name in the *name* field, and take note of the *groupId* for the community.

Next, go to your browser and go to the following URL:

```
http://<server name>:<port number>/software_catalog?<Group ID>
```

For example, if you are on the same machine as your Liferay instance, and that instance is running on port 8080, and your group ID from the database is 10148, you would use the following URL:

```
http://localhost:8080/software_catalog?10148
```

If you have configured everything properly, an XML document should be returned:

```
<plugin-repository>
<settings/>
        <plugin-package>
<name>My Summary</name>
<module-id>oldcomputers/download-portlet/4.3.4.1/war</module-id>
<modified-date>Fri, 23 Nov 2007 17:07:33 -0500</modified-date>
        <types>
<type>portlet</type>
</types>
        <tags>
<tag>documentlibrary</tag>
<tag>4.2</tag>
</tags>
<short-description>My Summary portlet</short-description>
<long-description>My Summary portlet</long-description>
<change-log>Initial Version</change-log>
<download-url>http://localhost/my-summary-portlet-4.3.4.1.war</download-url>
<author>Rich Sezov</author>
<screenshots/>
        <licenses>
<license osi-approved="true">MIT License</license>
</licenses>
        <liferay-versions>
<liferay-version>4.3.4</liferay-version>
</liferay-versions>
</plugin-package>
</plugin-repository>
```

Save this document to a file called *liferay-plugin-package.xml* and put this file on your HTTP server where you uploaded your portlet .war file. You can then give out the URL to the directory which holds this file on your web site, and anyone with an instance of Liferay will be able to point their Plugin Installer portlets to it.

MANUALLY CREATING A SOFTWARE CATALOG

If you do not wish to use the Software Catalog portlet to create your software catalog, you can create it manually by creating the XML file that the Software Catalog portlet would normally generate. Note that if you do this, you will not have a graphical user interface to your software that end users can use to download your software manually: you will have to build this yourself. Keep in mind that many instances of Liferay Portal sit behind a firewall without access to the Internet. Because of this, if you are making your software available to Internet users, some of them will have to download it manually. In this case, the Software Catalog portlet is the easiest way to provide a user interface for downloading your software.

To manually create a software catalog, obtain the DTD for the XML file from Liferay's source code. You will find this DTD in the *definitions* folder in the Liferay source. It is a file called *liferay-plugin-package_4_3_0.dtd*. Use this DTD with a validating XML editor (a good, free choice is JEdit) to create your software catalog manually.

CONNECTING TO A SOFTWARE CATALOG

If there is a software catalog of plugins that you would like to point your instance of Liferay to, all you need is the URL to the catalog. Once you have the URL, go to your Plugin Installer portlet and click the *Configuration* tab. You will see that there are two fields in which you can enter URLs to plugin repositories: *Trusted Plugin Repositories* and *Untrusted Plugin Repositories*. Currently, the only difference between the two is to provide a visual cue for administrators as to which repositories are trusted and untrusted.

Enter the URL to the repository to which you wish to connect in one of the fields and click *Save*. The portlet will connect to the repository and items from this repository will be shown in the list.

Liferay Services Oriented Architecture

Liferay includes a utility called the *Service Builder* which is used to generate all of the low level code for accessing resources from the portal database. This utility is further explained in the *Liferay Developer's Guide*, but it is mentioned here because of its feature which generates interfaces not only for Java code, but also for web services and JavaScript. This means that the method calls for storing and retrieving portal objects are all the same, and are generated in the same step.

Because the actual method calls for retrieving data are the same regardless of how one gets access to those methods (i.e., locally or through web services), Liferay provides a consistent interface for accessing portal data that few other products can match. The actual interfaces for the various services will be covered in the *Liferay Developer's Guide*, but before they can be used there are steps that need to be taken to enable users to access those services remotely.

In the default *portal.properties* file, there is a section called **Main Servlet**. This section defines the security settings for all of the remote services provided by Liferay. Copy this section and paste it into your custom *portal-ext.properties* file, and you can configure security settings for the Axis Servlet, the Liferay Tunnel Servlet, the Spring Remoting Servlet, the JSON Tunnel Servlet, and the WebDAV servlet.

By default, a user connecting from the same machine Liferay is running on can access remote services so long as that user has the permission to use those services in Liferay's permissions system. Of course, you are not really "remote" unless you are accessing services from a different machine. Liferay has two layers of security when it comes to accessing its services remotely. Without explicit rights to both layers, a remote exception will be thrown and access to those services will not be granted.

The first layer of security that a user needs to get through in order to call a method from the service layer is servlet security. The *Main Servlet* section of the *portal-ext.properties* file is used to enable or disable access to Liferay's remote services. In that section of the properties file, there are properties for each of Liferay's remote services.

You can set each service individually with the security settings that you require. For example, you may have a batch job which runs on another machine in your network. This job looks in a particular shared folder on your network and uploads documents to your community's document library portlet on a regular basis, using Liferay's web services. To enable this batch job to get through the first layer of security, you would modify the *portal-ext.properties* file and put the IP address of the machine on which the batch job is running in the list for that particular service. For example, if the batch job uses the Axis web services to upload the documents, you would enter the IP address of the machine on which the batch job is running to the *axis.servlet.hosts.allowed* property. A typical entry might look like this:

```
axis.servlet.hosts.allowed=192.168.100.100, 127.0.0.1, SERVER_IP
```

If the machine on which the batch job is running has the IP address 192.168.100.100, this configuration will allow that machine to connect to Liferay's web services and pass in user credentials to be used to upload the documents.

The second layer of security is Liferay's security model that it uses for every object in the portal. The user ID that accesses the services remotely must have the proper permission to operate on the objects it will be accessing. Otherwise, a remote exception will be thrown. The Portal Administrator will need to make use of Liferay's usual means of granting access to these resources to the user ID that will be operating on them remotely.

For example, say that a Document Library folder called *Documents* has been set up in a community. A group has been created, called *Document Uploaders*, which has the rights to add documents to this folder. Your batch job will be accessing Liferay's web services in order to upload documents into this folder. In order for this to work, you will have to call the web service using a user ID that is a member of this group (or that has individual rights to add documents to this folder). Otherwise, you will be prevented from using the Web Service.

To call the web service using credentials, you would use the following URL syntax:

```
http://" + userIdAsString + ":" + password + "@<server.com>:<port>/tunnel-web/secure/axis/"
+ serviceName
```

The user ID is the user's ID from the Liferay database. This may be obtained by logging in as the user and clicking *My Account* from the Dock. In the top left corner of the portlet that appears is the user ID.

For example, to get Organization data using a user that has the ID of *2* with a password of *test*, you would use the following URL:

```
http://2:test@localhost:8080/tunnel-web/secure/axis/Portal_OrganizationService
```

Note: In older versions of Liferay, this password had to be the encrypted version from Liferay's database.

In summary, accessing Liferay remotely requires the successful passing of two security checks:

1. The IP address must be pre-configured in the server's *portal-ext.properties* file.

2. The user ID being used must have permission to access the resources it is attempting to access.

Accessing Liferay's WSDL

After configuring the security settings properly, your first step in obtaining access to remote web services is to access the WSDL. If you are on a browser on the same machine Liferay is running on, you can do this by accessing the following URL:

```
http://localhost:<port number>/c/wsrp
```

If, for example, you are running on Tomcat on port 8080, you would specify this URL:

```
http://localhost:8080/c/wsrp
```

If you are on a different machine from the Liferay server, you will need to pass in your user credentials on the URL to access the WSDL:

```
http://<user ID>:<password>@<server
name>:<port number>/c/wsrp
```

Note that this URL construction does not appear to work on Internet Explorer; you will have to use another browser such as Firefox. In any case, once you successfully browse to this URL, you should see the screen to the right.

WSDL for each service is available by clicking on the *WSDL* link next to the name of the service. There are many services; one for each of the services available from the Liferay API.

Illustration 64: Liferay Web Services List

Once you click on one of the *WSDL* links, the Web Service Definition Language document will be displayed. This document can be used to generate client code in any language that supports it. You can either save the document to your local machine and then generate the client code that way, or use your tool to trigger Liferay to generate the document dynamically by using one of the URLs above.

For further information about developing applications that take advantage of Liferay's remote services, please see the *Liferay Developer's Guide*.

4. Advanced Configuration

Liferay Portal is a robust, enterprise-ready portal solution. As such, it is fully ready to support mission-critical, enterprise applications in an environment configured for multiple redundancy and 24/7 up times. The product, however, like other products of its kind, does not come configured this way out of the box, and so there are many steps that need to be taken in order to configure it this way.

This chapter will cover these topics in detail. Because Liferay runs on so many different Java EE application servers, it will be impossible to cover all of the differences between these application servers. For this reason, we will cover the configuration of Liferay only. As an example, we will cover how to connect Liferay to an LDAP directory, but we will not cover how that directory is initially set up. Please consult the documentation for your particular application server to see how you can configure LDAP directories, multiple clusters, and single sign-on products.

We will, however, cover the configuration of Liferay for a number of advanced scenarios, such as

- Clustering and Distributed Caching

- Single Sign-On (multiple implementations)

- Integration with Lightweight Directory Access Protocol (LDAP) Servers

- Integration with Chat Services

- Liferay Workflow

- Deploying Customized versions of Liferay

- Performance Testing and Tuning

During this discussion, we will mention a number of other open source products upon which Liferay relies for much of this functionality. These products all have their own documentation which should be consulted for a fuller view of what these products can do. For example, Liferay uses Ehcache for its caching mechanism. We will cover how to configure Ehcache to enable various caching functionality in

Liferay, but will refer you to that product's documentation for further information about that product.

Sometimes Liferay supports multiple products which perform the same function. There are, for example, multiple implementations of single sign-on functionality, and Liferay supports several of them. We will leave it up to you to select which product best fits the needs of your project without recommending one product over another.

With all of that said, let's get started configuring Liferay for the enterprise.

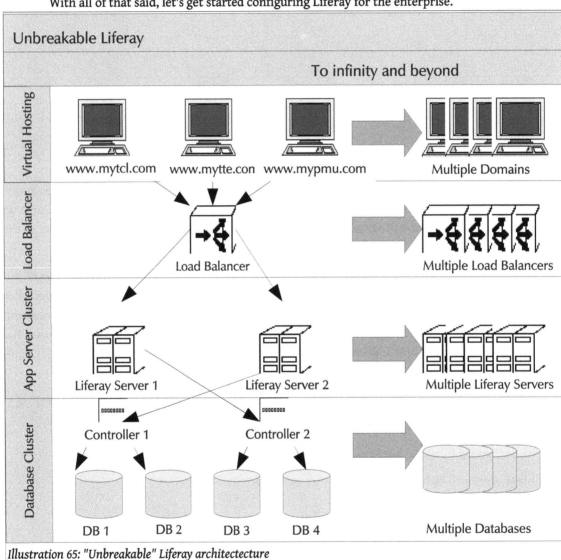

Illustration 65: "Unbreakable" Liferay architectecture

Liferay Clustering

Once you have Liferay installed in more than one node on your application server, there are several optimizations that need to be made. At a minimum, Liferay should be configured in the following way for a clustered environment:

- All nodes should be pointing to the same Liferay database

- Jackrabbit, the JSR-170 content repository, should be:

    o   On a shared file system available to all the nodes (not really recommended, though), or

    o   In a database that is shared by all the nodes

- Similarly, Lucene, the full text search indexer, should be:

    o   On a shared file system available to all the nodes (not really recommended, though), or

    o   In a database that is shared by all the nodes

- The hot deploy folder should be a separate folder for all the nodes, and plugins will have to be deployed to all of the nodes individually. This is best done via a script.

Many of these configuration changes can be made by adding or modifying properties in your *portal-ext.properties* file. Remember that this file overrides the defaults that are in the *portal.properties* file. The original version of this file can be found in the Liferay source code or can be extracted from the *portal-impl.jar* file in your Liferay installation. It is a best practice to copy the relevant section that you want to modify from *portal.properties* into your *portal-ext.properties* file, and then modify the values there.

All Nodes Should Be Pointing to the Same Liferay Database

This is pretty self-explanatory. Each node should be configured with a data source that points to one Liferay database (or a database cluster) that all of the nodes will share. This ensures that all of the nodes operate from the same basic data set. This means, of course, that Liferay cannot (and should not) use the embedded HSQL database that is shipped with the bundles. It is also best if the database server is a separate physical box from the server which is running Liferay.

Jackrabbit Sharing

Liferay uses Jackrabbit, which is a project from Apache, as its JSR-170 compliant document repository. By default, Jackrabbit is configured to store the documents on the local file system upon which Liferay is installed, in the *$HOME/liferay/jackrabbit* folder. Inside this folder is Jackrabbit's configuration file, called *repository.xml*.

To simply move the default repository location to a shared folder, you do not need to edit Jackrabbit's configuration file. Instead, find the section in *portal.properties* labeled **JCR** and copy/paste that section into your *portal-ext.properties* file. One of the properties, by default, is the following:

```
jcr.jackrabbit.repository.root=${resource.repositories.root}/jackrabbit
```

Change this property to point to a shared folder that all of the nodes can see. A new Jackrabbit configuration file will be generated in that location.

Note that because of file locking issues, this may not be the best way to share Jackrabbit resources. Instead, to enable better data protection, you should redirect Jackrabbit into your database of choice. You can use the Liferay database or another database for this purpose. This will require editing Jackrabbit's configuration file.

The default Jackrabbit configuration file has sections commented out for moving the Jackrabbit configuration into the database. This has been done to make it as easy as possible to enable this configuration. To move the Jackrabbit configuration into the database, simply comment out the sections relating to the file system and comment in the sections relating to the database. These by default are configured for a MySQL database. If you are using another database, you will likely need to modify the configuration, as there are changes to the configuration file that are necessary for specific databases. For example, the default configuration uses Jackrabbit's *DbFileSystem* class to mimic a file system in the database. While this works well in MySQL, it does not work for all databases. For example, if you are using an Oracle database, you will need to modify this to use *OracleFileSystem*. Please see the Jackrabbit documentation at http://jackrabbit.apache.org for further information.

Once you have configured Jackrabbit to store its repository in a database, the next time you bring up Liferay, the necessary database tables will be created automatically. Jackrabbit, however, does not create indexes on these tables, and so over time this can be a performance penalty. To fix this, you will need to manually go into your database and index the primary key columns for all of the Jackrabbit tables.

All of your Liferay nodes should be configured to use the same Jackrabbit repository in the database. Once that is working, you can create a Jackrabbit cluster (please see the section below).

Lucene Sharing

Lucene, the search indexer which Liferay uses, should also be in a shared configuration for a clustered environment. This means that you will need to either share the index on the file system or in the database.

The Lucene configuration can be changed by modifying values in your *portal-ext.properties* file. Open your *portal.properties* file and search for the text *Lucene*. Copy that section and then paste it into your *portal-ext.properties* file.

If you wish to store the Lucene search index on a file system that is shared by all of the Liferay nodes, you can modify the location of the search index by changing the *lucene.dir* property. By default, this property points to the */liferay/lucene* folder inside the home folder of the user that is running Liferay:

```
lucene.dir=${resource.repositories.root}/lucene/
```

Change this to the folder of your choice. To make the change take effect, you will need to restart Liferay. You can point all of the nodes to this folder, and they will use the same index.

Like Jackrabbit, however, this is not the best way to share the search index, as it could result in file corruption if different nodes try reindexing at the same time. A better way is to share the index via a database, where the database can enforce data integrity on the index. This is very easy to do; it is a simple change to your *portal-ext.properties* file.

There is a single property called *lucene.store.type*. By default this is set to go to the file system. You can change this so that the index is stored in the database by making it the following:

```
lucene.store.type=jdbc
```

The next time Liferay is started, new tables will be created in the Liferay database, and the index will be stored there. If all the Liferay nodes point to the same database tables, they will be able to share the index.

Hot Deploy

Plugins which are hot deployed will need to be deployed separately to all of the Liferay nodes. Each node should, therefore, have its own hot deploy folder. This folder needs to be writable by the user under which Liferay is running, because plugins are moved from this folder to a temporary folder when they are deployed. This is to prevent the system from entering an endless loop, because the presence of a plugin in the folder is what triggers the hot deploy process.

When you want to deploy a plugin, copy that plugin to the hot deploy folders of all of the Liferay nodes. Depending on the number of nodes, it may be best to create a script to do this. Once the plugin has been deployed to all of the nodes, you can then make use of it (by adding the portlet to a page or choosing the theme as the look and feel for a page or page hierarchy).

All of the above will get basic Liferay clustering working; however, the configuration can be further optimized. We will see how to do this next.

Distributed Caching

Liferay 4.3.1 and higher uses **Ehcache**, which has robust distributed caching support. This means that the cache can be distributed across multiple Liferay nodes running concurrently. Enabling this cache can increase performance dramatically. For example, say that two users are browsing the message boards. The first user clicks on a thread in order to read it. Liferay must look up that thread from the database and format it for display in the browser. With a distributed Ehcache running, this thread can be pulled from the database and stored in a cache for quick retrieval. Say then that the second user wants to read the same forum thread and clicks on it. This time, because the thread is in the local cache, no trip to the database is necessary, and so retrieving the data is much faster.

This could be done by simply having a cache running separately on each node, but the power of *distributed* caching allows for more functionality. The first user can post a message to the thread he or she was reading, and the cache will be updated across all of the nodes, making the new post available immediately from the local cache. Without that, the second user would need to wait until the cache was invalidated on the node he or she connected to before he or she could see the updated forum post.

Configuring distributed caching requires the modification of the *portal-ext.properties* file as well as one or more other files depending on what you want to cache. The first thing you will want to do is determine where on your server you will want to store your cache configuration files. This will have to be somewhere on Liferay's class path, so you will need to find where your application server has stored the deployed version of Liferay, and create a folder in Liferay's *WEB-INF/classes* folder to store the files. Because the original, default files are stored inside of a .jar file, you will need to extract them to this area and then tell Liferay (by use of the *portal-ext.properties* file) where they are.

For example, say you are running Liferay on Tomcat. Tomcat stores the deployed version of Liferay in *<Tomcat Home>/webapps/ROOT*. Inside of this folder is the folder structure *WEB-INF/classes*. You can create a new folder in here called *myehcache* to store the custom versions of the cache configuration files. Copy the files from the */ehcache* folder—which is inside the *portal-impl.jar file*—into the *myehcache* folder you just created. You then need to modify the properties in *portal-ext.properties* that point to these files. Copy / paste the **Hibernate** section of *portal.properties* into your *portal-ext.properties* file and then modify the *net.sf.ehcache.configurationResourceName* property to point to the clustered version of the configuration file that is now in your custom folder:

```
net.sf.ehcache.configurationResourceName=/myehcache/hibernate-clustered.xml
```

Now that Liferay is pointing to your custom file, you can modify the settings in this file to change the cache configuration for Hibernate.

Next, copy / paste the *Ehcache* section from the *portal.properties* file into your *portal-ext.properties* file. Modify the properties so that they point to the files that are in your custom folder. For example:

```
ehcache.multi.vm.config.location=/myehcache/liferay-multi-vm.xml
```

If you are going to enable distributed clustering, uncomment the following line and point it to your custom version of the file:

```
ehcache.multi.vm.config.location=/myehcache/liferay-multi-vm-clustered.xml
```

You can now take a look at the settings in these files and tune them to fit your environment and application.

Alternatively, if your Liferay project is using the extension environment to make customizations to Liferay, you can place your cache configuration in the extension environment. The settings there will override the default settings that ship with Liferay. If you wish to do this, you can create new versions of the files in *ext-impl/classes/ehcache*. The files should be postfixed with *-ext.xml*. For example, the custom version of *hibernate.xml* should be called *hibernate-ext.xml*, and the custom version of *liferay-multi-vm-clustered.xml* should be called *liferay-multi-vm-clustered-ext.xml*. You can then modify the files and tune them to fit your environment / application, and they will be deployed along with the rest of your extension environment.

Hibernate Cache Settings

By default, Hibernate (Liferay's database persistence layer) is configured to use Ehcache as its cache provider. This is the recommended setting. The default configuration, however, points to a file that does not have clustering enabled. To enable clustering, copy the *Hibernate* section from *portal.properties* into your *portal-ext.properties* file. To enable a clustered cache, comment out the default file (*hibernate.xml*) and uncomment the clustered version of the file, making sure that you change the path so that it points to your custom version of the file:

```
net.sf.ehcache.configurationResourceName=/myehcache/hibernate-clustered.xml
```

Next, open this file in a text editor. You will notice that the configuration is already set up to perform distributed caching through a multi-cast connection. It is likely, however, that the configuration is not set up optimally for your particular application. You will notice that by default, the only object cached in the Hibernate cache is the User object (*com.liferay.portal.model.impl.UserImpl*). This means that when a user logs in, his or her User object will go in the cache so that any portal operation that requires access to it (such as permission checking) can retrieve that object very quickly from the cache.

You may wish to add other objects to the cache. For example, a large part of your application may be document management using the Document Library portlet. In this case, you may want to cache Document Library objects, such as *DLFileEntryImpl* in order to improve performance as users access documents. To do that, add another block to the configuration file with the class you want to cache:

```
    <cache
            name="com.liferay.portlet.documentlibrary.model.impl.DLFileEntryImpl"
            maxElementsInMemory="10000"
            eternal="false"
     timeToIdleSeconds="600"
            overflowToDisk="true"
    >
      <cacheEventListenerFactory
                    class="net.sf.ehcache.distribution.RMICacheReplicatorFactory"
                    properties="replicatePuts=false,replicateUpdatesViaCopy=false"
                    propertySeparator=","
            />
            <bootstrapCacheLoaderFactory class="net.sf.ehcache.distribution.RMIBootstrap-
CacheLoaderFactory" />
        </cache>
```

Your site may use the message boards portlet, and those message boards may get a lot of traffic. To cache the threads on the message boards, configure a block with the MBMessageImpl class:

```
<cache
            name="com.liferay.portlet.messageboards.model.impl.MBMessageImpl"
            maxElementsInMemory="10000"
            eternal="false"
     timeToIdleSeconds="600"
            overflowToDisk="true"
    >
      <cacheEventListenerFactory
                    class="net.sf.ehcache.distribution.RMICacheReplicatorFactory"
                    properties="replicatePuts=false,replicateUpdatesViaCopy=false"
                    propertySeparator=","
            />
            <bootstrapCacheLoaderFactory class="net.sf.ehcache.distribution.RMIBootstrap-
CacheLoaderFactory" />
```

```
</cache>
```

Note that if your developers have overridden any of these classes, you will have to specify the overridden versions rather than the stock ones that come with Liferay Portal.

As you can see, it is easy to add specific data to be cached. Be careful, however, as too much caching can actually reduce performance if the JVM runs out of memory and starts garbage collecting too frequently. You will likely need to experiment with the memory settings on your JVM as well as the cache settings above. You can find the specifics about these settings in the documentation for Ehcache.

CLUSTERING JACKRABBIT

If you are using the Document Library, by default you are using the JSR-170 document repository, which is the Apache product *Jackrabbit.* You have already configured basic data sharing among nodes by moving its configuration into a database. The next thing you need to do is configure clustering for Jackrabbit, so that each node knows about data being entered into the repository by other nodes.

You can find the Jackrabbit configuration file in *<Liferay User Home>/liferay/jackrabbit.* The file is called *repository.xml.* You have likely already edited this file when you modified the configuration to move the data into the database.

At the bottom of this file is a cluster configuration that is commented out. If you are using a MySQL database, you can uncomment this section and use it as-is. You will need to change the cluster ID for each node so that they don't conflict with one another.

If you are using another database, the only changes necessary are the connection, credentials, and schema settings. Modify them according to your database of choice and then save the file. This is all it takes to set up clustering for Jackrabbit.

Single Sign-On

Single Sign-On solutions allow you to provide a single log in credential for multiple systems. This allows you to have people authenticate to the Single Sign-On product and they will be automatically logged in to Liferay and to other products as well.

Liferay at the time of this writing supports several single sign-on solutions. Of course if your product is not yet supported, you may choose to implement support for it yourself by use of the extension environment—or your organization can choose to sponsor support for it. Please contact sales@liferay.com for more information about this.

Central Authentication Service (CAS)

CAS is an authentication system that was originally created at Yale University. It is a widely-used open source single sign-on solution, and was the first SSO product to be supported by Liferay.

Please follow the documentation for CAS to install it on your application server of choice. You can use the version that Liferay provides on our web site or the official version from the JA-SIG web site. The reason for the difference is simply that newer versions require JDK 5 and above only. If you are using JDK 5 on your server, you should be able to use the newer versions of CAS and the client. If you are using 1.4, you will need to use the version of CAS that we provide, as well as the older Yale client.

Your first step will be to copy the CAS client .jar file to Liferay's library folder. On Tomcat, this is in *<Tomcat Home>/webapps/ROOT/WEB-INF/lib*. Once you've done this, the CAS client will be available to Liferay the next time you start it.

The CAS Server application requires a properly configured Secure Socket Layer certificate on your server in order to work. If you wish to generate one yourself, you will need to use the *keytool* utility that comes with the JDK. Your first step is to generate the key. Next, you export the key into a file. Finally, you import the key into your local Java key store. For public, Internet-based production environments, you will need to either purchase a signed key from a recognized certificate authority (such as Thawte or Verisign) or have your key signed by a recognized certificate authority. For Intranets, you should have your IT department pre-configure users' browsers to accept the certificate so that they don't get warning messages about the certificate.

To generate a key, use the following command:

```
keytool -genkey -alias tomcat -keypass changeit -keyalg RSA
```

Instead of the password in the example (*changeit*), use a password that you will be able to remember. If you are not using Tomcat, you may want to use a different alias as well. For First and Last name, enter *locahost*, or the host name of your server. It cannot be an IP address.

To export the key to a file, use the following command:

```
keytool -export -alias tomcat -keypass changeit -file server.cert
```

Finally, to import the key into your Java key store, use the following command:

```
keytool -import -alias tomcat -file %FILE_NAME% -keypass changeit -keystore
$JAVA_HOME/jre/lib/security/cacerts
```

If you are on a Windows system, replace $JAVA_HOME above with %JAVA_HOME%. Of course, all of this needs to be done on the system on which CAS will be running.

Once your CAS server is up and running, you can configure Liferay to use it. This is a simple matter of changing a few properties in your *portal-ext.properties* file. Find the **CAS** section in the default *portal.properties* file and paste it into your *portal-ext.properties* file. Enable CAS authentication, and then modify the URL properties to point to your CAS server:

```
##
## CAS
##

    #
    # Set this to true to enable CAS single sign on. NTLM will work only if
    # LDAP authentication is also enabled and the authentication is made by
    # screen name. If set to true, then the property "auto.login.hooks" must
```

```
# contain a reference to the class
# com.liferay.portal.security.auth.CASAutoLogin and the filter
# com.liferay.portal.servlet.filters.sso.cas.CASFilter must be referenced
# in web.xml.
#
cas.auth.enabled=true


#
# A user may be authenticated from CAS and not yet exist in the portal. Set
# this to true to automatically import users from LDAP if they do not exist
# in the portal.
#
cas.import.from.ldap=false


#
# Set the default values for the required CAS URLs.
#
cas.login.url=https://localhost:8443/cas-web/login
cas.logout.url=https://localhost:8443/cas-web/logout
cas.service.url=http://localhost:8080/c/portal/login
cas.validate.url=https://localhost:8443/cas-web/proxyValidate
```

Change *localhost* in the properties above to point to your CAS server. Save the file and then start Liferay. From the Dock, click the *Sign In* link. You will be directed to the CAS server to sign in to Liferay.

OpenID

OpenID is a new single sign-on standard which is implemented by multiple vendors. The idea is that multiple vendors can implement the standard, and then users can register for an ID with the vendor they trust. The credential issued by that vendor can be used by all the web sites that support OpenID. Some high profile OpenID vendors are AOL (http://openid.aol.com/screenname), LiveDoor (http://profile.livedoor.com/username), and LiveJournal (http://username.livejournal.com). Please see the OpenID site (http://www.openid.net) for a more complete list.

The obvious main benefit of OpenID for the user is that he or she no longer has to register for a new account on every site in which he or she wants to participate. Users can register on *one* site (the OpenID provider's site) and then use those credentials to authenticate to many web sites which support OpenID. Many web site owners often struggle to build communities because end users are reluctant to register for so many different accounts. Supporting OpenID makes it easier for site owners to build their communities because the barriers to participating (i.e., the effort it takes to register for and keep track of many accounts) are removed. All of the account information is kept with the OpenID provider, making it much easier to manage this information and keep it up to date.

Liferay Portal can act as an OpenID consumer, allowing users to automatically register and sign in with their OpenID accounts. Internally, the product uses OpenID4Java (http://code.google.com/p/openid4java/) to implement the feature.

OpenID is enabled by default in Liferay, but can be disabled by changing the property *openid.auth.enabled* to false in your *portal-ext.properties* file.

Atlassian Crowd

Atlassian Crowd is a web-based Single Sign-On product similar to CAS. Crowd can be used to manage authentication to many different web applications and directory servers.

Because Atlassian Crowd implements an OpenID producer, Liferay works and has been tested with it. Simply use the OpenID authentication feature in Liferay to log in using Crowd.

Integration with LDAP Directories

Connecting Liferay to an LDAP directory has become much easier and is now a straightforward process. There are two places in which you can configure the LDAP settings: the *portal-ext.properties* file and the Enterprise Admin portlet—where the settings will get stored in the database. Note that if you use both, the settings in the database will override the settings in *portal-ext.properties*. For this reason, we recommend for most users that you use the Enterprise Admin portlet to configure the LDAP settings. The only compelling reason to use the *portal-ext.properties* file is if you have many Liferay nodes which will be configured to run against the same LDAP directory. In that case, for your initial deployment, it may be easier to copy the *portal-ext.properties* file to all of the nodes so that the first time they start up, the settings are correct. Regardless of which method you use, the settings are the same.

To configure the LDAP settings, add an Enterprise Admin to a page, and navigate to the LDAP page by selecting *Settings -> Authentication -> LDAP*. You will see the following screen:

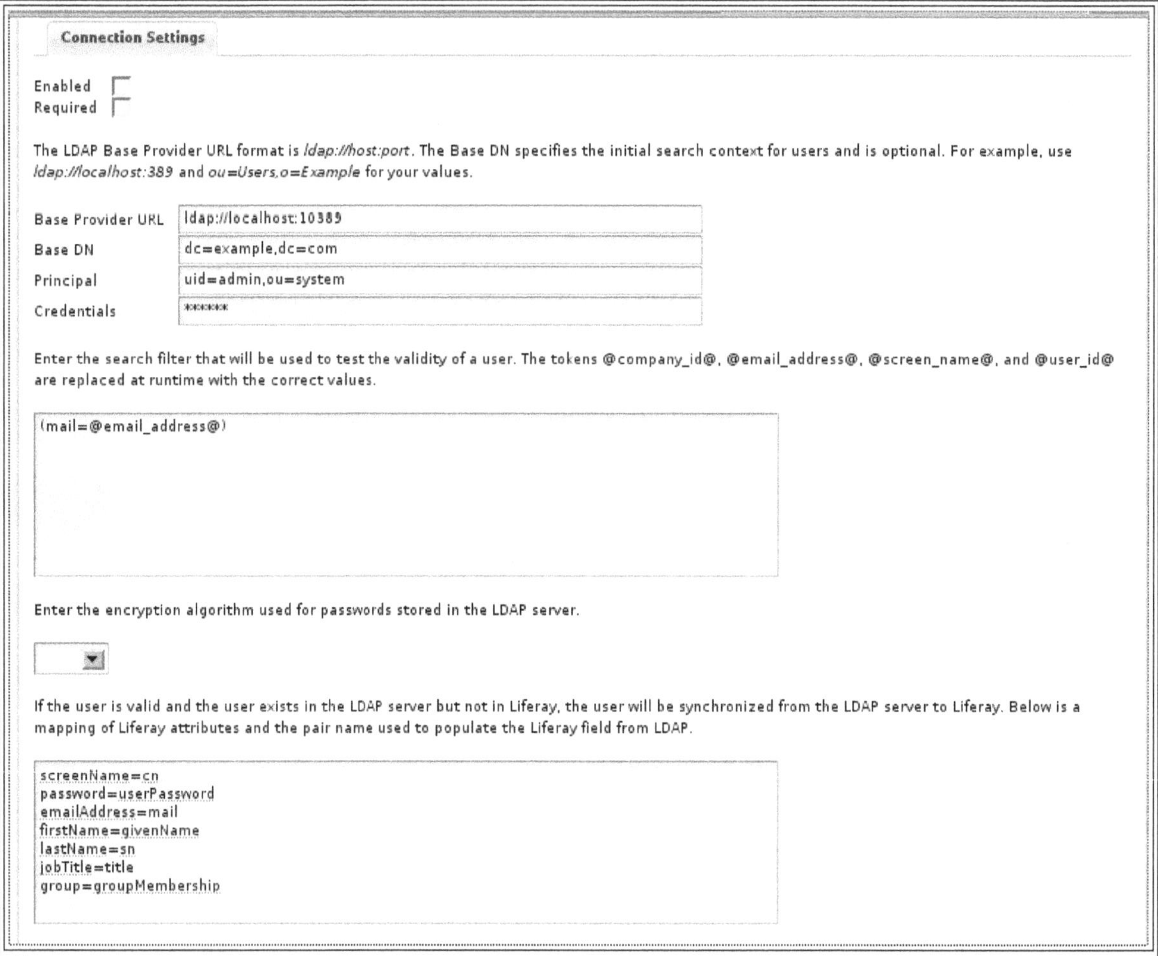

Illustration 66: LDAP Connection Settings

Enabled: Check this box to enable LDAP Authentication.

Required: Check this box if LDAP authentication is required. Liferay will then not allow a user to log in unless he or she can successfully bind to the LDAP directory first. Uncheck this box if you want to allow users that have Liferay accounts but no LDAP accounts to log in to the portal.

Base Provider URL: This tells the portal where the LDAP server is located. Make sure that the machine on which Liferay is installed can communicate with the LDAP server. If there is a firewall between the two systems, check to make sure that the appropriate ports are opened.

Base DN: This is the Base Distinguished Name for your LDAP directory. It is usually modeled after your organization. For a commercial organization, it may look something like: *dc=companynamehere,dc=com.*

Principal: By default, the administrator ID is populated here. If you have removed the default LDAP administrator, you will need to use the fully qualified name of the administrative credential you do use. You need an administrative credential because Liferay will be using this ID to synchronize user accounts to and from LDAP.

Credentials: This is the password for the administrative user.

This is all you need in order to make a regular connection to an LDAP directory. The rest of the configuration is optional: generally, the default attribute mappings are sufficient data to synchronize back to the Liferay database when a user attempts to log in.

Many organizations, however, prefer to run their LDAP directories in SSL mode, so that credential information is not passing through the network unencrypted. Liferay supports this as well, but you have to perform extra steps to share the encryption key and certificate between the two systems.

For example, if your LDAP directory happens to be Microsoft Active Directory on Windows Server 2003, you would take the following steps to share the certificate:

On the Windows 2003 Domain Controller, open the certificates mmc snapin. Export the Root Certificate Authority certificate by selecting *Certificates (Local Computer) mmc snapin -> Trusted Root Certification Authorities -> MyRootCACertificateName*. Right click this certificate and select *All Tasks -> export -> select DER encoded binary X.509 .CER*. Copy the exported *.cer* file to your Liferay Portal server.

As with the CAS install (see the above section entitled **Single Sign-On**), you will need to import the certificate into the cacerts keystore. The import is handled by a command like the following:

```
keytool -import -trustcacerts -keystore /some/path/jdk1.5.0_11/jre/lib/security/cacerts
-storepass changeit -noprompt
-alias MyRootCA -file /some/path/MyRootCA.cer
```

Once this is done, go back to the LDAP page in the Enterprise Admin portlet by selecting *Settings -> Authentication -> LDAP*. Modify the LDAP URL in the **Base DN** field to the secure version by changing the protocol to *https* and the port to 636 like the following:

```
ldaps://myLdapServerHostname:636
```

Save the changes. Your Liferay Portal will now use LDAP in secure mode for authentication.

Search Filter: The search filter box can be used to determine the search criteria for user logins. By default, Liferay uses the email address as a user login name. If you have changed this setting—which can be done on the *General* tab that's next to the *LDAP* tab in the Enterprise Admin portlet—you will need to modify the search filter here, which has by default been configured to use the email address attribute from LDAP as search criteria. For example, if you changed Liferay's authentication method to use the screen name instead of the email address, you would modify the search filter so that it can match the entered login name:

```
(cn=@screen_name@)
```

Encryption Algorithm: Liferay supports two encryption algorithms for synchronizing the password: *MD5* and *SHA*. Choose the algorithm (if any) you are using in your LDAP directory for storing passwords.

Attribute Mapping: The next field allows you to define mappings from LDAP attributes to Liferay fields. Though your LDAP user attributes may be different from LDAP server to LDAP server, there are five fields that Liferay requires to be mapped in order for the user to be recognized. You must define a mapping to thecorresponding attributes in LDAP for the following Liferay fields:

- screenName

- password

- emailAddress

- firstName

- lastName

The Enterprise Admin portlet provides default mappings for commonly used LDAP attributes. You can also add your own mappings if you wish.

LDAP Server: The next field is a drop-down field allowing you to select special support for particular LDAP servers. If you are using one of these servers, select it. If you are using a different LDAP server, leave this field blank.

Import Enabled: Check this box to cause Liferay to do a mass import from your LDAP directory. If you want Liferay to only synchronize users when they log in, leave this box unchecked. Definitely leave this unchecked if you are working in a clustered environment.

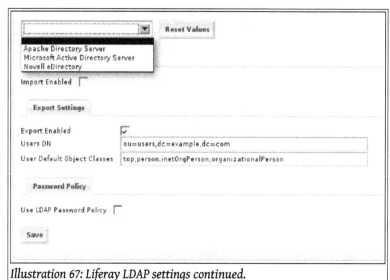

Illustration 67: Liferay LDAP settings continued.

If you check the box, several other options will become available.

Import on Startup Enabled: Check this box to have Liferay run the import when it starts up.

Import Interval: The import runs on a schedule. Select how often you want the import to run.

Export Enabled: Check this box to enable Liferay to export user accounts from the database to LDAP. Liferay uses a listener to track any changes made to the User object and will push these changes out to the LDAP server whenever the User object is updated. Note that on every login, fields such as *LastLoginDate* are updated. When export is enabled, this has the effect of causing a user export every time the user logs in.

Users DN: Enter the location in your LDAP tree where the users will be stored. When Liferay does an export, it will export the users to this location.

User Default Object Classes: When a user is exported, the user is created with the listed default object classes. To find out what your default object classes are, use an LDAP browser tool such as JXplorer, to locate a user and view the Object Class attributes that are stored in LDAP for that user.

Use LDAP Password Policy: Liferay uses its own password policy by default. This can be configured on the *Password Policies* tab of the Enterprise Admin portlet. If you want to use the password policies defined by your LDAP directory, check this box. Once this is enabled, the *Password Policies* tab will display a message stating that you are not using a local password policy. You will now have to use your LDAP directory's mechanism for setting password policies. Liferay does this by parsing the messages in the LDAP controls that are returned by your LDAP server. By default, the messages in the LDAP controls that Liferay is looking for are the messages that are returned by the Fedora Directory Server. If you are using a different LDAP server, you will need to customize the messages in Liferay's *portal-ext.properties* file, as there is not yet a GUI for setting this. See below for instructions describing how to do this.

Once you have completed configuring LDAP, click the *Save* button.

LDAP Options Not Available in the GUI

Though most of the LDAP configuration can be done from the Enterprise Admin portlet, there are several configuration parameters that are only available by editing *portal-ext.properties*. These options will be available in the GUI in future versions of Liferay Portal, but for now they can only be configured by editing the properties file.

If you need to change any of these options, copy the LDAP section from the *portal.properties* file into your *portal-ext.properties* file. Note that since you have already configured LDAP from the GUI, any settings from the properties file that match settings already configured in the GUI will be ignored. The GUI, which stores the settings in the database, always takes precedence over the properties file.

```
ldap.import.method=[user,group]
```

If you set this to *user,* Liferay will import all users from the specified portion of the LDAP tree. If you set this to *group,* Liferay will search all the groups and import the users in each group. If you have users who do not belong to any groups, they will not be imported.

```
ldap.error.password.age=age
ldap.error.password.expired=expired
ldap.error.password.history=history
ldap.error.password.not.changeable=not allowed to change
ldap.error.password.syntax=syntax
ldap.error.password.trivial=trivial
ldap.error.user.lockout=retry limit
```

These properties are a list of phrases from error messages which can possibly be returned by the LDAP server. When a user binds to LDAP, the server can return *controls* with its response of success or failure. These controls contain a message describing the error or the information that is coming back with the response. Though the controls are the same across LDAP servers, the messages can be different. The properties described here contain snippets of words from those messages, and will work with Red Hat's Fedora

Directory Server. If you are not using that server, the word snippets may not work with your LDAP server. If they don't, you can replace the values of these properties with phrases from your server's error messages. This will enable Liferay to recognize them.

Integration with Chat Services

Liferay includes a Chat Portlet which allows users to access instant messaging services via an Ajax interface in a portal page. This allows organizations to provide an internal chat service which members of the portal can use to communicate with each other. The Chat portlet requires access to a chat server in order to work. You can use any chat server that supports the Extensible Messaging and Presence Protocol (XMPP), better known as Jabber.

Though it is beyond the scope of this book to describe how to set up a Jabber server, a few things are important to note. Part of the specification allows for a technology known as *gateways* to other chat services. This allows a Jabber server to become a gateway to other instant messaging protocols, such as Yahoo! Instant Messenger, AOL Instant Messenger, MSN Messenger, or Google Talk (which is just a Jabber service itself). This becomes important when organizations choose which ports to open on their firewalls. Using a Jabber server with a gateway to a different instant messaging service allows administrators to open the instant messaging ports just for the Jabber server and not for the entire network, and users still get access to their external instant messaging accounts. Additionally, there are a number of open source Jabber servers available, allowing administrators to set up an internal instant messaging service at no cost for software licenses. Liferay has been tested with the *Openfire* Jabber server.

Once you have set up your XMPP (Jabber) server, it is a straightforward task to connect Liferay to it. There are a few properties which need to be customized in your *portal-ext.properties* file:

```
reverse.ajax.enabled=true
```

This allows for both push and pull communication to occur between the chat portlet and the chat server. If this weren't enabled, users would not be able to initiate chat sessions with other users.

Set the following to true to enable communication with a chat server.

```
jabber.xmpp.server.enabled=true
```

Enter the IP address to your server.

```
jabber.xmpp.server.address=localhost
```

Enter the host name of your server.

```
jabber.xmpp.server.name=localhost
```

Enter the port number on which the Jabber server is listening. The one below is the default.

```
jabber.xmpp.server.port=5222
```

Enter the password for the *admin* user on the Jabber server.

```
jabber.xmpp.user.password=L1f3RayJabb3r
```

Restart Liferay. Users should now be able to add the Chat portlet to their pages and use the chat service from within Liferay.

Workflow

The workflow portlet allows a user to define any number of simple to complex business processes/workflows, deploy them, and manage them through a portal interface. The power of this portlet is that it allows users to create forms-based data entry applications that are fully integrated with Liferay's permissions system. They have knowledge of users, groups, and roles without writing a single line of code—it only requires the creation of a single XML document.

The portlet relies on Apache ServiceMix or Mule to function as an Enterprise Service Bus (ESB) that acts as a broker between the portal and a workflow engine. Essentially, the portal provides a generic interface through which workflow services are requested via normal HTTP calls. The requests are routed through the ESB which in turn calls a workflow engine implementation that the user has defined in the ESB configuration. By default, Liferay provides an implementation of JBoss' jBPM workflow engine.

Installation and Test

Because the default implementation of the workflow portlet depends on one of the ESB packages and jBPM, the installation requires more than just the normal portal bundle. The following provides detailed instructions for deploying the software required by the workflow portlet. Once that is done, we will test it with a simple process.

1. We will assume if you have gotten this far that you already have an instance of Liferay running in your application server. If not, download one of the bundles and follow the instructions in chapter 2 to install it.

2. Download liferay-portal-mule-web-<*version corresponding to your version of Liferay*>.war and liferay-portal-jbpm-web-<*version corresponding to your version of Liferay*>.war, and rename them to *mule-web.war* and *jbpm-web.war* respectively.

3. Use your application server's deployment tools to deploy these two web applications from step 2 to your application server.

4. Make sure the following property in *portal-ext.properties* is set to the following:

```
jbi.workflow.url=http://localhost:8080/mule-web/workflow
```

5. Restart your application server after making the change to the above property.

6. Login to the portal as the portal administrator. The default credentials are *test@liferay.com/test*.

7. Add the *Workflow* portlet to a page.

8. Click on the *Definitions* tab.

9. Click on the *Add* button.

10. Copy and paste the contents of *jbpm-web.war/WEB-INF/definitions/datatypes_definition.xml* into the text area and click the *Save New Version* button.

11. Click on the *Add Instance* icon.

12. From the *Instances* tab, click on the *Manage* icon next to *Enter data*.

13. Fill out the form and click the *Save* button; alternatively, you can test the various error checking capabilities by inputting incorrect values and clicking the *Save* button.

14. Eventually, enter correct values and click the *Save* button.

15. From the *Instances* tab, click on the *Manage* icon next to *View Data*.

16. Confirm that all the data was entered correctly and click the *Finished* button.

17. Confirm that the instance is now in the *End* state.

Using Different Databases

The default implementation of jBPM uses an HSQL database found in *jbpm-web.war/WEB-INF/sql/jbpm.**. To change the location of the HSQL database, change the value of the *hibernate.connection.url* property in *jbpm-web.war/WEB-INF/classes/hibernate.cfg.xml*. The location is relatively addressed from where ever the startup script for your server is located.

To use a database other than HSQL, first create the database schema using one of the SQL create scripts supplied in the *jbpm-web.war/WEB-INF/sql* directory. Then uncomment the corresponding hibernate connection properties block in *jbpm-web.war/WEB-INF/classes/hibernate.cfg.xml*.

Technical Explanations

Since the default implementation of the workflow portlet relies heavily on the capabilities of jBPM, this section gives a technical overview of jBPM and explains how it integrates into Liferay using jBPM Process Definition Language (JPDL) formatted XML files. It does not, however, give an in depth view of jBPM. For that, please refer to the jBPM user guide (http://docs.jboss.com/jbpm/v3/userguide).

PROCESS DEFINITIONS

Before the workflow portlet can be used, business processes must be defined. Business processes in jBPM are defined by XML documents known as *process definitions* which are written in jBPM Process Definition Language (JPDL). This XML format specifies entities such as the process roles (known as *swimlanes*), the various states in the process (known as *nodes*), the tasks associated with each node, the roles associated with each task, the transitions from one node to the next, the variables associated with each task's form, the external actions executed on entry or exit of a node, and many others. For an in depth understanding of process definitions and JPDL, refer to JBoss' jBPM user guide at the link above.

There are three sample process definition XMLs that are packaged with the portlet. They can be found in *jbpm-web.war/WEB-INF/definitions*. We used one in the quick start section above to create a sample workflow. An explanation of each is included below.

INTEGRATING WITH USERS, COMMUNITIES, AND ROLES

In JPDL, there is the notion of process roles called *swimlanes*. Swimlanes can be associated with Liferay users, communities, and roles via the IdentityAssignmentHandler class.

```
<swimlane name="approver">
    <assignment class="com.liferay.jbpm.handler.IdentityAssignmentHandler" config-
type="field">
        <type>user</type>
        <companyId>10095</companyId>
        <id>10112</id>
    </assignment>
</swimlane>
```

In the XML above, the *approver* swimlane is associated with the Liferay user that has a User ID of *10112* and belongs to a Company ID of *10095*. You can also associate a Liferay user with a swimlane by email address as shown in the following XML snippet.

```
<swimlane name="shipper">
    <assignment class="com.liferay.jbpm.handler.IdentityAssignmentHandler" config-
type="field">
        <type>user</type>
        <companyId>10095</companyId>
        <name>test.lax.2@liferay.com</name>
    </assignment>
</swimlane>
```

In the XML above, the *shipper* swimlane is associated with the Liferay user that has an email address of "test.lax.2@liferay.com" and belongs to a Company ID of *10095*.

```
<swimlane name="salesman">
    <assignment class="com.liferay.jbpm.handler.IdentityAssignmentHandler" config-
type="field">
        <type>community</type>
        <companyId>10095</companyId>
        <id>3</id>
    </assignment>
</swimlane>
```

In the XML above, the *salesman* swimlane is associated with any Liferay user that belongs to a Community with the Group ID of *3* (which defaults to the *Support* community if you are using the embedded HSQL database that comes with the Liferay Portal bundles) and Company ID of *10095*. In other words, the salesman swimlane is assigned to the pool of *Support* users. If one of these users were to manage a salesman task, he/she would automatically be assigned to all other salesman tasks in the workflow.

```
<swimlane name="accountant">
    <assignment class="com.liferay.jbpm.handler.IdentityAssignmentHandler" config-
type="field">
        <type>community</type>
```

```
    <companyId>10095</companyId>
    <name>Support</name>
  </assignment>
</swimlane>
```

The XML above shows an alternative way to associate the *accountant* swimlane with the Support community using the actual community's name. Since community names must be unique per Company ID, this format accomplishes the same results as the previous XML.

```
<swimlane name="user_admin">
  <assignment class="com.liferay.jbpm.handler.IdentityAssignmentHandler" config-
type="field">
    <type>role</type>
    <companyId>10095</companyId>
    <id>1001</id>
  </assignment>
</swimlane>


<swimlane name="user_interviewer">
  <assignment class="com.liferay.jbpm.handler.IdentityAssignmentHandler" config-
type="field">
    <type>role</type>
    <companyId>10095</companyId>
    <name>User Interviewer</name>
  </assignment>
</swimlane>
```

The two XML snippets above are very similar to the Group XML snippets. Both associate their respective swimlanes with a role, but the first XML does so using the Role ID, and the second XML does so using the role's unique name.

DATA TYPES AND ERROR CHECKING

Currently, jBPM doesn't have support for variable data types. However, data types have been dealt with in the workflow portlet by incorporating them into the names of the controller variables. The table below shows the data types supported by the portlet as well as the syntax for the variable names:

Data Type	Syntax	Description
Checkbox	checkbox:name:checkedValue	name = the caption next to the checkbox checkedValue = the value assigned to the variable if the checkbox is checked
Date	date:name	name = the caption next to the date selector object
Email	email:name	name = the caption next to the text input field
Number	number:name	name = the caption next to the text input field
Password	password:name	name = the caption next to the text input field
Phone	phone:name	name = the caption next to the text input field
Radio Button	radio:name:option1,option2,...*	name = the caption next to the radio buttons option1,option2,...* = a comma-delimited list of options that represent the different radio button options
Select Box	select:name:option1,option2,...*	name = the caption next to the select box option1,option2,...* = a comma-delimited list of options that represent the different options in the select drop-down
Text	text:name	name = the caption next to the text input field
Textarea	textarea:name	name = the caption next to the textarea input field

Note that for all name and option values, the values should be entered in the XML in lowercase with hyphens used between words:

```
radio:are-you-hungry:yes,no,a-little-bit
```

In addition, you should register the corresponding display values in the *Language.properties* file:

```
are-you-hungry=Are you hungry?
yes=Yes
no=No
a-little-bit=A little bit
```

This will ensure that the values are displayed correctly in the portlet to the user.

By default, all variables are readable and writable by the user. Therefore, they can be defined as follows:

```
<variable name="textarea:comments" />
```

However, if variables should only be readable or writable, or if variables are required, these must be specified in the variable definition:

```
<variable name="text:name" access="read,write,required" />
```

```
<variable name="date:birthday" access="read" />
```

Variables of data type Date, Number, Email, and Phone are validated in the service call. Also, required fields are validated to ensure a value of some kind was submitted. If invalid values are submitted, the user is returned to the original form and error messages are displayed next to the invalid input fields.

Refer to the sample definition *jbpm-web.war/WEB-INF/definitions/datatypes_definition.xml* for examples of all data types in use in a single form.

SAMPLE PROCESS DEFINITIONS

The best way to understand JPDL is to look over the 3 sample XML files included with the workflow portlet. They can be found in *jbpm-web.war/WEB-INF/definitions/*. Below is a quick summary of each:

datatypes_definition.xml – a good guide to follow to understand how to use each of the data types described in the section above

holiday_definition.xml – a simple workflow that allows an employee to make a holiday request with a start and end date, and then a manager can either approve, reject, or send the request back for review

websale_definition.xml – a more complex workflow that emulates an online auction site in which control of the workflow passes through various roles. It is the most complicated of the 3 workflows, but it demonstrates almost all of the BPM features offered by jBPM

Notes:

- The JPDL definition XMLs can be created through a graphical design tool offered by JBoss, but that is beyond the scope of this document (see http://docs.jboss.com/jbpm/v3/gpd for a detailed explanation) and is also beyond the scope of the portal.

- For nodes that have tasks associated with them, each of the variables in the controller will be converted to a form element that the user must update.

- For nodes that have tasks associated with them, each of the transitions out of the node is represented as a button in the task's form. The transition's *name* attribute should always be in lowercase with hyphens between words and registered in *Language.properties*. The display value is used as the button's name.

- Many of the action handler classes found in the *com.liferay.jbpm.handler* package are just place holders that output relevant text to the console. Conceivably, these classes could perform operations such as sending out emails, initiating batch processes, updating legacy systems, etc.

- The websale workflow demonstrates the following jBPM concepts, all of which are discussed in further detail in the jBPM user guide (http://docs.jboss.com/jbpm/v3/userguide):

  o Events

  o Beanshell scripting

- ○ Swimlanes
- ○ Tasks
    - ■ Assigment(User/Pool)
    - ■ Controllers
    - ■ Variables
    - ■ Timers
- ○ Node Types
    - ■ State
    - ■ Task
    - ■ Fork
    - ■ Join
    - ■ Decision
- ○ Transitions
- ○ Actions

WARNING MESSAGES

If you have warning messages turned on for your server, in your console you may see some variant of the following message output several times when jBPM is called:

```
WARN  [org.hibernate.engine.StatefulPersistenceContext] Narrowing proxy to class org.jbpm.-
graph.node.TaskNode - this operation breaks ==
```

According to the following post on the JBoss forums (from Koen Aers, one of the key contributors to the jBPM project), this is not an error and is not of significance. He explains the reason this warning is thrown here: http://www.jboss.com/?module=bb&op=viewtopic&t=73123. Basically, the issue boils down to Hibernate doing lazy loading of the class. After a query, a collection is returned which holds a collection of stubs of the class. When a particular instance is retrieved, Hibernate goes and gets it from the database and replaces the stub with an actual instance, thereby breaking the == operator.

Administration

Once you have defined your business processes by successfully writing process definitions for them, the next step is to deploy your business processes. Once they are deployed, users can manage the life of each process instance as control is passed from one role to the next. This section is meant for end users who will actually be executing predefined process definitions.

DEPLOYING WORKFLOWS

Once the user logs in to the portal and adds the workflow portlet to her page, he or she will see something similar to the following:

Illustration 68: Default view of the Workflow Portlet

If she clicks on the "Definitions" tab, he or she will see the following:

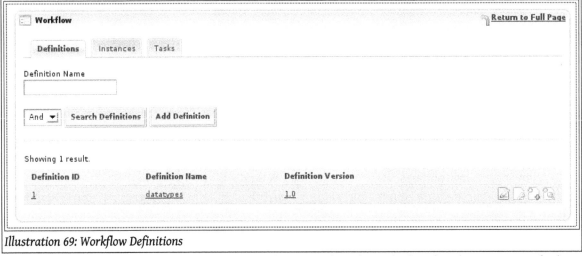

Illustration 69: Workflow Definitions

The *Definitions* tab displays all of the workflows that have been deployed in the system. To deploy a workflow, click on the *Add Definition* button. The user will see the following screen:

Illustration 70: Adding a Workflow Definition

At this point, the user can paste in the contents of a definition XML (see *jbpm-web.war/WEB-INF/definitions* for examples) and click the *Save New Version* button. If the XML is invalid, an error message will be displayed. If the XML is valid, it will be deployed, the user will be returned to the *Definitions* tab, and a success message will be displayed.

Because business processes may change over time, every version of the workflows is maintained. To edit an existing version, click on the *Edit* icon next to the definition name. Update the XML in the text area, and click the *Save New Version* button. The new version number will be incremented by 1 from the previous version. To start a new instance of a workflow definition, click on the *Add Instance* icon. A new instance will appear on the *Instances* tab. To view all the instances of a particular definition, click on the *View Instances* icon. Finally, the user can also search for a definition by name using the *Definition Name* input box.

MANAGING INSTANCES

After a definition is deployed and an instance of that definition is started, it is up to the user to manage the life cycle of the instance. Instance management is controlled from the *Instances* tab. Below is an example of what the user might see:

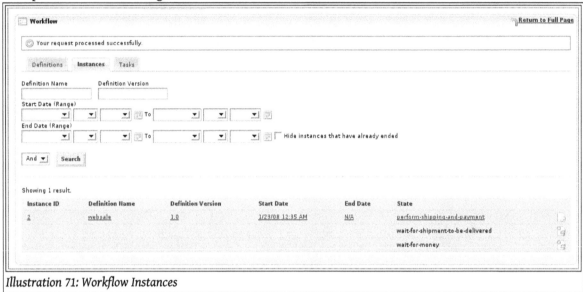

Illustration 71: Workflow Instances

The *Instances* tab displays every instance of every version of every workflow deployed in the system. They are listed alphabetically by **Definition Name** followed by **Start Date** in descending order. The search form at the top of the screen allows the user to find specific instances to manage. In particular, the *Hide instances that have already ended* check box allows the user to display only active, running instances. The date ranges also allow the user to search by *Start Date* and/or *End Date* (**NOTE:** Date ranges are inclusive of the day. For example, if the *Start Date* range was set to January 23, 2008 – January 23, 2008, then only instances that were started between January 28, 2008, 12:00am to January 28, 2008, 11:59pm would be displayed). The first row for each instance describes the state of the instance. Any subsequent rows in the instance define tasks associated with the current state. Often times, the current state and current task have the same name. In the example screen shot above, notice that web sale version 1.0 is currently in the "Perform shipping and payment" state, and it has two outstanding tasks associated with it – "Wait for shipment to be delivered" and "Wait for money."

The right-most column in the results table displays what actions the current user can perform on the given instance in its current state. The table below shows all of the possible actions and what each means:

Action	Explanation
Blank	3 possibilities: ● The user doesn't have the appropriate role / swimlane to perform an action on the instance in its current state ● The user doesn't have permissions to perform an action ● The instance has already ended
Manage icon ( )	The user directly has the appropriate role / swimlane to perform an action or the user belongs to a group which has the appropriate role / swimlane. If the user clicks on the "Manage" icon, she will be taken to a form which must be submitted to complete the task. See section 3.3 for more details
Signal icon ( )	The instance is currently in a wait state and must be "signalled" to continue. Typically, signals come from eternal processes (e.g., the arrival of a package, the successful update of a legacy system, etc.) and are not manually entered by a user. However, in the case that user intervention is required, the "Signal" icon is available.
Waiting on sibling tokens to complete	This only occurs when the process has forked into multiple subprocesses. In order for the main process to continue, all of the subprocesses must complete. As each of the subprocesses completes, they will go into this state. Once all subprocesses complete, the main process will continue like normal.

MANAGING TASKS

Task management is controlled from the "Tasks" tab. Below is an example of what the user might see:

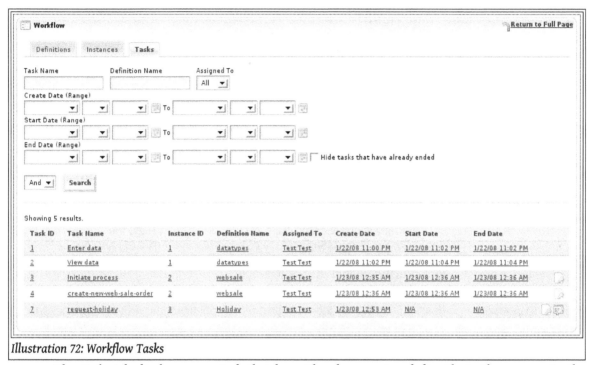

Illustration 72: Workflow Tasks

The *Tasks* tab displays every task that has either been assigned directly to the user or to the group/role pool that the user belongs to. They are listed by **Create Date** in ascending order, and the tasks assigned directly to the user are listed before the tasks assigned to the user's pool (if the **Assigned To** column is blank, that means the task is open to the pool). The search form at the top of the screen allows the user to find specific tasks to manage. In particular, the *Hide tasks that have already ended* check box allows the user to display only active tasks. The date ranges also allow the user to search by task *Create Date*, *Start Date*, and/or *End Date*. The user can also choose to only display tasks assigned directly to her, tasks assigned to her pool, or all tasks assigned to either by using the *Assigned To* drop-down.

The right-most column in the results table displays what actions the current user can perform on the given task. It will either be blank or the *Manage* icon. The logic to determine which of these will be displayed is exactly the same logic described in the table in the section above labeled **Data Types and Error Checking**.

If the user clicks the *Manage* icon, a form similar to the following will be displayed:

Illustration 73: Workflow Form

These task forms are generated from the control variables associated with the task and defined in the definition XML. Depending on the data type, the corresponding element is created in the form. Required fields are denoted by a red asterisk. If the user submits the form with invalid data, she will be returned to the form with error messages next to each of the invalid fields. If all data is valid and the user submits the form, she will be returned to the *Tasks* tab with a success message displayed.

Future Enhancements

LOGGING

Currently, the workflow portlet has no notion of logging other than the ability to review all of the tasks that a user has assigned to them or has completed. However, jBPM provides rather robust logging functionality so administrators/users can monitor every action that has ever been taken in a particular workflow.

The only reason logging functionality has not been built out in the current release is because the Liferay development team is not sure what the most effective logging metrics would be to the end user. If you or your organization has logging requirements, please submit them to the Liferay Forums, and we will review those requirements for possible inclusion in future versions of the Workflow portlet.

CUSTOMIZABLE FRONT-END

Though the workflow portlet's strength is that it can provide a forms-based data entry application virtually on-the-fly, it is obvious that there is not much control over what the forms look like when they are rendered by the portlet. To address this concern, the Liferay development team plans to create style sheets and templates that can be applied to the vanilla forms. The functionality would be very similar to how XSL style sheets are currently applied to Journal Articles in the Liferay Journal Content Management System. This enhancement would give organizations flexibility in layout and UI design of their forms.

FILE UPLOAD DATA TYPE

There have already been several requests to add a file data type to provide a means for users to upload files that are associated with workflow tasks. This will definitely be a future enhancement.

Frequently Asked Questions

HOW DO YOU WRITE A NEW PROCESS DEFINITION?

The best way to learn how to write a new process definition is to use one of the sample definition XMLs (found in *jbpm-web.war/WEB-INF/definitions/*) as a starting point. In particular, *websale_definition.xml* demonstrates most of the BPM features offered by jBPM. For an exhaustive explanation of JPDL, visit JBoss' documentation at http://docs.jboss.com/jbpm/v3/userguide/jpdl.html. There is also a graphical JPDL designer available at http://labs.jboss.com/jbossjbpm/downloads.

WHY ARE THERE "DUPLICATE FILE" EXCEPTIONS WHEN I CHANGE DATABASES FOR JBPM?

Since we are using ServiceMix as the service broker for our workflow implementation (by default, we are using jBPM), we cannot rely on the workflow engine to maintain versions of our process definitions. Therefore, we maintain the process definition XMLs as system documents in our document library. The XMLs are named based on their definition IDs, and the definition IDs are maintained in the jBPM database. Therefore, if you were to switch databases to a new instance, the definition IDs would also be reset, and when the system tries to store the process definition XML, it will find a duplicate XML already exists. The only way to ensure that this exception does not occur is by clearing out the *<User Home>/liferay/jackrabbit* folder before switching databases. However, be warned that this will delete ALL the files that are stored in your Document Library. It is recommended that once you decide on a jBPM database that suits your needs, you should only use that database.

Deploying A Customized Liferay

As described in the *Installation* chapter of this book, Liferay allows for complete customization of the portal through the Extension Environment. Deploying the extension environment to a server requires one of two scenarios:

- The Liferay development tools (JDK, Ant, etc.) are installed on the server, the Liferay Portal source code is available on the server, and the extension environment is checked out to a directory on the server

- On a client machine which contains the Liferay development tools, a drive can be mapped or a folder mounted which points to the installation directory on the server

Once one of these two requirements have been met, deploying to the server becomes as easy as deploying locally to the developer's machine.

If you will be deploying the extension environment directly on the server, you will have to configure two new configuration files which define the settings for the deployment. In the extension environment, create a file called *app.server.<username>properties*, where *<username>* is the user name of the account under which the server executable runs. If, for example, you have a Glassfish server running under the user name of *glassfish*, your file would be called *app.server.glassfish.properties*. This file will override the default values which are found in *app.server.properties*. You will need to configure two properties in this file: the server type and the server path.

The server type should be one of the following:

```
app.server.type=geronimo-tomcat
app.server.type=glassfish
app.server.type=jboss-jetty
app.server.type=jboss-tomcat
app.server.type=jetty
app.server.type=jonas-jetty
app.server.type=jonas-tomcat
app.server.type=oc4j
app.server.type=resin
app.server.type=tomcat
```

The path property is similar to the server type. It should look like this:

```
app.server.<server name>.dir
```

Replace <server name> with the server type above. For example, if you are using Glassfish, your property would be:

```
app.server.glassfish.dir=/home/glassfish/glassfish-v2
```

The value of the property should be the fully qualified path to the server directory.

Next, create another file similar to the first one called *release.<username>.properties*. Again, substitute *<username>* with the user name the server runs under and under whose credentials you will be doing the deployment. This file will override the default values found in *release.properties.*

This file requires two properties:

```
lp.source.dir
lp.ext.dir
```

Set the value for the *lp.source.dir* property to be equal to the fully qualified directory name for where you have installed the Liferay Portal source. Set the value for the *lp.ext.dir* property to be equal to the fully qualified directory name for where you have installed the Extension Environment you have checked out from your source code repository. For example:

```
lp.source.dir=/home/glassfish/lportal/portal
lp.ext.dir=/home/glassfish/lportal/ext
```

Once you have set up these two properties files, run the following Ant task:

```
ant deploy
```

Your customized Liferay will be automatically compiled and deployed to your application server.

If you will be deploying a customized Liferay from a client machine, you will need to map a drive (on Windows) or a folder on your file system (Mac or Linux) to the server. Once you have done this, follow the same procedure outlined above, with the exception that the *<username>* should be the user name of the user logged in to the client, not the user name on the server. You will not need to change the *release.<user-*

name>.properties file; only the *app.server.<username>.properties* file will need to be modified.

If you are using a developer's machine to do the deployment, these configuration files will already exist. Modify the *app.server.<username>.properties* file to match the application server type and location of the directory in which it is installed from your mapped drive or folder. Then run the above Ant task to deploy the extension environment.

Note that this second method is not a best practice, as it enables changes to be made locally on a developer's machine which can then be deployed directly to a server without source code management being done first. It is better to have developers check in all their code, version that code, and then pull that version from your source code management software to deploy it to a server.

Performance Tuning

Once you have your portal up and running, you may find a need to tune it for performance, especially if your site winds up generating more traffic than you'd anticipated. There are some definite steps you can take with regard to improving Liferay's performance.

Memory

Memory is one of the first things to look at when you want to optimize performance. If you have any disk swapping, that will have a serious impact on performance. Make sure that your server has an optimal amount of memory and that your JVM is tuned to use it.

There are three JVM command switches that control the amount of memory it will use.

```
-Xms
-Xmx
-XX:MaxPermSize
```

These three settings control the amount of memory available to the JVM initially, the maximum amount of memory into which the JVM can grow, and the separate area of the heap called Permanent Generation space.

The first two settings should be set to something reasonable. For example, by default, the Tomcat start script, called *catalina.sh* (or *catalina.bat*) sets the options to

```
-Xms128m -Xmx1024m -XX:MaxPermSize=128m
```

This is perfectly reasonable for a moderately sized machine or a developer machine. These settings allow the JVM to initially take 128MB of RAM, grow up to 1024MB of RAM, and have a PermGen space of 128MB. If, however, you have Liferay on a server with 4GB of RAM and you are having performance problems, the first thing you might want to look at is increasing the memory available to the JVM. You will be able to tell if memory is a problem by running a profiler (such as Jprobe or YourKit) on the server. If you see Garbage Collection (GC) running frequently, you will definitely want to increase the amount of memory available to the JVM.

Issues with PermGen space can also affect performance. PermGen space contains long-lived classes, anonymous classes and interned Strings. Hibernate, in particular—which Liferay uses extensively—has been known to make use of PermGen space. If you increase the amount of memory available to the JVM, you may want to increase the amount of PermGen space accordingly.

Properties File Changes

There are also some changes you can make to your *portal-ext.properties* file once you are in a production environment.

Set the following to false to disable checking the last modified date on server side CSS and JavaScript.

```
last.modified.check=false
```

Set this property to true to load the theme's merged CSS files for faster loading for production. By default it is set to false for easier debugging for development. You can also disable fast loading by setting the URL parameter *css_fast_load* to *0*.

```
theme.css.fast.load=true
```

Set this property to true to load the combined JavaScript files from the property *javascript.files* into one compacted file for faster loading for production. By default it is set to false for easier debugging for development. You can also disable fast loading by setting the URL parameter *js_fast_load* to *0*.

```
javascript.fast.load=true
```

Servlet Filters

Liferay comes by default with 15 servlet filters enabled and running. It is likely that for your installation, you don't need them all. Two filters that you can disable without any impact are the *Compression Filter* and the *Strip Filter*. These filters are responsible for shrinking the size of the response (to save bandwidth). The Strip Filter removes whitespace from the response object, and the Compression Filter compresses it. This obviously requires some processing, and so disabling these two filters can enhance performance.

To disable a servlet filter, simply comment it out of your *web.xml* file.

If there is a feature supported by a servlet filter that you know you are not using, you can comment it out as well to achieve some performance gains. For example, if you are not using CAS for single sign-on, comment out the CAS Filter. If you are not using NTLM for single sign-ons, comment out the Ntlm Filter. If you are not using the Virtual Hosting for Communities feature, comment out the Virtual Host Filter. The fewer servlet filters you are running, the less processing power is needed for each request.

Portlets

Liferay comes pre-bundled with many portlets which contain a lot of functionality, but not every web site that is running on Liferay needs to use them all. In *portlet.xml* and *liferay-portlet.xml*, comment out the ones you are not using. While having a loan calculator, analog clock, or game of hangman available for your users to add to pages is nice, those portlets may be taking up resources that are needed by custom portlets you have written for your site. If you are having performance problems, commenting out some of the unused portlets may give you the performance boost you need.

5. Maintaining A Liferay Portal

Maintaining a running implementation of Liferay Portal is not much different from maintaining the application server environment upon which it is running. There are, however, several factors which administrators should be aware of when they are responsible for a running instance of Liferay. This chapter will cover these issues, outlining for system administrators some specifics about keeping a running Liferay instance stable and secure.

This chapter will cover the following topics:

● Liferay Monitoring using Google Analytics

● Backing Up a Liferay Installation

● Changing Logging Levels

The discussion on back up will cover what parts of Liferay should be backed up. We will not cover specific backup software or procedures; generally, most organizations have standards for doing backups of their systems, and Liferay as a Java EE application fits well into these standards.

Liferay Monitoring Using Google Analytics

Liferay includes built-in support for Google Analytics, allowing administrators to make use of Google's tool set for analyzing site traffic data. When you sign up for Google Analytics, a snippet of code is provided which needs to be added to your web pages in order to allow Google's system to register the page hit. It can be a tedious process to add this code to every page on a site, especially if it is a large site and there is a lot of user-generated content.

This problem can be solved in Liferay by putting Google's code into a custom theme written especially for the site on which the portal is running. Doing this, however, requires that a theme developer make specific changes to the theme, and it prevents users from using the many freely available themes that are available for Liferay "out of the box."

Because of this, support for Google Analytics has been built into Liferay, and can be turned on through a simple user interface. This allows Liferay Administrators to make use of Google Analytics on a community by community basis and turn it on and off when needed.

To enable Google Analytics support, go to the Manage Pages screen for the community for which you want to enable support. You can do this through the Communities portlet or by clicking the *Manage Pages* link in the Dock while you are on a page in the community. Click the top level link on the left side to go to the settings for all pages of the community.

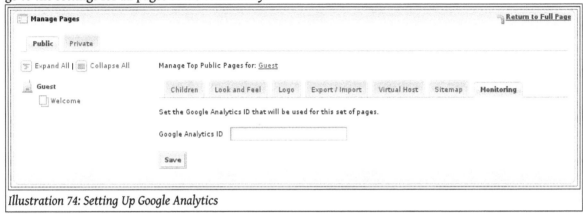

Illustration 74: Setting Up Google Analytics

Click the **Monitoring** Tab. Put your Google Analytics ID (which should have been provided to you when you signed up for the service) in the field and click *Save*. All of the pages in the community you selected will now have the Google Analytics code in them and will be tracked.

Backing Up A Liferay Installation

Once you have an installation of Liferay Portal running, you will want to have proper backup procedures in place in case of a catastrophic failure of some kind. Liferay is not very different from any other application that may be running in your application server, but there are some specific components that need to be backed up in addition to your regular backup procedures for your application server.

Source Code

If you have extended Liferay or have written portlet or theme plugins, they should be stored in a source code repository such as Subversion, CVS, or Git. This repository should be backed up on a regular basis to preserve your ongoing work.

If you are extending Liferay with the Extension Environment, you will want to make sure that you also store the version of the Liferay source on which your extension environment is based. This allows your developers convenient access to all of the tools they need to build your extension and deploy it to a server.

Liferay's File System

Liferay's configuration file, *portal-ext.properties*, gets stored in the *WEB-INF/classes* folder in the location to which your application server deployed Liferay. At a minimum, this file should be backed up, but it is generally best to back up your whole application server.

Liferay also stores configuration files, search indexes, cache information, and the default Jackrabbit document repository in a folder called *liferay*. This folder resides in the home directory of the user ID under which Liferay is running. On Unix-based systems, this folder will likely be in */home/<user id>*. This folder should be backed up also.

Database

Liferay's database is the central repository for all of the Portal's information and is the most important component which needs to be backed up. You can do this by either backing up the database live (if your database allows this) or by exporting the database and then backing up the exported file. For example, MySQL ships with a *mysqldump* utility which allows you to export the entire database and data into a large SQL file. This file can then be backed up. In case of a database failure, it can be used to recreate the state of the database at the time the dump was created.

If you are using Liferay's Document Library extensively, it is likely that you have configured Jackrabbit to store documents in a database rather than the file system. In this case, the Jackrabbit database should be backed up also.

Liferay's Logging System

Liferay uses Log4j extensively to implement logging for nearly every class in the portal. If you need to debug something specific while a system is running, you can use the **Admin** portlet to set logging levels by class dynamically.

The Admin portlet appears in the Admin section of the *Add Content* menu. Add this portlet to an administrative page somewhere in your portal.

To view the log levels, select the *Server* tab, then the *Log Levels* tab.

You will then see a paginated list of logging categories. These categories correspond to Liferay classes that have log messages in them. By default, all categories are set to display messages only if there is an error that occurs in the class. This is why you see ERROR displayed in all of the drop down list boxes on the right side of the portlet.

Each category is filtered by its place in the class hierarchy. For example, if you wanted to see logging for a specific class that is registered in the Admin portlet, you would browse to that specific class and change its log level to something that is more descriptive, such as DEBUG. Once you click the *Save* button at the bottom of the list, you will start seeing DEBUG messages from that class in your application server's log file.

If you are not sure which class you want to see log messages for, you can find a place higher up in the hierarchy and select the package name instead of an individual class name. If you do this, messages for every class lower in the hierarchy will be displayed in your application server's log file.

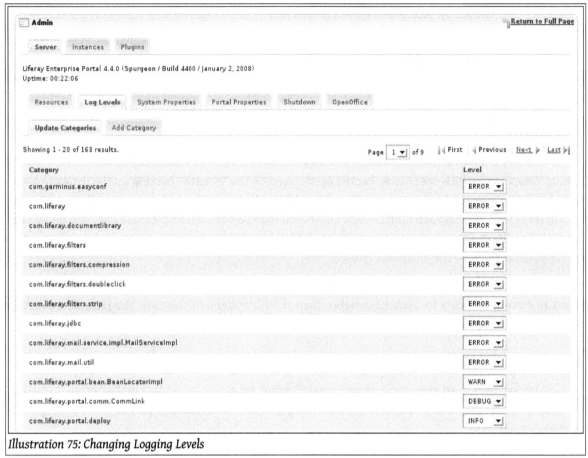

Illustration 75: Changing Logging Levels

Be careful when you do this. If you set the log level to DEBUG somewhere near the top of the hierarchy (such as *com.liferay*, for example), you may wind up with a lot of messages in your log file. This could make it difficult to find the one you were looking for, and causes the server to do more work writing messages to its log file.

If you are working in the extension environment or have created a plugin and want to set the log level for one of your own classes, you can register that class (so long as it uses Log4J to do its logging) with the Admin portlet so that you can control the log levels more easily.

You will first need to implement Log4J logging in your class, with a statement such as the following (taken from Liferay's JCRHook class):

```
private static Log _log = LogFactory.getLog(JCRHook.class);
```

You would then use this *_log* variable to create log messages in your code for the various logging levels:

```
_log.error("Reindexing " + node.getName(), e1);
```

To enable your logging messages to appear in your server's log file via the Admin portlet, click the *Add Category* tab on the same *Log Levels* page.

Illustration 76: Adding a Logging Category

You will see that you can add a logging category to the Admin portlet. Simply put in the fully qualified name of your class or of the package that contains the classes whose log messages you want to view, choose a log level, and then click the *Save* button. You will now start to see log messages from your own class or classes in the server's log file.

6. APPENDIX: DOCUMENTATION LICENSE

Creative Commons License

License

will not be considered an Adaptation for the purpose of this License. For the avoidance of doubt, where the Work is a musical work, performance or phonogram, the synchronization of the Work in timed-relation with a moving image ("synching") will be considered an Adaptation for the purpose of this License.

b. **"Collection"** means a collection of literary or artistic works, such as encyclopedias and anthologies, or performances, phonograms or broadcasts, or other works or subject matter other than works listed in Section 1(f) below, which, by reason of the selection and arrangement of their contents, constitute intellectual creations, in which the Work is included in its entirety in unmodified form along with one or more other contributions, each constituting separate and independent works in themselves, which together are assembled into a collective whole. A work that constitutes a Collection will not be considered an Adaptation (as defined below) for the purposes of this License.

c. **"Creative Commons Compatible License"** means a license that is listed at http://creativecommons.org/compatiblelicenses that has been approved by Creative Commons as being essentially equivalent to this License, including, at a minimum, because that license: (i) contains terms that have the same purpose, meaning and effect as the License Elements of this License; and, (ii) explicitly permits the relicensing of adaptations of works made available under that license under this License or a Creative Commons jurisdiction license with the same License Elements as this License.

d. **"Distribute"** means to make available to the public the original and copies of the Work or Adaptation, as appropriate, through sale or other transfer of ownership.

e. **"License Elements"** means the following high-level license attributes as selected by Licensor and indicated in the title of this License: Attribution, ShareAlike.

f. **"Licensor"** means the individual, individuals, entity or entities that offer(s) the Work under the terms of this License.

g. **"Original Author"** means, in the case of a literary or artistic work, the individual, individuals, entity or entities who created the Work or if no individual or entity can be identified, the publisher; and in addition (i) in the case of a performance the actors, singers, musicians, dancers, and other persons who act, sing, deliver, declaim, play in, interpret or otherwise perform literary or artistic works or expressions of folklore; (ii) in the case of a phonogram the producer being the person or legal entity who first fixes the sounds of a performance or other sounds; and, (iii) in the case of broadcasts, the organization that transmits the broadcast.

h. **"Work"** means the literary and/or artistic work offered under the terms of this License including without limitation any production in the literary, scientific and artistic domain, whatever may be the mode or form of its expression including digital form, such as a book, pamphlet and other writing; a lecture, address, sermon or other work of the same nature; a dramatic or dramatico-musical work; a choreographic work or entertainment in dumb show; a musical composition with or without words; a cinematographic work to which are assimilated works expressed by a process analogous to cinematography; a work of drawing, painting, architecture, sculpture, engraving or lithography; a photographic work to which are assimilated works expressed by a process analogous to photography; a work of applied art; an illustration, map, plan, sketch or three-dimensional work relative to geography, topography, architecture or science; a performance; a broadcast; a phonogram; a compilation of data to the extent it is protected as a copyrightable work; or a work performed by a variety or circus performer to the extent it is not otherwise considered a literary or artistic work.

i. **"You"** means an individual or entity exercising rights under this License who has not previously violated the terms of this License with respect to the Work, or who has received express permission from the Licensor to exercise rights under this License despite a previous violation.

j. **"Publicly Perform"** means to perform public recitations of the Work and to communicate to the public those public recitations, by any means or process, including by wire or wireless means or public digital performances; to make available to the public Works in such a way that members of the public may access these Works from a place and at a place individually chosen by them; to perform the Work to the public by any means or process and the communication to the public of the performances of the Work, including by public digital performance; to broadcast and rebroadcast the Work by any means including signs, sounds or images.

k. **"Reproduce"** means to make copies of the Work by any means including without limitation by sound or visual recordings and the right of fixation and reproducing fixations of the Work, including storage of a protected performance or phonogram in digital form or other electronic medium.

2. Fair Dealing Rights. Nothing in this License is intended to reduce, limit, or restrict any uses free from copyright or rights arising from limitations or exceptions that are provided for in connection with the copyright protection under copyright law or other applicable laws.

3. License Grant. Subject to the terms and conditions of this License, Licensor hereby grants You a worldwide, royalty-free, non-exclusive, perpetual (for the duration of the applicable copyright) license to exercise the rights in the Work as stated below:

a. to Reproduce the Work, to incorporate the Work into one or more Collections, and to Reproduce the Work as incorporated in the Collections;

b. to create and Reproduce Adaptations provided that any such Adaptation, including any translation in any medium, takes reasonable steps to clearly label, demarcate or otherwise identify that changes were made to the original Work. For example, a translation could be marked "The original work was translated from English to Spanish," or a modification could indicate "The original work has been modified.";

c. to Distribute and Publicly Perform the Work including as incorporated in Collections; and,

d. to Distribute and Publicly Perform Adaptations.

e. For the avoidance of doubt:

i. **Non-waivable Compulsory License Schemes.** In those jurisdictions in which the right to collect royalties through any statutory or compulsory licensing scheme cannot be waived, the Licensor reserves the exclusive right to collect such royalties for any exercise by You of the rights granted under this License;

ii. **Waivable Compulsory License Schemes.** In those jurisdictions in which the right to collect royalties through any statutory or compulsory licensing scheme can be waived, the Licensor waives the exclusive right to collect such royalties for any exercise by You of the rights granted under this License; and,

iii. **Voluntary License Schemes.** The Licensor waives the right to collect royalties, whether individually or, in the event that the Licensor is a member of a collecting society that administers voluntary licensing schemes, via that society, from any exercise by You of the rights granted under this License.

The above rights may be exercised in all media and formats whether now known or hereafter devised. The above rights include the right to make such modifications as are technically necessary to exercise the rights in other media and formats. Subject to Section 8(f), all rights not expressly granted by Licensor are hereby reserved.

4. Restrictions. The license granted in Section 3 above is expressly made subject to and limited by the following restrictions:

a. You may Distribute or Publicly Perform the Work only under the terms of this License. You must include a copy of, or the Uniform Resource Identifier (URI) for, this License with every copy of the Work You Distribute or Publicly Perform. You may not offer or impose any terms on the Work that restrict the terms of this License or the ability of the recipient of the Work to exercise the rights granted to that recipient under the terms of the License. You may not sublicense the Work. You must keep intact all notices that refer to this License and to the disclaimer of warranties with every copy of the Work You Distribute or Publicly Perform. When You Distribute or Publicly Perform the Work, You may not impose any effective technological measures on the Work that restrict the ability of a recipient of the Work from You to exercise the rights granted to that recipient under the terms of the License. This Section 4(a) applies to the Work as incorporated in a Collection, but this does not require the Collection apart from the Work itself to be made subject to the terms of this License. If You create a Collection, upon notice from any Licensor You must, to the extent practicable, remove from the Collection any credit as required by Section 4(c), as requested. If You create an Adaptation, upon notice from any Licensor You must, to the extent practicable, remove from the Adaptation any credit as required by Section 4(c), as requested.

b. You may Distribute or Publicly Perform an Adaptation only under the terms of: (i) this License; (ii) a later version of this License with the same License Elements as this License; (iii) a Creative Commons jurisdiction license (either this or a later license version) that contains the same License Elements as this License (e.g., Attribution-ShareAlike 3.0 US); (iv) a Creative Commons Compatible License. If you license the Adaptation under one of the licenses mentioned in (iv), you must comply with the terms of that license. If you license the Adaptation under the terms of any of the licenses mentioned in (i), (ii) or (iii) (the "Applicable License"), you must comply with the terms of the Applicable License generally and the following provisions: (I) You must include a copy of, or the URI for, the Applicable License with every copy of each Adaptation You Distribute or Publicly Perform; (II) You may not offer or impose any terms on the Adaptation that restrict the terms of the Applicable License or the ability of the recipient of the Adaptation to exercise the rights granted to that recipient under the terms of the Applicable License; (III) You must keep intact all notices that refer to the Applicable License and to the disclaimer of warranties with every copy of the Work as included in the Adaptation You Distribute or Publicly Perform; (IV) when You Distribute or Publicly Perform the Adaptation, You may not impose any effective technological measures on the Adaptation that restrict the ability of a recipient of the Adaptation from You to exercise the rights granted to that recipient under the terms of the Applicable License. This Section 4(b) applies to the Adaptation as incorporated in a Collection, but this does not require the Collection apart from the Adaptation itself to be made subject to the terms of the Applicable License.

c. If You Distribute, or Publicly Perform the Work or any Adaptations or Collections, You must, unless a request has been made pursuant to Section 4(a), keep intact all copyright notices for the Work and provide, reasonable to the medium or means You are utilizing: (i) the name of the Original Author (or pseudonym, if applicable) if supplied, and/or if the Original Author and/or Licensor designate another party or parties (e.g., a sponsor institute, publishing entity, journal) for attribution ("Attribution Parties") in Licensor's copyright notice, terms of service or by other reasonable means, the name of such party or parties; (ii) the title of the Work if supplied; (iii) to the extent reasonably practicable, the URI, if any, that Licensor specifies to be associated with the Work, unless such URI does not refer to the copyright notice or licensing information for the Work; and (iv) , consistent with Ssection 3(b), in the case of an Adaptation, a credit identifying the use of the Work in the Adaptation (e.g., "French translation of the Work by Original Author," or "Screenplay based on original Work by Original Author"). The credit required by this Section 4(c) may be implemented in any reasonable manner; provided, however, that in the case of a Adaptation or Collection, at a minimum such credit will appear, if a credit for all contributing authors of the Adaptation or Collection appears, then as part of these credits and in a manner at least as prominent as the credits for the other contributing authors. For the avoidance of doubt, You may only use the credit required by this Section for the purpose of attribution in the manner set out above and, by exercising Your rights under this License, You may not implicitly or explicitly assert or imply any connection with, sponsorship or endorsement by the Original Author, Licensor and/or Attribution Parties, as appropriate, of You or Your use of the Work, without the separate, express prior written permission of the Original Author, Licensor and/or Attribution Parties.

d. Except as otherwise agreed in writing by the Licensor or as may be otherwise permitted by applicable law, if You Reproduce, Distribute or Publicly Perform the Work either by itself or as part of any Adaptations or Collections, You must not distort, mutilate, modify or take other derogatory action in relation to the Work which would be prejudicial to the Original Author's honor or reputation. Licensor agrees that in those jurisdictions (e.g. Japan), in which any exercise of the right granted in Section 3(b) of this License (the right to make Adaptations) would be deemed to be a distortion, mutilation, modification or other derogatory action prejudicial to the Original Author's honor and reputation, the Licensor will waive or not assert, as appropriate, this Section, to the fullest extent permitted by the applicable national law, to enable You to reasonably exercise Your right under Section 3(b) of this License (right to make Adaptations) but not otherwise.

5. Representations, Warranties and Disclaimer

UNLESS OTHERWISE MUTUALLY AGREED TO BY THE PARTIES IN WRITING, LICENSOR OFFERS THE WORK AS-IS AND MAKES NO REPRESENTATIONS OR WARRANTIES OF ANY KIND CONCERNING THE WORK, EXPRESS, IMPLIED, STATUTORY OR OTHERWISE, INCLUDING, WITHOUT LIMITATION, WARRANTIES OF TITLE, MERCHANTIBILITY, FITNESS FOR A PARTICULAR PURPOSE, NONINFRINGEMENT, OR THE ABSENCE OF LATENT OR OTHER DEFECTS, ACCURACY, OR THE PRESENCE OF ABSENCE OF ERRORS, WHETHER OR NOT DISCOVERABLE. SOME JURISDICTIONS DO NOT ALLOW THE EXCLUSION OF IMPLIED WARRANTIES, SO SUCH EXCLUSION MAY NOT APPLY TO YOU.

6. Limitation on Liability. EXCEPT TO THE EXTENT REQUIRED BY APPLICABLE LAW, IN NO EVENT WILL LICENSOR BE LIABLE TO YOU ON ANY LEGAL THEORY FOR ANY SPECIAL, INCIDENTAL, CONSEQUENTIAL, PUNITIVE OR EXEMPLARY DAMAGES ARISING OUT OF THIS LICENSE OR THE USE OF THE WORK, EVEN IF LICENSOR HAS BEEN ADVISED OF THE POSSIBILITY OF SUCH DAMAGES.

7. Termination

a. This License and the rights granted hereunder will terminate automatically upon any breach by You of the terms of this License. Individuals or entities who have received Adaptations or Collections from You under this License, however, will not have their licenses terminated provided such individuals or entities remain in full compliance with those licenses. Sections 1, 2, 5, 6, 7, and 8 will survive any termination of this License.

b. Subject to the above terms and conditions, the license granted here is perpetual (for the duration of the applicable copyright in the Work). Notwithstanding the above, Licensor reserves the right to release the Work under different license terms or to stop distributing the Work at any time; provided, however that any such election will not serve to withdraw this License (or any other license that has been, or is required to be, granted under the terms of this License), and this License will continue in full force and effect unless terminated as stated above.

8. Miscellaneous

a. Each time You Distribute or Publicly Perform the Work or a Collection, the Licensor offers to the recipient a license to the Work on the same terms and conditions as the license granted to You under this License.

b. Each time You Distribute or Publicly Perform an Adaptation, Licensor offers to the recipient a license to the original Work on the same terms and conditions as the license granted to You under this License.

c. If any provision of this License is invalid or unenforceable under applicable law, it shall not affect the validity or enforceability of the remainder of the terms of this License, and without further action by the parties to this agreement, such provision shall be reformed to the minimum extent necessary to make such provision valid and enforceable.

d. No term or provision of this License shall be deemed waived and no breach consented to unless such waiver or consent shall be in writing and signed by the party to be charged with such waiver or consent.

e. This License constitutes the entire agreement between the parties with respect to the Work licensed here. There are no understandings, agreements or representations with respect to the Work not specified here. Licensor shall not be bound by any additional provisions that may appear in any communication from You. This License may not be modified without the mutual written agreement of the Licensor and You.

f. The rights granted under, and the subject matter referenced, in this License were drafted utilizing the terminology of the Berne Convention for the Protection of Literary and Artistic Works (as amended on September 28, 1979), the Rome Convention of 1961, the WIPO Copyright Treaty of 1996, the WIPO Performances and Phonograms Treaty of 1996 and the Universal Copyright Convention (as revised on July 24, 1971). These rights and subject matter take effect in the relevant jurisdiction in which the License terms are sought to be enforced according to the corresponding provisions of the implementation of those treaty provisions in the applicable national law. If the standard suite of rights granted under applicable copyright law includes additional rights not granted under this License, such additional rights are deemed to be included in the License; this License is not intended to restrict the license of any rights under applicable law.

Creative Commons Notice

Creative Commons is not a party to this License, and makes no warranty whatsoever in connection with the Work. Creative Commons will not be liable to You or any party on any legal theory for any damages whatsoever, including without limitation any general, special, incidental or consequential damages arising in connection to this license. Notwithstanding the foregoing two (2) sentences, if Creative Commons has expressly identified itself as the Licensor hereunder, it shall have all rights and obligations of Licensor.

Except for the limited purpose of indicating to the public that the Work is licensed under the CCPL, Creative Commons does not authorize the use by either party of the trademark "Creative Commons" or any related trademark or logo of Creative Commons without the prior written consent of Creative Commons. Any permitted use will be in compliance with Creative Commons' then-current trademark usage guidelines, as may be published on its website or otherwise made available upon request from time to time. For the avoidance of doubt, this trademark restriction does not form part of the License.

Creative Commons may be contacted at http://creativecommons.org/.

7. COLOPHON

This book was physically created using entirely open source software. This book was mentally created in several steps.

It was initially outlined in a small notebook (paper, not a computer) on a plane flying from Philadelphia to Los Angeles in order to help the author (actually, General Editor, since there have been contributors of material) focus his thoughts for an interview at Liferay. It was then presented to two of the partners at Liferay during the interview, and may have contributed to the General Editor actually landing the job—which, in the General Editor's view, is a very good thing.

A couple of months later, it was rehashed electronically in outline form among a small group of Liferay employees (including said General Editor) until the final list of content was considered complete. This seemed like a big accomplishment at the time, but paled in comparison to the work of actually documenting all of the things we'd decided to include.

The writing and editing process took a period of five months of mostly full time work. It would have taken much longer except for the fact that many fantastic contributions came unsolicited from many different people. I have endeavored to give credit to everyone who made a contribution (it's on the copyright page), but if I missed somebody—which would not be surprising—please let me know so your name is not left out of the next edition! I cannot express enough how wonderful it is to be surrounded by so many talented people who do everything they can to make this product the best it can be—even when a particular task is not their primary job.

The text and layout were accomplished using OpenOffice.org 2.3 running on multiple distributions of Linux. There are clues on the General Editor's blog as to why this had to happen. The file is one large document, rather than a multi-linked master document. It's just easier to manage that way. The PDF was exported directly from OpenOffice.org.

All of the fonts used in the creation of this book are open source fonts that are freely available. The body text font is Gentium Book Basic, created by SIL International. It can be found here: http://scripts.sil.org/cms/scripts/page.php?site_id=nrsi&item_id=Gentium.

The font for the titles is MgOpen Modata. The text on the cover of the book is MgOpen Cosmetica, and the text used in tables is MgOpen Moderna. This font was also used for the title on the front cover. These fonts were originally created by Magenta Ltd. and then released under an open source license. They can be found here: http://www.ellak.gr/fonts/mgopen/index.en.html.

The font used for source code is Liberation Mono, created by Red Hat, Inc. The Liberation fonts can be found here: https://www.redhat.com/promo/fonts.

Screen shots that were taken by the General Editor were taken using Ksnapshot, an excellent screen shot program that is part of the KDE desktop. Other screen shots were taken by the contributors using unknown software. Drawings inside the book (such as the Unbreakable Liferay diagram) were created in OpenOffice.org draw, using some stencils from Dia (http://www.gnome.org/projects/dia). Some drawings and screen shots were touched up using the GIMP.

The cover of the book was done in a combination of programs. The picture was touched up and given its drop shadow via the GIMP (http://www.gimp.org). The Liferay logo was converted from a PDF into a Scalable Vector Graphics file by pdf2svg (http://www.cityinthesky.co.uk/pdf2svg.html). This was then touched up in Karbon14 (http://www.koffice.org/karbon) and then imported into InkScape (http://www.inkscape.org), which was used to design the front cover. You may be wondering why it had to be done this way: this will remain a mystery. The front cover was exported to PDF format using InkScape's exporter.

The picture on the front cover is a picture of Crepuscular Rays. These are rays of sunlight which appear to spring from a hidden source—usually from behind a cloud, but can also appear diffused through trees. The rays are actually parallel, and it is perspective that makes them appear to converge at the Sun. Also known as God's rays, crepuscular rays can be spectacular and certainly seemed appropriate for the cover of a book about a product called *Liferay* Portal. This great shot was taken by none other than Liferay's CEO, Bryan Cheung, in Langen, Germany, near the offices of Liferay's European headquarters.

Rich Sezov, March 2008

INDEX